The Eagle of Toledo: The Life and Times of Federico Bahamontes

RECKLESS

THE LIFE AND TIMES OF LUIS OCAÑA

ALASDAIR FOTHERINGHAM

B L O O M S B U R Y
LONDON • NEW DELHI • NEW YORK • SYDNEY

First published in Great Britain 2014

Copyright © 2014 by Alasdair Fotheringham

The moral right of the author has been asserted

Bloomsbury Publishing plc
50 Bedford Square
London
WC1B 3DP

www.bloomsbury.com
Bloomsbury is a trademark of Bloomsbury Publishing Plc

Bloomsbury Publishing, London, New Delhi, New York and Sydney

A CIP catalogue record for this book is available from the British Library

Hardback ISBN 978 1 4088 4602 5
Export Trade Paperback ISBN 978 1 4088 4601 8

10 9 8 7 6 5 4 3 2 1

Typeset by Saxon Graphics Ltd, Derby
Printed and bound in Great Britain by CPI Group (UK) Ltd, Croydon CR0 4YY

For my mother

CONTENTS

INTRODUCTION

THE EXCEPTION TO THE RULE

Bernard Thévenet, the double Tour de France winner, says Luis Ocaña once told him why he quit the race in 1975.

By stage 11, for the first time since taking the Tour in 1973, Luis Ocaña was back on track in a three-week stage race. Fifth overall and 7'00" down on his nemesis Eddy Merckx does not sound exceptional, but in comparison to 1974, when Ocaña never even made it to the Tour after a bizarre accident in the Tour de l'Aude – then a men's race – saw him fracture his arm then take a low-key exit from his team BIC at the end of the season, this was a major improvement.

However, after stage 11's 242-kilometre trek to Albi eastwards through hilly terrain from Tarbes, Thévenet says Ocaña felt restless. Very restless, in fact: to the point where Ocaña told him he decided to sneak out of the hotel that evening and drive home for the night – around 300 kilometres each way.

Sitting behind a steering wheel for a total of seven hours' driving was hardly the recommended way of resting after a seven and a quarter hour stage of the hardest endurance event on the planet. But, as countless people have observed, once Ocaña had an idea in his head there was no driving it out.

This became clear again when Ocaña reached his home near Mont-de-Marsan to find it empty, the doors locked, the windows shuttered and bolted. And that he had left his door key in Albi.

So – according to Thévenet – Ocaña refused, as he would do so often, to give up. Instead he decided to break in, climbing up

1

onto the roof and trying to get in that way. Having managed to jemmy open a skylight, he then fell heavily through the rafters, injuring his knee so badly he could barely drive back to the team hotel. Starting the next day's stage was out of the question and Ocaña abandoned.

According to the team, Ocaña pulled out because of sunstroke. According to his soigneur, Emilio Cruz, Ocaña left because he 'had a knee injury that year in the Tour and none of us could work out how it got there'. According to his team-mate José Luis Viejo, Ocaña had to quit because of a 'wound in his groin that was so big the only way he could pedal, he said, was by stuffing a lump of steak in to ease the pain and even then the pain got too much for him'. According to Ocaña's widow, Josiane, Thévenet's version of events – the drive back to Mont-de-Marsan, the break-in and so on – is completely false.

Whether or not Thévenet's tale contains a grain of truth – and neither he nor Josiane has a vested interest in inventing, or denying it, after all – is impossible to tell. But ultimately it does not matter: the tale of why Ocaña abandoned the Tour lingers in the memory because there is so much in it that could be true, so much that was typical of him: wild impetuosity and individuality combined with a degree of stubbornness that led Ocaña, time and again, into a spiral of self-destruction. And, with time, the myth has become larger than anything Ocaña did or did not achieve.

But it was those very same factors – the bloody-mindedness, the impulsive decision-making, the determination not to let circumstances get the better of him – that enabled Ocaña, too, to be remembered as the only rider who took on and conclusively beat Eddy Merckx in the Tour de France, whilst the Belgian was at the peak of his powers. That honour goes to him and to him alone. Nobody else got knocked back as often as Luis Ocaña. But nobody else got back up, so determined to try again, either.

1

THE HOLE IN THE CEILING

These days, Luis Ocaña's home village of Priego in Spain is picturesque almost to the point of caricature. It is too far from Cuenca, the capital of a hilly agricultural region of pine forests, vast hidden canyons and huge stretches of uncultivated ochreous soil, to have suffered from the rash of high-rise flats that has scarred most dormitory towns in Spain since its countryside began to empty with a vengeance in the 1960s. On one side of the village, perched over a huge gorge containing one crumbling tower – all that remains of a sixteenth-century castle – such building remains in any case, thankfully, fairly impractical.

So Priego has stayed much as it was when Ocaña and his family left it in 1951, when he was nearly seven, first for eastern Spain and then France: a huddle of sun-bleached, mostly two-storey houses and badly tarmacked winding streets around a stubby, thick-walled Renaissance church, still the tallest building in the area. Rather than the supermarket you find in almost every Spanish village, Priego has to make do with a traditional version – a shop in the central square selling everything under the sun, from fly spray and sweets in huge jars to ham cuts and Dora Explorer dolls in cellophane packages.

What catches the eye most of all, though, is the proliferation of metre-high drystone dividing walls, rather than fences, between the village houses: a reminder of the harshness of the surrounding landscape, and the fact that Ocaña and his family left Priego because his parents, Luis and Julia, agricultural workers and the children of agricultural workers, could not afford to stay there any longer. As is so often the case, the factors that make Priego such a picture postcard village today – isolation and just a few cottage industries like tiny ceramics and reed-basket workshops – made life difficult for dozens of families eking out a living at subsistence level half a century before.

'We were all poor, but the Ocaña family were one level below the rest of us,' recalls José Luis Romero, now a successful builder who lived with his family 'in a house just 20 metres away from Luis' as a child. He describes the Ocañas' house – two storeys, close to the central square and near the village knacker's yard – as 'a real tumbledown affair, very small'. In their house, animals, as in others in the village, would be stabled on the ground floor and the family would live on the first.

'I can remember they had one light bulb and one cable for the whole of it. When they'd finished at the bottom half of the house for the night, there was a hole in the first-floor ceiling so they could pull the light bulb up on a wire and that way they could see upstairs while they were going to bed.' There was no mains water or internal sanitation, little furniture, virtually no heating, little food, only a few houses with electricity in the village. 'There was one rich family and there was a rumour going round that the kid would get to sleep in a real cot. The rest of us weren't sleeping in donkeys' troughs – not quite – but almost.'

By the time Ocaña was four he had a brother and sister, Antonio and Amparo. Eventually there would be six Ocaña children, but in an era when international observers estimated that Spain had up to a 50 per cent working-class infant mortality rate, the fourth to be born, Marino, died at just two months old. Romero says that there was never actually a famine in the village – unlike in the towns after Spain's Civil War of 1936 to 1939, rural Spain fared comparatively well in the so-called 'Years of Hunger' – but 'we were never too far off being hungry'.

Just one economic rung further down, however, Ocaña recounts in his biography having to share his food with his brothers and sisters – and his stomach rumbling after each meal. Meat, he says, was a luxury they rarely enjoyed. 'They would have lived off their working of the fields, getting firewood,' says Romero. 'Some of us had a pig or a donkey and some olive trees. They owned two or three hectares, where you'd plant cereals and have, above all, a vegetable garden, for cucumbers and tomatoes. Essentially we were agriculturally self-sufficient. And if you had bread, you ate it, but not many people had it.

'It was a poor village in a poor region, and that's despite the fact that it was the most important village in the area, with its own market, law courts and so on. Although that's all moved to Cuenca now.' Many of the fields outside Priego have gone back to nature again, because 'people don't care for them any more'.

Romero is one of the very few people left alive who recalls Luis Ocaña prior to the family following the well-trodden path of exile from Priego. 'Luis was just one of the dozens of kids who'd be roaming round the village playing games. I can remember he was exceptionally snotty – it used to reach down to his middle at times!' He also recalls Ocaña with 'terrible scabs and scars on his knees, but that was just because the roads were so badly paved and whenever you fell you'd cut yourself a lot'.

Even then, he was not a person who accepted authority lightly. 'At [primary] school, if I was someone who got into trouble, then he was one of those who'd play up to the teacher even more.' Within two years of his starting school, though, the Ocañas had gone. 'I can remember when they quit the village, a lorry came round for the furniture – and the donkeys.' Ocaña's father's family in particular were not pleased with their son's decision to leave for France, 'but when Luis became a cyclist and started winning the Tour, that changed quick enough'.

Ocaña's house itself collapsed years ago; all that now remains is empty wasteland. 'New foundations were put down and the local cycling Federation came round' – about 18 years ago – 'and [1988 Tour winner] Pedro Delgado, too, so Pedro could lay the first stone of a house or building that was supposed to act as some kind of clubhouse for local cyclists there. But it's never been built,' Romero says sadly.

Still standing, though, is Luis Ocaña's tower house, built for him by Romero shortly after Ocaña won the Tour in 1973. A solid stone construction that is still inhabited – to judge by the full washing lines stretching from the highest crenellation to another opposite – it stands on a promontory high above the gorge. However, Ocaña had to sell the building when he ran into tax problems in Spain after retiring, and, on top of that, he had to deal with amateur burglars. 'He put all the furniture in store because kids were breaking in there half the time when he was away,' Romero says. 'He'd come back from his home [near Mont-de-Marsan] often enough, maybe two or three times a year, but they'd still get in there.'

As a builder, it was only natural that Romero should construct the now weather-worn monument, made out of local stone and iron, of Ocaña on his bike close to the village's dilapidated central park. On it there is a roll call of his major victories, inside it an urn containing half of his ashes. (Appropriately enough for a rider with such deeply entwined French and Spanish roots, the remainder were scattered at Nogaro, Ocaña's final French residence.) Most of the family – like Luis' mother, who returned from France in old age – have either died or now left for Cuenca or gone further afield and Ocaña's siblings remain in France. Only a few cousins – such as one on his mother's side, Virginia, who runs a fruit and vegetable shop – now remain in Priego. 'Somebody always leaves flowers there at the memorial, but nobody knows who,' Romero adds.

There is also an Avenida Luis Ocaña, a broad avenue running almost the entire length of the more recently built upper edge of the village. In the windswept cemetery just above Priego, the name Ocaña may not be on any of the crypt doors – that would be reserved for the better-off families – but it is present in force on a cluster of gravestones in one corner, mingled with Romeros and Caballeros. The name Ocaña can also be seen on a small cross, jammed between two graves, that acts as an indication that the plots for future burials already belong to that family. Curiously enough, Pernia – Ocaña's mother's name – is not so well represented, even if the Pernias were equally as much of a 'clan' as the Ocañas in Priego.

'There are at least five different families here all called the same,' says Adelina, herself a Pernia and serving at the bar of that name in the centre of the village. The bar has a photograph of a besuited and grinning Ocaña standing among the olive groves outside the village. Adelina was apparently friends with the rider but that is as far as the connection goes: 'we're not related to him'.

The food on offer locally is substantial fare – thick vegetable soups or slabs of pork in garlic, suitable for long days in the fields but not for the faint-hearted: in one bar they offer 'half a lamb's head' as a *tapa* (snack) with each drink. Yet if the food is robust enough, the village itself seems to be sinking: when the Ocaña family left, Priego's population stood at 3,000, and was dropping fast. Forty years later, it continues to shrink with just under half that total remaining.

Where once there were more than three dozen potters, each with their own shop, now there are only four and the basket makers have almost all gone, too. The tourist information boards informing walkers of Priego's three rivers within the village bounds, its numerous vultures and their nests on adjoining cliffs in the gorge, and the three religious celebrations a year that mark the village's social highpoints are all partly destroyed, tatty affairs. A second park halfway down the valley contains swings and benches marooned in long reed grass. 'We've still got 19 bars,' one local businessman tells me, 'though heaven knows how. Most of the young people here are unemployed. When people ask me how the village gets by economically, I ask myself the same question.'

Although claims exist to the contrary, Romero insists that the departure of Ocaña was not, as was the case for hundreds of thousands of families in Spain, precipitated by Luis' parents having any allegiance with the losing side in the Civil War. 'He was a Nationalist, we all were round here,' he recalls. But supporting Franco did not in any case guarantee anyone a decent living and even if Romero recalls 'a certain degree of dissatisfaction within the family when they left', like so many other Spanish rural families of the time, and even today, the Ocañas had no real choice.

In 1951, Luis' father began the first of a series of moves that would eventually see the Ocañas settle in France. A friend found him a job working as a miner in the tunnels that were being blasted for hydroelectric stations in the Aran Valley in the Spanish Pyrenees, close to the source of the River Garonne. Less than a decade before, Aran had witnessed the one serious military challenge made by the Republicans to dislodge Franco from power after losing to him in the Civil War: but it ended, once again, in absolute defeat and exile in France and beyond. Seven years later, the Ocañas were to follow the same path as the defeated Republicans back into the neighbouring country – but, according a very close family source, for economic rather than political reasons.

First, though, the family quit Priego, when Ocaña's father decided the mining work was stable enough for the entire family to make the 300-kilometre move north-east to the Aran Valley. Their first house, in the hamlet of Vila close to the skiing town of Vielha, was in an even worse state than the one they had left behind in Priego, but at least the family now had one stable income. And, with time, as Ocaña's father switched from mining to building jobs, his monthly pay packet improved slightly as well: given that there was another mouth to feed when Luis' little brother (also christened Marino) appeared, this was probably just as well.

Luis' school problems continued, however. After falling out so badly with the teacher in Vila that one day he came home covered in bruises from the beating she had given him, the Ocañas decided to take drastic action. At seven they decided Luis was old enough to make a daily lone six-kilometre hike, on foot and across country, to a different school, run by monks this time, in nearby Vielha. The journey itself was demanding, particularly when the snowdrifts towered over his head in winter and with no money in the family to spare to buy Luis a warm coat. But occasionally Ocaña would be able to hitch a lift on the back of a lorry taking workers and building materials to the hydroelectric plants, and at least Ocaña's education was no longer marred by conflicts with his teachers.

Perhaps understandably given his hour-long trudge to and from school, Ocaña first became captivated by the idea of cycling when travelling between Vielha and Vila. From the back of one of the works lorries, Ocaña watched a cyclist making the most of the vehicle's wake, giving him an opportunity to witness man and machine working in unison for some time. Tellingly, given his future obsession with bike technology, as he recounts it in his autobiography, he was as much struck by the frame itself – shiny grey chrome – as by the rider's 'smooth cadence and elegant poise on the bike ... one day I dreamed of being like him'.

Duly inspired, Ocaña's first bike ride came a few days later when he 'borrowed' one left at a crossroads near his home for a quick spin. Almost immediately, and not surprisingly given his lack of riding experience, he had a spectacular crash.

'It was this beautiful bike, with a red frame, left where we used to wait for the lorry lifts to school,' Ocaña would later recall. 'Every day it was there, and every day I would stare at it. One day I couldn't resist any longer and I grabbed it and got on it. But I almost immediately crashed into somebody, we both took a good knock when we fell.' While it would be overstating it to claim the accident was an omen for his future career, the young Ocaña's desire to push the boat out with no regard for personal safety was certainly a foretaste of things to come.

***

The 15-kilometre D2 road from the bustling market town Aire-sur-l'Adour to Le Houga in south-west France is hardly a spectacular affair. A *départemental*, or back road, running mostly along the border of the Landes region – miles and miles of huge, somewhat eerie, silent pine forests on the flatlands south of Bordeaux and the slightly hillier Gers province a little further east – it snakes gently past well-established bungalows, broad cabbage fields and a handful of vineyards producing Armagnac. There are fields with wire fences containing small, sturdy geese sitting in sociable groups, blissfully unaware of their approaching fate as producers of the *foie gras* delicacy that is a staple of the local economy.

But what really catches the eye is the grassy banking, rising perhaps six or seven metres, of an oval-shaped structure on the outskirts of Aire-sur-l'Adour. Nearby, a vast green hangar that acts as a sports hall gives a clue to its purpose. The banking houses the local outdoor velodrome for Aire-sur-l'Adour's club, the Vélo Club Aturin. And the simple words on the plaque at the tiny but sturdy-looking ticket office at the gate give away the name of the local star: *Merci Luis Ocaña*, they read, and, given that the D2 was the road which Ocaña rode countless times from his home in Le Houga to his first cycling club at Aire-sur-l'Adour, the velodrome's builders could hardly have chosen a more appropriate location.

Le Houga was the final destination of the Ocaña family after leaving Priego eight years earlier. Ocaña was 15 and now had four younger brothers and sisters, with a fifth sibling still to come. In between was a three-year-spell at Magnan, a hilltop village five kilometres east of Le Houga but far smaller, with just 500 inhabitants.

While not particularly appealing these days – its most noticeable defining characteristic is an A road heaving with farm traffic that splits it into two equally unremarkable halves – Ocaña nonetheless described Magnan as 'paradise'. His family had not come there to appreciate the views, or lack of them, though; rather, he recalled it as 'the first place I had lived in where we could fill our stomachs to the brim with food'.

The family's arrival in a foreign country had followed an almost identical pattern to their leaving Priego for Vielha – first Luis *padre* heading off alone to check out both the job and living conditions, then some six months later the rest of the family joining him. The contact this time came via one Uncle Candido, married to one of his mother's sisters and living in France for a few years: the employment was in the headquarters of a farming collective, first as a woodcutter and later as a warehouseman.

Uncle Candido had more to offer than just a job: to Ocaña's delight, he discovered that his cousins, Angele and Marie, and their parents had no fewer than four bikes. For Luis, bikes became a means of finding solitude, away from the constant racket and mayhem of a cramped family home filled with noisy children. 'When I rode away in the forest and the birds sang,' Ocaña would later say, 'it felt as if they were singing me their best romantic song, following me down the road. This was one of the rare moments of my childhood when I actually felt happy.'

If home was noisy bedlam, school for Ocaña was no refuge. Spanish immigrants were numerous in the south of France at the time and, despite Ocaña quickly learning French, racism – in his case, in the shape of bullying and being spat at at school – was prevalent. Unlike the previous Spanish winner of the Tour de France, Federico Bahamontes, who started riding a bike purely as a way of boosting his black-market dealings by transporting goods from the countryside to Toledo, for Ocaña the bike was something that put the material world – of exile, rejection and that nagging fear of poverty – at a greater distance. At the same time, after years of being uprooted from one village to another, not to mention one country to another, when on the bike it was Ocaña who, for the first time in his life, was in control of his own destiny. His bike, in short, embodied glorious, inconsequential freedom – and that was something, throughout his life, that he was never prepared to change or sacrifice, no matter the cost.

Small wonder, then, that as soon as Ocaña started making money, albeit a pittance helping his father at carpentry and local woodcutters after he quit school at 14, one of his first purchases was a cream-coloured Automoto bike. His opportunities to use it, though, risked being increasingly limited: having learned the basics of the trade with his father, Ocaña began serving an apprenticeship with a local carpenter, Michel Ducos, in Aire-sur-l'Adour.

For all their different backgrounds and attitudes to racing, Bahamontes played an unconscious part in inspiring Ocaña to move towards stepping up his game in the sport. In the winter of 1959, Ocaña's father took his family on their first trip back to Priego for eight years, and from there they went on to Madrid to watch Bahamontes and other great stars of the time in action at the capital's velodrome. Ocaña, by then 14, described himself as starstruck: 'Spain was at Bahamontes' feet … and I myself drew a picture of Bahamontes from the photos in the program and stuck it to my bike.'

The next step in moving away from carpentry and into more serious bike racing was his obtaining, at 16, a racing licence. Ocaña did this despite opposition from his parents, who could not see the point of him wasting his time on sport, but with the full backing – bizarrely enough – of Michel Ducos, his employer. Ducos was a huge cycling fan, to the point where he cast a blind eye if Ocaña stayed out too long on one of the daily lunchtime or evening training rides that he would carry out religiously after 6 p.m. each day. In the end Ocaña faked his parents' signature on his first racing licence – a cadet's licence with the Aire-sur-l'Adour club after his father refused to cooperate – and after Ducos gave him five months' pay in advance he then purchased his first racing bike.

Ocaña's talent did not take long to shine through. Like his hero Bahamontes, who won the second race in which he took part, Ocaña missed out on his first ever race but hit the bull's-eye at the next attempt.

As chance would have it, that victory was in Bretagne-de-Marsan, the same village where, eight years later, he would buy a plot of land in 1968 for the construction of his first family home. Ocaña had no way of knowing but, as he raised his arms in victory that day, rather than being 'the Spaniard from Cuenca' he had turned a definitive corner towards both a career in cycling and gaining the nickname he would have all his life: the 'Spaniard of Mont-de-Marsan'.

2

OCAÑA OR OCANA?

The notebooks are all in order. Page after page, Pietro Cescutti has kept everything he used as Luis Ocaña's trainer when he was an amateur, from 1964 to 1967. And behind him, on the middle of his brightly lit cellar wall and perfectly preserved under a plastic wrapping, hangs the yellow jersey Cescutti received at the foot of the 1973 Champs-Elysées podium when Luis Ocaña stepped down, unzipped it and handed it to him. As the greatest possible prize cycling has to offer, there can be no more powerful reminder of what a bike rider who had passed through Cescutti's hands could then achieve, 40 years before.

Cescutti, now in his nineties, briefly touches the plastic as we walk in, not it seems particularly reverentially but, rather, out of habit. The notebooks, start lists and prize lists which act as landmarks on the pathway of Ocaña's amateur career from 1964 to 1967 are in a bulging, shiny white folder in a cupboard underneath. Among them, in perhaps five or six dozen, neatly stapled pages of A4 paper, are all the typed-out instructions he gave Ocaña as a coach: not just the training programmes for his off-season in his final years as an amateur, but everything from a specific series of instructions on how to eliminate the 'dead point' – the point at each revolution of the pedals where no energy is transmitted – down to what he could or could not eat.

There, too, are sheafs of paper containing the abandoned projects for his star protégé: the joint investment and building plans for the hotel for Mont-de-Marsan, for example, and all the application forms for Ocaña to change nationality from Spanish to French. In other, smaller folders are those of other professional riders Cescutti guided through the years and up the rungs of the Stade Montois cycling club in Mont-de-Marsan. But the thickest is Ocaña's or, as Cescutti's version of his name on the front cover of the folder has it, Ocana, with no tilde (the 'gn' sound in English) over the n, making for a French version of the same name.

As for the training, in the early months of 1964, for example – when Ocaña was not yet 20 and had only started his first season with Cescutti – the intensity is anything but high: each week, from 1 January, when his training programme started, he has just 40 kilometres mid-week and another 40 on the Saturday. However, bearing in mind that he would be doing a full day of intense physical labour in the carpentry shop, as experienced British sports director and former pro rider John Herety says, 'There is no need whatsoever for any more than that. At that age and doing that much work, you wouldn't want any more.' However, if the programme is fairly minimalist, the tone is not at all light-hearted: 'Ride with an easy gear, 45x20,' reads a terse side note, before recommending Ocaña get the ride in on a Wednesday so that 'in case of bad weather' it can be pushed forward to Thursday or Friday.

Up until the end of January, the number of kilometres rises by ten each week, with the gearing also becoming slightly tougher. Then, in February, Cescutti adds in another factor: sprint series every two or three kilometres on an extra 15-kilometre ride each Saturday. At this point the detail is suddenly much richer: apart from the gearing he should use, also clearly marked are the distances (100 metres each time, building up to 200 metres by the beginning of March), different circuits he should use and even how he should breathe between the sprint efforts: in through the nose and out through the mouth.

Far stricter, in Cescutti's book at least, is diet – and the eating process from beginning to end. Some of his theories seem bizarre – as little drinking as possible during the meal (with the word 'during' underlined), for example, or having no milk with your coffee. But they are nothing if not thorough. 'Watch your dental hygiene, teeth and the workings of your stomach' is how he rather delicately puts it, after advising Ocaña to 'eat slowly, chewing each mouthful'.

The number of foodstuffs that are strongly recommended *not* to be consumed takes up nearly two-thirds of a page. Everything from powdered milk to mutton, red meat, packet soups and snails is on the banned list. ('All molluscs' is added in again a little later, as if just to reinforce the point about the dangers of consuming a stray *escargot*.) This is followed by strict advice against courgettes, cucumbers, peas, sauerkraut, under-ripe fruit, overfresh bread, too cold drinks, crêpes, chocolate … 'Do not trust fizzy drinks,' it sternly warns. It comes almost as a relief to find that Ocaña does get the green light for a portion of rice pudding in the mornings – but only if he is racing.

Mixed in with three pages of advice on diet are ideas well ahead of their time. For example, Ocaña is barred from eating a steak for breakfast when in a race – as many riders did. Rather, the instructions tell him to eat light snacks at intervals during it, so as 'not to tax your digestion'.

When I ask Cescutti who had helped him to build up such innovative ideas and all his other knowledge, he looks somewhat irritated at the suggestion he might have had help: 'nobody. It all came down to experience.' That experience was accumulated over years as the President of the Mont-de-Marsan club, 'and just about every other job in it, too, at one point or another.

'When I die, I have left instructions that I will send it all over to Josiane,' Cescutti – still without an ounce of excess fat on him and still, until very recently, going on bike rides – says without looking remotely worried at the prospect.

But it is clear – from the shelves of documents on Ocaña and his racing, the palmarès of his professional career, the bike frames and the jersey taking pride of place – that, as Ocaña's sporting 'godfather' in so many ways, the Spaniard still lives on inside him. It does not seem to matter that it is more than 45 years since they first met and 20 since Ocaña died. In fact, with a painting by Ocaña on the wall (and another upstairs in the living room); with those naturalisation papers in perfect order and ready to be handed over for processing by the corresponding department of 1960s French state bureaucracy; and an ancient single bed, still made up, in Cescutti's basement for a stray Spanish rider to sleep over when necessary, it truly feels as if a small, brightly lit window back to half a century ago remains stubbornly, and perhaps painfully, wedged open.

***

Cescutti's own life story could fill a book, even prior to meeting Ocaña. His parents were Italian émigrés who arrived in France in 1922 when he was just one year old. As masons, his father and many of his compatriots found plenty of work in the north of the country repairing buildings destroyed in the First World War. After his father befriended a businessman from the Landes, when the post-war construction boom finally started to diminish, Cescutti's parents came south to see what work they could get through their business acquaintance and they ended up living in Mont-de-Marsan.

'I can remember seeing my first Tour de France there in 1933 or 1934 when it came through the town,' Cescutti recalled. 'I was impressed by the masks of dust and sweat, their black welder's glasses, the two spare tyres criss-crossing their backs, their metal drinks cans hanging from the handlebar tape ... by those following cars and the boss, Henri Desgrange, looking like a Roman emperor standing erect in his Hotchkiss car, by the atmosphere and the applause of the crowd who were looking to recognise the favourites of the time: [1931 and 1934 Tour winner Antonin] Magne,

[25-time Tour stage winner] André Leduc, [1933 Tour winner] Georges Speicher ... the crowd were held back by a double cordon of Senegalese troops, with their fez hats and leggings, channelling the course through the town.'

As part of the local cycling club when the Second World War broke out – 'I won three races in 1938' – Cescutti is one of the few riders left who can provide a record of what it was like racing in France during the early part of the German occupation. 'Races were thin on the ground in 1940 and 1941 and far apart. No cars to get to them and rationed food. We'd be up early, kit and race grub in a knapsack, for Bayonne, Bordeaux, Dax or Langon. The race would almost always be for all categories, 120–150 kilometres long, often on untarmacked roads and with no broomwagon! Coming back we'd have done maybe 300–350 kilometres riding in one day, getting back to Mont-de-Marsan in the pitch dark between 10 p.m. and midnight and then we'd have one last race – with the gendarmes [enforcing the curfew] breathing down our backsides!'

Aged 20, Cescutti left France to join De Gaulle's troops in North Africa. Captured as he attempted to cross Spain, he then spent four months in a Spanish concentration camp in Miranda del Ebro and only got out, he claims, when Britain and De Gaulle agreed to pay General Franco 'a generous supply of oil in order to let us French who wanted to go to Africa leave the country'. As a result of this oil-for-men deal, Cescutti and 1,500 other Frenchmen then travelled by train to Lisbon before taking a French boat to Casablanca. Eight months in Morocco and four months in England, training north of Hull in Yorkshire as a sapper, then followed – 'I can speak Eeenglish very well,' he says mid-interview with an accent that would have done Inspector Clouseau proud – after which came a landing at Utah Beach, in Normandy, on 31 July 1944, 'in the Leclerc Second DB [Free French Armoured Brigade] where we linked up with General Patton's Americans'.

Although there were some considerable regrets that the Second DB were not involved in the D-Day landings, 'we took part in the liberation of Paris and Strasbourg, where we were among the first in there. And from there we went on to the Berchtesgaden where I was one of the first to get into Hitler's residence at the Berghof. General Leclerc had stopped his troops about a kilometre out and, as he thought it might be mined, he sent us sappers ahead to clear them.

'But the whole place had been bombed out two days before by the Americans. Only the wine cellar was left,' he says with a smile. So too, fortunately, were its contents and Cescutti waves his head around to indicate the rather sozzled state in which he and his fellow troops celebrated VE-Day inside Hitler's residence a few days later.

Cescutti came through the war with life and limbs intact, but he paid a high price nonetheless: his digestive system was in pieces. 'I had contracted marsh fever and jaundice while in North Africa. I couldn't eat properly and, when I got home, I couldn't race any more. So I decided to do for other young riders what I was no longer able to do for myself.'

Cycling for him was all but inescapable, even at home. He married Rolande Danné, today a beaming, charmingly voluble 91-year-old and back in 1947 and 1948 a double women's Hour Record holder as well as the winner of a 350-kilometre Pyrenean marathon across the Aspin, Tourmalet, Aubisque and the Peyresourde. 'Day *and* night,' she archly points out, with what could be the slightest hint of a wink.

Then Cescutti became the trainer for Mont-de-Marsan's Stade Montois in the late 1940s. This was the town's main sports club, with 25 different sports specialities, particularly rugby, with a history stretching back to the nineteenth century. The 1950s and 1960s were the cycling branch's heyday, with the club taking 65 wins, 31 of them first category in 1952, reaching its all-time record of 31 events in a single year in 1955. In the 1960s, it had eight first-category riders at amateur level (most French clubs would have one or two at most) and around five times that number in the lower ranks.

For more than 50 years, too, the Stade Montois has produced a string of solid middle-ranking professionals: Christian Leduc, a criterium specialist in the 1960s, André Romero, twice the Best Young Rider of the Tour de France in the 1970s, and Gilbert Chaumaz, a domestique with Bernard Hinault at Renault-Elf and winner of the Mont Faron time trial in the 1977 Tour Méditerranéen ahead of Eddy Merckx, Van Impe and Poulidor. As for the club's greatest ever star, however, Ocaña was one of six Stade Montois riders who turned pro in a single year, 1968 – again a record.

As their top coach, Cescutti would keep his eye on up and coming riders from all over the region, not just Mont-de-Marsan, to bring them into the club. Ocaña, having won six to eight races a year with the Aire-sur-l'Adour VC Aturin in his late teens, was another prime candidate for a spot of inter-club 'poaching'.

Getting Ocaña on board was no easy task, however, given that Ocaña's father remained so strongly opposed to his son's racing, but Cescutti finally offered a combined package of apprenticeship at Mont-de-Marsan – six days a week with another carpenter, M. Dupéyron, and a day off for training or racing. Asked by Luis' father, presumably in a very sarcastic tone, if his son would 'be paid for enjoying himself', Cescutti finally managed to convince him by insisting that Ocaña would continue with his carpentry career, 'at which Luis was very good, as well as being an *artiste* when he was painting'.

He also pointed out that other great riders such as Jacques Anquetil, despite humble working-class beginnings like Ocaña's, had ended up as champions – and multimillionaires. Cescutti even pushed the boat out and claimed that Ocaña had it in him to win the Tour de France. After much deliberation, Luis' parents finally gave their consent, although his father, who had an almost unhealthy (if understandable, given how poor their life had been) obsession with his children having stable jobs, pointed out that his son still owed nine days' work to M. Ducos and would have to do them before changing employers.

So for the next three years Ocaña's 'home' was a cheap hotel room in Mont-de-Marsan. 'No palace' was his own laconic description of his new digs. Le Houga was close enough for Ocaña to see a lot of his family but, at 19, it was another major shift towards independence and his professional cycling career. If Luis' parents represented the big obstacle to convincing Ocaña to leave the family nest, Ocaña himself needed little persuasion. 'I'd seen him in third-category [amateur] races while he was at Aire [sur-l'Adour]. I kept an eye because he was a good rider, eh?' Cescutti says. 'But at Aire he didn't have team-mates to work for him, he was alone. Come to Stade Montois, I said, and you'll get riders to help you.

'Over the next three years he moved up to first category and then [in 1967] he became an *indépendant* – allowed, as a top amateur, to take part in a certain number of professional races. In Ocaña's case this was at Mercier with sports director Antonin Magne, former double winner of the Tour de France and director for French greats Raymond Poulidor in the 1960s and, a decade before, Louison Bobet.

Magne was a character in his own right, both eccentric and brilliant – he used to dress up in a Breton smock to remind riders of his roots. But Cescutti, who proudly lists the six Stade Montois riders he guided to professional status, remains furious with him for failing to recognise Ocaña's full talent and signing him.

'If Magne had listened to me then Ocaña would have won the Tour de France as a Frenchman, because I had prepared all the documents for his nationalisation.

'Ocaña wanted to turn pro, but Magne didn't want to know. He said that Ocaña wasn't mature enough', which, given that

21

Ocaña was 23, seems surprising. But instead, 'Fagor were waiting in the wings and hired him, on condition he stayed Spanish. If Magne had listened to me then he wouldn't have been "the Spaniard of Mont-de-Marsan" but "Ocana" – with no ñ – "of Mont-de-Marsan".'

In any case, without Cescutti, Ocaña would almost certainly never have moved up the ladder from promising junior and second-category amateur to professional. It was not only that Cescutti made sure Ocaña had the opportunity to race; without Cescutti's basic advice and his ability to communicate with one of the sport's most un-cooperative stars, there is a very strong case for saying Ocaña would never have been as successful.

When asked about his role in setting Ocaña en route to stardom, it is typical of Cescutti that he plays down his role, but there is no doubt he held the key. 'I found him a job here as a joiner and I got him to come over and live in Mont-de-Marsan so I could keep a close eye on him,' he says baldly.

'But he was *difficult* to give advice to,' he adds, stressing heavily the word 'difficult'. 'I would tell him to do one thing but he would do the opposite.' Ocaña, he says, *'faisait des conneries'*, a French expression that is hard to translate – perhaps 'pissed about' is the closest. 'And then when he came back he would say' – and here he puts on an accent of a Spaniard speaking, as Ocaña did, with the thick south-west French accent of the Landes on top of his original language – '"*quel bordel* [what a shambles], you were right".' And he cackles with laughter at the memory.

Was Ocaña very Spanish, then, despite living so long in France? 'He had more the spirit of a *matador* than of a *chanteur*' is how Cescutti recalls it, 'a very proud man.'

Their relationship, starting off with Ocaña's seven years in the Stade Montois, seems to have been very close but formal. Ocaña would always address Cescutti, his senior in age, as 'vous' rather than 'tu', for example. But Cescutti, even while maintaining a distance, knew Ocaña well enough to be able to develop his weak points and iron out the inconsistencies to become a good all-rounder. Equally crucially, as the light training programme for January 1964 shows, Cescutti – having seen that stage racing was Ocaña's forte – did not try to push him too hard, too soon in that area. And as for track, which 'Luis didn't like', he didn't push him at all. Cescutti was aware that a softly-softly approach, rather than shouting him out, was definitely more effective when it came to keeping Ocaña on board.

'He was a born attacker, so I tried to motivate him about his time trialling, to get that as honed as possible. He could climb, he was good on the flat. It was only his sprinting that let him down. I advised him about everything, from diet to tactics.' More than anything else, Cescutti – like sports director Maurice De Muer later on – possessed something that always seemed to push Ocaña up another notch in terms of performance: he understood him well. But he agrees, slightly sadly and slightly proudly, that it was attacking more than winning that Ocaña liked.

There was never any question of trying to switch him over towards the Classics, though. 'Above all he felt best in races where you had to race, recover in the evening and race again every day' – in other words, stage racing. 'And *voilà*,' Cescutti says, as if once again seeing that particular option closed off for his former protégé.

Teaching Ocaña how to attack more effectively on a mountain climb, though, was one area where Cescutti had a big influence and, lesson duly learned, Ocaña would apply that particular tactic when the roads steepened throughout his career. 'I taught him to accelerate slowly and steadily when he tried to attack, rather than "sprinting" with a sudden effort that would be harder to maintain. All sorts of different tricks.' He would equally try to rein in Ocaña from getting overambitious and pushing himself too hard, teaching him 'not to use such huge gears as he sometimes wanted to in time trials'. He was also aware, he says, that training Ocaña involved a delicate balance between strengthening his time trialling – an exercise in self-control if ever there was – without smothering his desire to launch unpredictable, all-out attacks – in other words, the spontaneity that so unnerved his rivals.

'He was a real tough nut, though, be it for training or racing. But he wasn't so good at moving in the bunch, he always needed' – as Cescutti had promised him as part of the 'poaching operation' – 'two or three riders to protect him.'

But, although there were two or three support staff at the Stade Montois, with Ocaña's boss, M. Perol, occasionally lending a hand, it is no exaggeration to say that the person that held the club together was Cescutti, from providing race tactics right down to driving the riders to races as far afield as Bayonne. And it was Cescutti who persuaded Ocaña that he could turn professional, given that Ocaña 'was not really too sure'. That the Italian does not take all the credit for converting Ocaña into a rider capable of taking on Merckx – saying that it was De Muer, his director at BIC, and Ocaña who delved into technological advances as deeply as they could, including the use of titanium frames – only lends more credence to Cescutti's positioning himself as central to Ocaña's progress in other areas.

But Ocaña was not one to forget his debts, Cescutti insists. 'Maybe others made some proposals to try and "poach" him back, but he never answered them.' And the greatest proof of that loyalty was that, when he won in Paris, it was Cescutti who received the final yellow jersey of the race.

'When he won the Tour de France, three days before the race was finished, he called me to go up to Paris so that I could follow the race with De Muer in the lead team car,' he says proudly, 'as well as the celebrations that followed. He always remembered, Luis, where he had come from.'

During the four years as an amateur with Cescutti, Ocaña accelerated the speed with which he jumped upwards through the ranks – from second category in 1964 to Hors Catégorie (the level beyond first category) in January 1965. But what impresses the most is the dramatic improvement in quality of his victories and placings in the face of much tougher opposition. Whereas previously in the VC Aturin he would take part mainly in local events round Mont-de-Marsan, as early as spring 1965 Ocaña's name began to pop up in semi-professional events, like the Mont Faron hill climb – previously the private domain of another Spaniard, no less a figure than Federico Bahamontes – where Luis secured a notable fifth (and also secured rival Jacques Anquetil's autograph at the same time). At the GP de France in Laval, 600 kilometres further north, near Rennes, Ocaña took second behind one of Britain's most promising time triallists of the era, Peter Hill – who later raced the Tour de France with the GB selection in 1967. At the amateur GP Nations – France's biggest single time trial event in the Parc des Princes velodrome in Paris and at the time a sprawling day-long competition with all kinds of professional and amateur events – Ocaña finished seventh in his category.

1966 saw him spread his wings yet further, taking his first victory in Spain, the Vuelta a Bidasoa, one of the Basque Country's most prestigious amateur stage races. Both in Mont Faron and in the GP Nations, he went two places better than in 1965: third on the hill climb and fifth in the Paris race.

His final season as an amateur saw Ocaña diversify to the point where he took wins in the GP Nations as well as one of France's most difficult events at that level, the Tour du Roussillon. Most surprisingly of all, given his dislike of track racing, was a Madison victory at Palma de Mallorca with – and this again is an indication of his rising status – none other than Jacques Anquetil as a partner. But the most impressive achievement was the brief spell that he raced with the pros at the Midi Libre – thanks to Mercier's co-sponsoring of both a professional squad and the Stade Montois – where, in one of the toughest warm-up events for the Tour de France, he took sixth.

More than results, though, for Cescutti what defined Ocaña in one crucial way and the thing that separated him from the rest throughout his entire life 'was the way he considered Merckx. He was the only one who thought of Merckx as the man who had to be beaten. And *voilà*,' he says with simple finality: Merckx was somebody who caused him both to raise his game and to stand out from the rest. But that did not mean the two were similar in his eyes.

According to Cescutti – and this is perhaps the crucial difference between the two greatest riders of their generation – Ocaña was prepared to recognise his own limitations, was prepared to recognise he was 'only human'. Merckx, once described as 'half man, half bike', was not. 'Ocaña could accept he could be beaten, Merckx never did. Luis could never understand that that bloody bastard always wanted to win everything, always to win everything. He never left anything to anyone, not even in the criterium, whereas Luis knew how to give races as "presents" to other riders.'

As for the legacy that Ocaña left behind at the Stade Montois, his name acted as a huge draw for riders across France. Cescutti recounts that Chaumaz, who grew up in the Savoie on the other side of the country, 'wrote to me saying he wanted to be in Ocaña's club and he turned up one day at the clubhouse with a suitcase in one hand and a bike in the other. Two years later he was a pro. All because he wanted to come to the club which had had Ocaña as a member.' Nor was Ocaña the last Spanish émigré to pass through his hands: Romero, born in Granada in 1950, moved to Mont-de-Marsan with his parents in the 1960s and was inspired by Ocaña's example to start racing. He rode in the same team as Ocaña, BIC, in 1974 and even went one step further than Ocaña by taking French nationality.

Although the Tour and the Vuelta are the races for which Ocaña is best remembered, in some ways his happiest era on the bike came when he was an amateur. Neither the bronchitis nor the perpetual liver problems had yet put in an appearance. And as Cescutti reports, Ocaña never had a single serious crash when he was an amateur. Rather than being famous for being unlucky, he had a reputation for completely the opposite. 'That came later,' Cescutti explains. He remains all too aware of the bad luck that bedevilled his most brilliant protégé, the missed opportunities and the wasted chances. Among them were the two Tours he feels that Ocaña could have won – 1971 and 1972 – as well as another Vuelta and another Dauphiné Libéré, and Cescutti's plan for Ocaña's French nationality (prepared right down to the letter of application to the local *député* [Member of Parliament], who had to give the naturalisation his blessing). For a man who had no choice but to live through cycling vicariously, that cannot be easy to accept – even now.

3

THE OTHER SIDE OF THE DOOR

'The most decisive moment of my career? When I threw a hammer at my boss' – Luis Ocaña, November 1977

According to Josiane, for her the worst parts of Ocaña's accident-plagued life were not the crashes in themselves. It was the moment when she would find herself standing outside a hospital ward door, still unaware of what her husband had managed to do to himself this time. 'I never knew what I'd find on the other side.'

The worst accident of all, she says, came after Ocaña had finished racing, when he was a TV commentator for the 1979 Tour de France. His injuries were so bad it was not until midnight that Josiane was told she could go through and see him. But as she made her solitary way towards a ward door in a hospital somewhere in the Alps, this time, she says, she was hardly able to imagine what condition her husband would be in. Because by rights he ought not to have been there: he should have been in the mortuary. And that she knew only too well, because she had seen the accident take place.

'It was the rest day in the Alps, it was on a kind of racing circuit.

'They were in teams of two, my husband was supposed to do the circuit on a motorbike and another guy in a car. And I was standing around with them for a while, and then they went off to the start and it seems like at the last minute my husband suddenly decided to get in the car as a co-pilot. Which was bad luck in itself, because why he did that I just don't know.

28

'Anyway, I was standing around with friends and not really paying much attention and suddenly I saw the car go hurtling down the mountain – the gendarmerie report later said it had fallen down 250 metres in one go – and I said to myself, "the people in that car are dead".

'So everybody was getting nervous, I started to say "my husband, where is he, I can't see him?" and I couldn't see him, I couldn't see him and, you know, you start to have a hunch about something, and then suddenly, in a flash, when I saw that everybody was looking at me, the people had started to find out and they were all looking at me, then I realised he had been inside the car …

'He had mainly head injuries, they had fallen 246 metres headlong and it was mainly his head which had taken … his head was three times its normal size, I never thought it could get back to normal, it was horrible. He had fractures in his arms, all over his upper body.

'When you look at it all, you realise that during his entire career, for all he crashed so often he never broke a single bone. And from then, in the 1979 Tour up until his death, he broke it all. Absolutely everything.

'Do you know what he said to me in that hospital bed? "Forgive me. Forgive me for all the suffering I've caused you." It was the one time in his entire life he said those words to me.'

***

Given the amount of anguish and stress Luis Ocaña was, unintentionally or otherwise, going to cause Josiane during their 29-year-long relationship, one thing was probably just as well – as quickly becomes clear when, half a century later, she lifts the lid on his painfully complex personality and the relentless episodes of bad luck and upheavals throughout his life. One thing Josiane Ocaña does not lack is strength of character.

At first glance, her wafer-thin figure, elegant looks and old-world courtesy do not suggest that. But the power of her personality comes through as she describes her husband with both passion and relentless clarity. And not a little regret.

The two had met by chance at a dance at a village fête near Mont-de-Marsan. Ocaña was not yet 21, Josiane 18. In his auto-biography, he recalls that she was wearing a blue dress exactly the colour of her eyes. She remembers, now, that she and her sister were drawn to a group of three male friends because one of them had clearly recently crushed his finger – in a door, as it turned out – and his hand looked very painful. But it was Luis, having ridden and won the village's annual bike race earlier that day, who asked her to dance.

The first test of Josiane's strength of character when it came to Ocaña was from her father, who ran a local transport business: 'very strict', as Josiane recalls him, and not even willing to let his daughter go out for walks with Ocaña unaccompanied. In turn, as she recalls, Ocaña would use her, and her alone, as an outlet for his unhappiness at the latent anti-Spanish racism he encountered in the Gers and the Landes regions.

The second test of her strength of character was Cescutti. He was initially opposed to the relationship on the grounds that Josiane would turn his man away from cycling because Ocaña – whom Cescutti realised was very taken with his own good looks – would be worried about smashing up his face in a crash. Only when he realised that Josiane backed her future husband's deter-mination to turn pro and stick to cycling did he give the couple his support. Cescutti's change of stance was so definitive that he was even one of the very few guests present when they married, in the 'cyclists chapel' of Notre-Dame-de-Cyclistes, in the hamlet of La Bastide d'Armagnac a few dozen kilometres north of Mont-de-Marsan on Christmas Eve 1966.

Such strong challenges are apt to force people to decide what they want from a very early stage in a relationship, and whether the game is the worth the candle. And Josiane was – to judge from their marrying barely a year later – as smitten as Luis, and as determined to stick with him. And stick with him she did, too, when Ocaña revealed in April 1967 that he *had* to turn professional the following year, because he had fallen out with his employer – big time.

The argument between Luis and his employer, over a seemingly trivial comment – but one which surely hid greater tensions between them – had turned violent, Ocaña recalled: 'I was bashing away at a ceiling halfway up a ladder and the boss was standing there, with his hands in his pockets, watching me work. And he said, "You're going to break the light bulb that's hanging down from the ceiling." And I kept on thwacking away and, of course, I broke the light bulb. And the next thing I knew, I'd thrown a hammer at my boss.'

The hammer missed, fortunately, but Ocaña was down the ladder and down the stairs in a flash, knowing that he was out of work. It was, he later said, the most decisive moment of his cycling career 'because there was no way back'.

As Josiane agrees, Ocaña had problems not just with one particular boss but with figures of authority in general, and 'having things imposed on him. You needed to be able to know how to bring him round.' As she did, and as did M. Cescutti. 'Whatever Monsieur Cescutti said, he applied it.'

After Ocaña found himself out of work, though, it was Josiane who first had to pick up the pieces. She went out and promptly got a job as a doctor's receptionist to try to resolve any financial worries – which had increased when she discovered she was pregnant that spring. Ocaña was left with no choice but to sign for a professional team, which, after Magne's humming and haaing at Mercier, ended up being Fagor in 1968.

Josiane's initial interest in cycling was minimal. 'The only connection my family had with it was through my father. He would occasionally go to a bike race for pleasure. But I can't say that he was a huge fan,' she says, still with the same piercing look in those blue eyes that so captivated her husband. 'As for me, I was even less so. When I met Luis, when he came up to me, I didn't even know he'd been in the bike race that afternoon.' Her reason for being at the Saint Pierre du Mont fête at all was purely thanks to an aunt and uncle who lived in the village and it had been a fluke that she'd ended up at the dance afterwards. 'I'd watched the race a bit with my dad, and for once he'd let me go out that evening.' Then, when Ocaña asked if she knew who'd won, she was forced to admit she had no idea. But by that point, for one party at least it didn't really matter what she said: Ocaña recounted later that within five minutes of meeting Josiane he was – impulsive as ever – already hopelessly in love.

At what point he told her he was Spanish hardly mattered – as Josiane recalls, it was very easy to guess. Ocaña would always speak French with a mixture of a Spanish accent and the regional burr of the Gers. 'When you combined the two, he really rolled his rs,' she recalls, and those piercing blue eyes briefly twinkle.

Socially, though, it proved harder for him to integrate. According to Josiane, the racist teasing and bullying and the spitting incidents he suffered in Magnan continued later into his teens, and 'it wasn't just in class. He was really, really affected by that, and he suffered all sorts of things that he could only tell me, particularly when he came here. Afterwards, that all changed, but' – as might be expected in such a proud individual – 'he never forgot it even so.'

Ocaña's language of choice for expressing his most intimate thoughts, though, was French: Josiane says he never spoke Spanish with her, even though she is fluent in it, and, although she wanted to live in Spain, it was Ocaña who preferred them to live near Mont-de-Marsan. Equally, when he first introduced himself it was as 'Louis, not Luis,' she recalls. 'And nobody around here called him Ocaña, ever. He was Ocana.

'So at least when I met him he considered himself more French than Spanish, although that changed later, when we went there more often. He was purely Spanish in character but, as his wife for 27 years, I think overall he was more French than Spanish.

'Remember that he came here when he was 12 and was educated here. And marrying a Frenchwoman helped reinforce all of that.'

But it was not just Ocaña, with French roots at least as deep as those linking him to his birth, who was split between two countries. His entire family, Josiane recalls, conversed in French at mealtimes at home, even his mother – who spoke it the least well.

As for how the Spanish rated their exile, Josiane believes that 'he was more valued in France than he was there. God knows I love the country, and he was given a lot of recognition when he won the Tour, he was "the Spaniard from Mont-de-Marsan" … but he wasn't appreciated enough.'

The perception that he was a foreigner, no matter which country he was in, persisted throughout his life. 'He was Spanish in France and French in Spain,' she says simply. Ocaña's autobiography neatly sums up the dichotomy: it is entitled *Luis Ocana*, with the Spanish version of his first name and the French version of his surname.

Josiane believes that one possible reason why Ocaña never wanted to live in Spain was, while on both sides of the border the fans wanted to claim him as one of their own, they considered him 'either too French or too Spanish for his own good. And you could say his career suffered a bit as a result of that.'

It was not just his home and adopted nations that inspired this mass of mixed feelings in him. 'He loved his Spanish family dearly, they were sacred for him', but when it came to his father, Josiane claims, Luis 'never wanted him to come and watch him in a bike race. It even got to the point where his dad would come [and spectate], and my husband wouldn't know about it.

'And let's say that the devotion my husband had for his father only appeared *after* his father had died. During the time he was alive, he never showed it. That's something I've never managed to understand about my husband.' Indeed, when Ocaña finally won the Tour, his first port of call was not taking part in an ultra-profitable criterium in Caen, as all the other Tour stars did, but to visit his father's grave in Mont-de-Marsan.

His relationship with his mother, Josiane says, was equally dysfunctional when it came to cycling. At home, either because Luis didn't want any support, as was the case with his father, or – in that of his mother – according to Josiane, because she was unable to give it, he had none. This helps explain, among other things, the importance of Cescutti.

Josiane gives an example of how disconnected Ocaña was from his family, despite his intense love for them: 'My husband was born in 1945 and the last of my parents-in-laws' children was born in 1965, so that's 20 years' difference and also the year I met him. And one day he and a friend came round and the friend said, "Okay, we've got to get a move on because we're going to the hospital maternity ward to see Luis' [new] little brother." And I had no idea.

'So I thought the friend was kidding me and, although he [Ocaña] then told me that he had a little brother called Michel, I still didn't believe it until I actually saw him.

'In those days it was pretty rare for women to have kids at 46, and what I'm trying to say is that his mother was a woman who was immersed in her family and everything else interested her very, very little. When the last one arrived, there was already another aged five, another aged seven, another nine, another 14 …' as well as Ocaña himself.

'Outside the house, nothing interested her: if her son rode a bike, she washed his socks after a race; that would have been about the extent of it [her interest]. He certainly didn't become a bike rider thanks to his mother.'

On the other hand, Josiane feels that the role played by Cescutti was fundamental. 'It was Cescutti who helped him, oversaw what he did, got everything for him right down to filling out start forms for races. If it hadn't been for Cescutti, perhaps he would never have become a professional.'

Cescutti's guidance had its limits, though, above all once Ocaña turned pro. Ocaña had followed the diet set by his club coach while in Mont-de-Marsan – 'Cescutti even made me go on a diet,' Josiane remembers. 'It was all very strict and my husband took it so seriously.' But the tales of Ocaña's huge appetite whenever he raced suggest that he took a very different attitude to eating and drinking once he was away from home.

Yet one thing did not change: his passionate Latin temperament, which, Josiane agrees, could not help but shine through from the first day of their relationship – and, as a cyclist, it was what dominated his approach to his entire career. 'He would criticise himself a lot. But at the end of the day, my husband's biggest problem was that he never raced to win, it was purely because he liked the battle.

'He had to be in a fight of some kind, once the race had started, that was it – *c'etait parti* – and the sports director could say what he liked, he wouldn't listen, he just did whatever he wanted and, afterwards, that produced one result or another.

'He always used to say he didn't race for a palmarès. If he had done that, if he had thought things through beforehand' – planning and executing a strategy during a race – 'then he would have had a lot more victories to his name.' Two adjectives sum him up both on and off the bike, she says: impulsive and stubborn. 'And once he'd made his mind up, nobody could stop him.'

One mistake fans and journalists often make is that, because a bike rider's racing style is so often an extension of his character, they think that at home riders are exactly the same. But Josiane says that it was not the case with her husband.

'He was a lot more calm, there weren't any arguments or rows here, whereas outside ...' – and at this point she utters that particularly dismissive French 'pfffff' to indicate that it was a very different story. 'I'm not wishing to boast, but I always tried to keep him on an even keel. When he came back from a race, after he'd told me everything over three or four hours, he'd then move on to another topic.' And if verbally taking a bike race apart for four hours does not actually sound like Ocaña was quick to get the sport out of his system, at least when he did so, cycling would be completely forgotten. Equally, according to Josiane, although Ocaña would be angry with himself if he had made a mistake while racing, he was in no way neurotic about it, at least 'never at home'.

However, two subjects did prove more difficult to tease out of his system: Merckx and Ocaña's recurrent bad luck. If the subject of 'the Cannibal' (as Merckx was known) came up, sometimes it was in a humorous way: Josiane recalls that they renamed their first dog, an Alsatian called Rex, Merckx – simply because Ocaña thought it was amusing to be able to order it around. 'He particularly liked telling it to lie at his feet.' But the subject of Merckx came up more often because, as Josiane says, 'it was a real, real war.

'Even for me it was hard because they didn't really become friends until almost the end of his life, when Eddy helped my husband with his business exporting our Armagnac to Belgium. Not in the slightest. There was never any friendship, none at all. People can say anything they like but right up until the final years, even after they had both stopped racing, they might say "hello" but it wasn't anything special.' Not even, Josiane says, the most famous reconciliation – on a plane to Lausanne in 1974 after a criterium – managed to heal the wounds. 'During their careers there was no warmth between them in the slightest.'

Merckx, then, was a painful but apparently inescapable topic, even at home in Mont-de-Marsan. But if Ocaña's misfortune at having Merckx as a rival was one issue that affected not just the Spaniard but every other bike rider of his generation, the bad luck which seemingly singled out Ocaña time after time was a different story.

Ocaña, she says, realised that he was seemingly pursued by ill fortune, that it was 'a little bit … set against him, he had no choice, he would even say, "Damn it, what have I done [to deserve so much bad luck]?" Whatever he did there was always a problem. When he won the Tour in 1973, he did five kilometres of the first stage and a dog runs out across the road and only one rider hits it. And why? I just don't know, that wasn't his fault, he'd done nothing then.'

'Just tell me why,' Josiane says, but she has never been able to come up with an answer. 'There was something, I don't believe in superstition and all of that, but I still wonder.' It was, as she says, 'a very long list' of misfortune.

One constant of his bad luck was his health issues, which Josiane says plagued him throughout his career. 'He was extremely fragile, that came principally from having delicate lungs … a real handicap.' But there were also, she reveals, liver problems from a very early age, with visits to doctors in San Sebastián and Bilbao to try to resolve them.

Asked if Ocaña had any regrets when he looked back on his career, Josiane shakes her head, but then remembers one – and it is not, perhaps surprisingly, anything to do with failing, finally, to beat Merckx outright in a Tour. Rather, it is the lack of recognition from the Tour – in the tangible, physical form of a trophy – that he most resented.

'It was in 1973, when he won the Tour. Normally you get a cup or an apartment, something, but my husband got nothing at all. Not even one tiny plaque. That really annoyed him, and when he thought about it he would get angry to a degree I've rarely seen in him particularly when it came to material things, which he wasn't at all bothered about normally.

'But that did really get him upset, it made him so angry. And so afterwards he said what had happened and they did give him a

plaque for the Tour' – which she shows me, a singularly unim-
pressive silver trophy about six inches tall – 'and that made him
even crosser.'

I tell her I am little puzzled that Ocaña was not more outspoken
more often, given his character. But, curiously, Ocaña was never
one to show his feelings when he won, Josiane says. 'There was
never any huge explosion of joy and I was surprised, too. But
perhaps because he won so often, it just became natural.' And
perhaps, too, as Josiane says, the real interest throughout his career
was not winning but the fight for the victory itself. Unless, of
course, the opponent who lost was a certain Belgian.

4

REMEMBERING 'CHEPAS'

One very wet, stormy winter evening in 2012, Ramón Mendiburu and Domingo 'Txomin' Perurena find themselves sitting side by side on a long bench in an almost deserted *txoco* (a Basque gastronomic club) deep in the province of Guipúzkoa.

Both now 70 or so, they have been an integral part of Spain's cycling fabric for more than half a century. Perurena, a winner of 158 races including the Tour's King of the Mountains jersey and 12 Vuelta a España stages, is now a bespectacled, bald and solemn-looking individual who arrives wearing a large *txapela* (a Basque beret) to protect his head from the torrential rain. Mendiburu, more dapper – his shirt collar turned up and with an expensive-looking neckerchief to keep out the winter chill – is best known for his work, post-retirement in 1970, first as Spanish national coach then as team director with the legendary KAS squad and co-director of the Vuelta a España in the 1980s.

At the *txoco*, as the wine flows and plate after plate of traditional Basque dishes appear from the kitchen, the two have little difficulty remembering their Fagor team-mate 'Chepas' (Humpy), as they affectionately nicknamed Ocaña for his slight humpback. (As quick as all pro cyclists to notice the pros and cons of pretty much anything in terms of racing, their first thought is that it was an automatic point in his favour because it enabled him to adopt a very hunched, ultra-aerodynamic position when riding on a time trial bike.)

Ocaña, as Perurena points out, hit the ground running as soon as he joined Fagor, his first fully professional team, in 1968, taking three stage wins in the Vuelta a Andalucía, one of Spain's key early season races. But his limitations also became clear almost as quickly.

'I remember most of us were in a training camp in Dénia that February and [Fagor director] Pedro Matxain would ring up each evening to see how the part of the team that had gone down to Andalucía was going,' recalls Perurena.

'Matxain would come back to the dinner table each time and say, "My God, he's won again, he's going brilliantly. It'll take a real cock-up for him to lose the race."

'And, sure enough, things got really messed up' – on a stage on the delta-like western Andalucía flatlands between Sevilla and Jerez de la Frontera – 'when the Belgians got to the front and the echelons started forming in the crosswinds. Luis got blown out the back, straight away.'

Ocaña lost 6'00" overall and, although he bounced back and captured the next day's stage (his third) to the coastal town of Algeciras with a solo victory, Belgium's Antoon Houbrechts' advantage of over 5'00" was unsurpassable. Still, third overall and three stages was hardly a bad haul for Ocaña's first race as a fully fledged professional.

'He could have won a whole lot more if he'd had his head screwed on the right way,' says Mendiburu, 'but there was no doubting he was a rider with a hell of a lot of class. And we could see that right from the start.'

There could be little doubt either that there was a gap to be filled in the uppermost echelons of Spanish cycling. Since Federico Bahamontes, Spain's only previous Tour winner in 1959, had finally quit in 1965, it had initially been hoped that Julio Jiménez, an almost equally talented climber, could fill the space left behind by 'the Eagle of Toledo'. But 'the Watchmaker of Avila', for all that he took three King of the Mountains titles on the trot and a second place overall in the Tour in 1967, was in no way a good enough all-rounder to take the race outright. Other Spanish riders like José Pérez Francés (third in the Tour in 1963 and 1966), Gregorio San Miguel or Patxi Gabica (Spain's most recent Vuelta a España winner when Ocaña turned pro) were all too inconsistent or had reached an upper limit of – in San Miguel's case – fourth and a single day's lead in the 1968 Tour.

Ocaña was talented, but when he signed for Fagor his future was unclear. 'Ocaña was a good-hearted lad, but so, so impetuous,' says Luis Otaño, another team-mate in the final year of his career at Fagor in 1968 and who had ridden the 1959 Tour de France as a team-mate of the victorious Bahamontes.

'He had a problem; he never paid any attention to what the directors said. Having said that, Matxain as the Fagor director was pretty average. He never gave anybody any advice as far as I know. Those days, it was sink or swim.'

Otaño first came across Ocaña by chance as an amateur at the inauguration of the San Sebastián Velodrome in August 1965 and the two became friends despite the age difference.

'He was only a kid and they put me up against him in a five-kilometre individual pursuit. Anquetil was there, too. So I beat Ocaña, but' – after slowing down deliberately so as not to humiliate his rival and to give the impression that it was more of a competition – 'only by ten lengths or so,' which was still presumably humiliating enough!

***

Three years later their paths crossed again and Otaño could see that Ocaña had still not matured in certain crucial ways. 'I rode with Ocaña in [his first race at] Andalucía and he was right out the back when the splits went, and that was it. He was still wet behind the ears then. He attacked everywhere and never listened to anyone.'

Apart from his impetuosity, individualism and natural talent, Ocaña's team had also noticed that his impulsiveness revealed itself in another way: in his appetite for food. Most bike riders are choosy to the point of obsessiveness about what they will or won't eat and how much; Lance Armstrong, who always used to weigh his food carefully before eating it, is one of the most extreme cases.

Ocaña, on the other hand, was the complete opposite. 'He'd eat absolutely everything,' says Perurena, 'and he wouldn't think about the consequences. If he wanted a watermelon, he wouldn't eat a slice: he'd eat the whole thing, and then live with whatever happened to his stomach.'

Fast-forward ten years and his ability to eat prodigious amounts of food in one sitting still created a huge impression. 'I remember one time Luis slept for an entire day,' says Agustín Tamames, who raced and roomed with him in his second last squad, Super Ser. 'And the hotel receptionist would go up with room service. First it was "knock-knock, breakfast", then "knock-knock, lunch" and so on. And she left the trays by the side of his bed. When he finally woke up, he ate the whole lot – breakfast, lunch and dinner – in one go!'

Ocaña's passion for art also caused heads to turn very early on. When staying in the Basque Country for training camps with Fagor, his team-mates were amazed to come across Ocaña standing beside the famous local sculptor Jorge de Oteiza, intently questioning him about the sculpture he was working on at the time at the Aranzazu sanctuary next to the team hotel. 'He was really good with carpentry, painting, handiwork of all kinds,' says Mendiburu.

And if that artistic bent impressed them, there must have been both a sense that Ocaña's errors would iron themselves out with time, and that what counted, above all, was that here was a real rough diamond. 'Luis had a heck of a temperament, but everybody knew he was the coming man,' says Perurena. 'One of the most amazing feats I've ever seen on a bike was what he did in the GP Llodio [one-day race] up here that first spring. This was at a time when the "war" between Fagor and [arch-rivals the top Basque squad] KAS was at its height, above all between the directors.

'And Luis got away and for all that the whole of the KAS squad were chasing him down, they couldn't bring him back. I remember [KAS director Dalmacio] Langarica drove past the front of the pack and up to Luis to see what was going on – and to check he wasn't getting any assistance from a motorbike. But he wasn't.'

There were other reasons for recalling Ocaña that day. He arrived so late from France for the start of the Llodio that he drove his car – an Opel with French plates, a rare enough sight in Spain as it was – at full speed through the crowds to the foot of the signing-on podium, and leapt out of it, leaving the keys in the ignition and the engine running as he then headed for the start line.

Driving style apart, Ocaña's death or glory style of racing appealed enormously to the fans. 'When he attacked, he never looked back,' says Perurena. 'These days I think the riders need rear-view mirrors the amount they turn round. When Luis went for it, it was with total confidence. He never looked back once, instead he just steadily accelerated and he was away.'

Following Ocaña's very promising start to the season in Andalucía and Llodio, the 1968 Vuelta, his first Grand Tour, was not nearly such a success – to the point where, in his autobiography, Ocaña does not even mention that he took part in it. But, in a tedious first week in which little happened but a series of bunch sprints, and when perhaps the most exciting moment came when German race leader Rudy Altig was fined 200 pesetas for stealing oranges from a tree mid-stage to quench his thirst, Ocaña survived reasonably well and even, on one day, got a top-three placing.

On stage eight's hilly route inland from the Mediterranean coast at Benidorm to Almansa, Ocaña had taken second behind lone stage winner Martín Piñera and had moved up to eighth overall. Although Piñera's late attack over a non-classified climb had made the Spaniard the hero of the day when he claimed the overall lead (and finally ended the monotony of several sprint stages), Ocaña's sudden charge for the line to pick up some time bonuses for second place had indicated improving form.

Then, on stage nine, disaster struck. On a 230-kilometre trek across the flat, exposed plateau of central Spain to the railway town of Alcázar de San Juan, Altig took advantage of strong cross-winds and an intermediate sprint mid-stage to break away. The peloton split into three and, after a ferocious pursuit lasting nearly two and a half hours, all the pre-race Spanish contenders – 1966 Vuelta winner Gabica, Perurena and the former race leader, the 37-year-old Piñera (or *El Abuelo*, Grandpa, as he was nicknamed) – were out for the count. (The local media put Ocaña down as one of the favourites but only, ironically, when he had no chance of winning.) Most of the Spanish riders lost 12'00" while Ocaña finished second to last, nearly 25'00" down.

It was of little comfort to Ocaña that his Fagor team-mate José María Errandonea – one of the few gifted Spanish time triallists of the time, and clear-headed enough to get into the Altig-driven move – had won in Alcázar de San Juan. 'Luis spent the last 30 kilometres with two KAS riders sitting on his back wheel,' Otaño said, 'and got to the finish exhausted.' Ocaña's failure to ask the two KAS riders for help was not in keeping with a long tradition in bike racing of collaboration between rivals when there are mutual interests at stake, be it in forging a breakaway or limiting the gap when dropped. On that stage, where all three riders were presumably aiming to expend as little energy as possible and survive, mutual interests were blindingly obvious. But, instead, Ocaña rode his own race, driving away at the front of the trio without them 'taking turns', ignoring the opposition and the effect of that on his own energy levels. As will become clear, rather than this being just a beginner's error, what was essentially a massive – and chronic – blind spot on Ocaña's part when it came to seeing the bigger picture during breaks became evident again in the 1969 Vuelta, with far more damaging consequences.

In the 1968 Vuelta, in any case, Ocaña was all but out for the count, but he showed what was to be his trademark spirit in such circumstances, and promised his team-mates that, after such a humiliating failure to get on the right side of the break in the crosswinds (a repeat of what had happened in Andalucía in February), he would not miss out on the following stage to Madrid.

In the first hour, one that again saw an ultra-fast start with the peloton constantly splitting and reforming, Ocaña was in the thick of the action and keeping true to his word. But then, to his immense frustration, when a pack of 31 riders finally went clear, he was not among them.

Instead, as Otaño recalls, 'Luis attacked and attacked at the start of the stage, on a road going through all those vineyards they have round there, but he'd gone so hard that he burned himself out in the first hour. And then he was so pissed off that he decided he'd abandon' – after less than 50 kilometres of racing.

'He'd come in the night before second to last and then swore black and blue that he would knock down half the peloton if he got blown out in another echelon,' recalls Jesús Aranzabal, another team-mate. 'And then, we–ell ...'

The freezing weather, with ten centimetres of snow making life very difficult for the peloton on the mountain passes outside the Spanish capital, can hardly have increased Ocaña's motivation, given his particular dislike, throughout his career, of cold weather. But his abandon was far more motivated by his annoyance at being unable to make an impact on the race. 'He couldn't do what he wanted, so he just quit' is how Otaño sees it.

Ocaña's 'hissy-fit' was probably aggravated even more by the fact that, prior to stage nine's debacle and stage ten's exit, he had begun to show some form. Yet, in a sudden reversal of fortune less than two days later, Ocaña was heading back to Mont-de-Marsan with precious little to show for his first major Tour experience – except that he had a dangerous tendency to overreact to adversity, regardless of the consequences, and also to ignore one of the basic rules of bike racing – you form an alliance with your rivals in a break, no matter what the cost to your pride, if it is to your mutual advantage.

It has to be said that, in terms of racing, Ocaña did not miss much in what was left of the Vuelta. In a dreary, otherwise uneventful second half, probably the most notable moment came when a bomb planted by the separatist organisation ETA in the Basque Country went off beside the race route. Fortunately, no one was injured but, after a two-hour delay, the riders dismounted, unwilling to continue. Tension built as the organisers pushed the riders' bikes through the debris caused by the explosion. At that point the best-placed Spaniard at the time, José Pérez Francés, came out with an unforgettable line: he would not race any more that day because 'I have already done my military service in Africa'. The stage was finally cancelled.

This stage had come after a spell of exceptionally freezing weather, with the 'high point' a blizzard on the descent of the notoriously dangerous Col de Pajares that ripped the peloton apart – unfortunately, however, with such poor weather, TV coverage was abandoned and nobody could see it happening. The racing as such had fizzled out well before the Vuelta reached a rain-drenched finale in Bilbao. It was eventually won by Italian stage race specialist Felice Gimondi, who took advantage of the relentless war between Fagor and KAS to claim the third of his four Grand Tour victories.

Dull it may have been, but Ocaña might have reaped the benefits: with strong form and a low position overall, at the very least a stage win was within his grasp. Instead, Ocaña's initial Vuelta performance revealed what were, in hindsight, a number of none too positive trademarks of his racing style: a promising start followed – not without some dramatic visual fireworks – by a dramatic and self-induced collapse of energy levels. Had Fagor director Matxain not had enough on his hands already when Ocaña abandoned (that day, too, Perurena was in the process of notching up Fagor's second straight stage win), Ocaña might not have been allowed to quit on what were clearly his own terms. Instead, a dangerous pattern in the way Ocaña tackled a major Tour was established very early on in his career.

***

Ocaña's next race, the Giro d'Italia, was to cast a similarly negative and extensive shadow over his career. According to Josiane, 'it was where he caught bronchitis, something that plagued him all his life, for the first time'.

Treated correctly and quickly in normal circumstances, i.e. not a bike race, and allowing time for convalescence, the illness would probably not have been such an issue. But in the Giro Ocaña's obstinate determination to complete the race and to battle on regardless proved to be seriously detrimental to his health. Ignoring his team doctor's recommendation, which was to abandon, Ocaña raced on, finally finishing an hour and a half down in 32nd place.

By that point the bronchitis had become chronic and it would return again and again throughout his career. 'I went to see him in his hotel in a Vuelta at a point when his rivalry with Merckx was at its height. It was a cold, rainy stage,' recalls his childhood friend Romero, 'and I only got up to his hotel room because I claimed to be his cousin – but when I did you could barely talk to him for all his coughing because of his bronchitis.'

Bronchitis was far being Ocaña's only problem. In a major pile-up in the first week of the Giro – in which another team-mate, José Antonio Momeñe, was so badly injured he had to abandon – Ocaña slammed into a milestone chest-first. He rode on, albeit with such severe bruising that he needed bandages around his upper body for the next five days. Factor in the additional pain caused by bronchitis and a severe case of haemorrhoids, and it becomes understandable why Ocaña was being given 14 painkilling injections a day. His courage in the face of physical pain once again becomes obvious. So, too, does Josiane's conviction that 'once Luis had an idea in his head' – in this case finishing the Giro – 'nobody could change his mind'.

The 1968 Giro wasn't all pain and suffering for Ocaña, however. In the third week, as his injuries eased, he also took a second place on stage 19 to Rome behind Italy's Luciano Dalla Bona at the end of a four-man breakaway. 'My team,' Ocaña said, 'were almost as surprised as me.' But the photographs showing the look of desperation on Ocaña's face (far chubbier then than in his later years) as a triumphant Dalla Bona crosses the line reveal how much it must have stung to have overcome his illness and injuries only to lose by such a narrow margin.

On a day that had started very promisingly with two Fagor riders, Ocaña and Ginés García joining forces with a pair of Italians early on, the Giro d'Italia had made its stately way down Rome's Via Aurelia. The four established a gap of 6'00" on the bunch, enough to guarantee them a crack at individual glory in Rome.

Both Ginés García and Ocaña attempted to drop Dalla Bona on the streets of Rome but the Italian, a former track 100-kilometre pursuit champion, was not to be shaken off and showed the greater resilience when it came to beating Ocaña in a technical drawn-out sprint. Given that the stage had been lost in a tactical battle so typical of track racing, one Spanish newspaper huffily observed that it was 'yet again, proof that we need more velodromes in Spain'.

Ocaña's second place was overshadowed, in any case, by a large-scale roadside fan protest, waving banners referring to doping, probably in response to the growing rumours (later confirmed) that a large number of riders had tested positive during the race. The fans' protest earned them a reprimand from the Federation doctor, Signore Frattini, as being 'unfair and not justified'; given the welter of positive tests – eight – that emerged from the Giro, this seems a bit rich.

Proving he was returning to form, Ocaña's also bagged fourth place on the Blockhaus summit finish on the penultimate day of the Giro. But once again this was no major overall bid; rather, it came after he formed part of a breakaway of six riders, none of them well placed on general classification, that took off midway through the relentlessly undulating stage. Although Eddy Merckx, clad in the pink leader's jersey, single-handedly shredded the chasing peloton after attacking at the foot of the climb deep in the mountains of Abruzzo, the six ahead stayed out of his reach.

Ocaña, who had crashed – further evidence of his bad luck – when almost within sight of the finish, nonetheless remounted and clawed his way past two of the breakaway riders to take fourth place. He might have done better but, before he had a chance to do so, the Spaniard ran out of road.

The 1968 Giro was in fact the first time that Ocaña's and Eddy Merckx's paths crossed. Once again, in his autobiography Ocaña all but ignores the fact that he raced the Giro, focusing instead on his increasing anxiety about his father (diagnosed with cancer) and his own ongoing battle with bronchitis. And, anyway, would Merckx, en route to his first major Tour win at nearly 23, have noticed the first-year Spanish pro who finished 1'14" ahead of him on the Blockhaus when he himself was just a day away from securing Belgium's first ever Giro victory?

Oddly enough, probably the moment when the fates of Merckx and Ocaña were most notably entwined in that Giro came at a point when neither of them was aware of it: on stage 12, the Tre Cime di Lavaredo summit finish. On that stage, Merckx pulled off a victory that would be remembered for generations, carving his way through the riders ahead of him on the ascent and, as William Fotheringham writes in his biography *Merckx: Half Man, Half Bike*, 'passing the lesser lights as if they were standing'.

'The images from Lavaredo are iconic … Merckx, bare-armed, barely visible through the driving snowflakes, several centimetres of snow on the roadsides [Favourites Gianni] Motta and [Italo] Ziloli finished more than four minutes behind, Gimondi at six minutes – incredible gaps for a single mountain top finish. Gimondi … was seen later on Italian television in tears, apologising for having let down the public … [Merckx] lest we forget … was not yet 23.'

Ocaña, still in his 22nd year, too, completed stage 25, 5'51" back. That was a far from abysmal result. But the extreme cold on that day (four below zero and snowing when Merckx finished), coupled with Ocaña's determination to lose as little time as possible, and thereby putting his body under maximum pressure, lowered his defences at a point when all the riders were feeling vulnerable. The result was predictable: bronchitis, an illness that, turning chronic as a result of his own refusal to abandon, would permanently handicap him throughout his battles with Merckx.

'It was a critical turning point for Merckx … he lost his fear of the mountains,' Fotheringham's biography claims. But for Ocaña, with hindsight, contracting bronchitis proved critical as well. And while Merckx triumphed, Ocaña could only curse his bad luck, the crashes, the injuries and the near misses and miscalculations, all of which, in the years to come, regularly formed part of the pattern of his career. In his first two Grand Tours, too, overestimating his own strength, a lack of tactical nous and ignoring the warning signs of illness or injury had led either to total defeat or to long-term damage. All too often, in later races, only the way these factors combined to bring about his downfall would change.

5

SPAIN'S NEXT CHAMPION?

The summit of the Ballon d'Alsace, the Vosges Mountains, eastern France, 5 July 1970: 17'25" after Eddy Merckx has triumphed on stage six of the Tour de France, Luis Ocaña reaches the finish line. But – bleeding heavily from a major crash some 70 kilometres before on the descent of the Col de Grosse Pierre, his eyes closed, unable to pedal and pushed along by half a dozen Fagor team-mates – he has no idea that he has done so.

'He was unconscious, we had to peel his hands off the handlebars at the finish,' says Perurena, one of those team-mates: 'These days they wouldn't have allowed Luis to continue after he crashed. And we shouldn't have tried either. But we didn't get a single fine. The photos of him that day are of a unique event.'

Evacuated to hospital by helicopter, Ocaña recovers enough to struggle on for another day and a half. But he is barely able to ride, often losing consciousness again, to the point where his team-mates have to push food between his lips to get him to eat. 'I remember his jersey was ripped to shreds by that crash and we didn't have a spare,' says Mendiburu another Fagor rider in the Tour that year. 'He rode for that day and a half with the back half of his jersey joined up with sticking plaster.'

As for the 'unique photos' of Ocaña as an inert, bloody, two-wheeled parcel surrounded for kilometre after kilometre by his team-mates, three of the four still in existence are on public view. They can be seen on the wall of a bar owned by Perurena's mother in a tiny village in a remote rural corner of the Basque Country. Like the final yellow jersey of the 1973 Tour sitting for 40 years on the wall of a house belonging to a nonagenarian Franco-Italian who came within a whisker of taking part in the D-Day landings and who celebrated Hitler's downfall in the Führer's wine cellar, this is an almost predictably unlikely location for one of the key fragments of Ocaña's story.

Merckx, meanwhile, takes his first solo win in the Tour that day, having reeled in early attackers of the calibre of 1968 champion Jan Janssen and French Tour hero Raymond Poulidor, and goes on to capture his first Tour by nearly 18'00" over 1967 winner Roger Pingeon – the biggest winning margin in 14 years.

***

Illness marked Ocaña's first year as a pro on more than just a personal level. It was no coincidence, perhaps, that Ocaña's father's drawn-out battle against cancer through the summer of 1968 saw Luis turn in steadily worse results.

The one exception to all this came in the Spanish National Championships. Held in late July in the shape of a 75-kilometre individual time trial in the Basque town of Mungia, Ocaña blasted away the opposition – almost all of them far more experienced than he – to the point where the closest, Antonio Gómez del Moral, was nearly 3'00" down and the bronze medallist, his team-mate Jesús Aranzabal, was almost 4'00" adrift.

The course was an exceptionally hard one, twisting, with numerous little climbs, and the extreme heat that day made it even tougher. Six pros found the going so difficult that they abandoned mid-race, an extremely rare occurrence in a time trial: that three of them were favourites – Patxi Gabica, José Pérez Francés and José Antonio Momeñe – caused consternation in the press. In contrast, the difficult conditions at the midway checkpoint did not prevent Ocaña from opening up a 64" gap on Gómez del Moral, his closest pursuer, and overtaking two more riders: Andrés Gandarias, another promising first-year pro who had recently taken ninth in the Tour de France, as well as Vuelta stage winner Angel Ibañez. Ocaña's two victims had started out respectively 2'00" and 4'00" before him. A third, Vicente López Carril, one of the most successful pros of the 1970s in Spain, was in his sights as Ocaña swept to the finish.

It was his first time trial triumph as a pro, and one of his most devastating in a career in which Ocaña's ability to race against the clock was one of his strongest suits. Very broadly speaking, when it comes to time trialling strategy there are two different schools of thought: 'measuring your strength' so that, should you have an unexpected drop in power, you still have some reserves to draw on, or going flat out from start to finish and hoping that your strength will carry you through, and to hell with any calculations. Ocaña – to judge by the frequent post-victory comments that always talk of 'going at 100 per cent' or 'giving it everything' – only knew how to apply the second tactic. But he had every intention of making his attempts at obliteration of his rivals even more complete. Apart from using huge gears even by 1970s standards (his 55x18 in the 1970 Dauphiné Libéré is a classic example), he was obsessed with acquiring the latest technological advantages: in the Tour's official *Guide Historique* to the race, in 1973 Ocaña appears as the rider who introduced titanium frames to the peloton, this with the assistance of a friend working at the space research programme in Toulouse, near his home at Mont-de-Marsan. 'At the time trial from Versailles to Paris in the 1973 Tour,' recalls team-mate Ramón Mendiburu, 'I picked up the bike he was going to use and it was [so light it was] like you hadn't picked anything up at all.'

Ocaña's forced smile on the podium as he donned a Basque *txapela*, as well as what appears to be an almost complete failure to talk to the press, was an indication that this was not a triumph he treasured for its significance to the Spanish fans. All the press seemed able to get from him was that his good form was due partly to coming out of the Giro in relatively good shape (despite the bronchitis) and partly to riding numerous kermesses (exhibition races) in Belgium during the Tour, where the constant acceleration on every lap of the city-centre circuits had further honed his condition for a twisting course such as the one at Mungia.

Much later, he would reveal the inspiration behind such a spectacular success: his father and his desire to bring him the Spanish national champion's jersey before he died. 'I had seen him clinging on to the walls of buildings on his way to work,' Ocaña later recalled, 'and he could barely speak but he still managed to utter some brief words of encouragement to me for the Championships.' Later, Ocaña would recall his father lying on the sofa and brushing the gold and red striped jersey with his fingertips, 'and for the first and last time I saw him cry. My victory could have been celebrated amid scenes of pure joy, but cruel fate would not let this happen.'

Sadly, Ocaña might have brought his father two Spanish champions' jerseys rather than one before he died. In the Spanish National 'Mountains' Road Race – another Championship event but, unlike the time trial, not considered to be the main event – held two days later in nearby Mondragón, Ocaña made it into the key break with Gregorio San Miguel. But a puncture as the race roared through the town of Bergara and the absence of team-mates (riders formed a one-man team in that particular event) or support vehicles in the race to give him a quick replacement tyre meant Ocaña was caught on the back foot at a critical moment. San Miguel won the event, and Ocaña took sixth.

Ocaña's father died just before he started racing in the World Championships, in Imola, Italy, on 1 September. 'We opted to say nothing to Luis until the race was completed,' Mendiburu recalls in very even tones, as if he has deliberately pre-drained what he is saying of any possibility of emotion, 'because we didn't want to affect his morale. And then, afterwards, I told him.'

Ocaña seemed to take it well, but only initially. 'After we'd flown to Madrid ... Jesus. We got in that Opel of his and we went flat out for the north. We stopped in Aranda [del Duero] to change tyres. [Ocaña was saying] 'these tyres are no good, these tyres are no good.' I took the wheel for a little bit, but when we got to my home [in the Basque Country] and I offered to go with him [to Mont-de-Marsan], it was "No, leave me alone!" And away he went.'

'My father was someone for whom work and duty were sacred,' said Ocaña in his autobiography and, although his relationship might have been a distant one during his childhood and adolescence, the final image he gives of the funeral – 'I visited his tomb alone to wipe my lips with some of the soil under which he was buried' – is one of reconciliation and perhaps regret, given what Josiane reveals, that that reconciliation had not come sooner.

***

Despite an uneven end to the season, and a liver complaint that gave him severe trouble in the off-season for the first time in his career, Fagor were impressed enough to offer Ocaña a second year's contract with the team. 'He didn't have a clue how much money to ask them for, though,' says Luis Otaño, his veteran team-mate at Fagor. 'So I told him to ask for a lot. He wouldn't believe he could do that at first, but then he named the price I'd said, and he got it. And that surprised him even more!' (It seems the old habits of cycling's fabled *omerta* die hard: Otaño will not reveal how much the sum was, even 45 years later.)

That Fagor wanted Ocaña after such a spectacular first season was understandable. But was it such an automatic choice for Ocaña to stay with the Spanish? Perurena is adamant that Fagor, despite Ocaña's differences of opinion with Matxain, were 'a bloody good team for him to be with. Bear in mind that I knew Fagor from when I was an amateur in 1965 and again as a new pro in 1966. And it's fair to say that Fagor were the ones who gave Spanish cycling a certain degree of dignity.'

This was harder than it sounds. By the time Ocaña signed for the team, Spain had come out of its darkest economic period, the 1950s, and the country was – globally – booming financially. But it has to be remembered that for the bulk of the population, many of whom had been on the brink of economic starvation ten years before, living conditions were so poor that there was a lot of catching up to do before Spain could be considered a modern nation.

Back in the 1960s, therefore, Spain was a long way behind other countries when it came to bike teams. According to Luis Balagué, Ocaña's lifelong friend and BIC team-mate, there were 'still only 30 or 40 professionals in Spain by the early seventies, maybe a fifth of the total in France'. But Fagor – 'pretty much a regional Basque team, with just two or three guys not from here, Madrid and other places,' as Otaño, himself from near San Sebastián, describes it – were one of the first to try to catch up with the foreign opposition, although KAS, one of Spain's most legendary squads, were not far behind.

Fagor held not one but two pre-season training camps, for example – an unheard of practice at the time in Spain – first at the ski resort of Candanchú in the Pyrenees ('only walking, they wouldn't let us ski in case we broke our legs. Besides, none of us knew how to ski anyway,' recalls Otaño), and later in Dénia on the Valencia coast ('we'd just decide for ourselves how many kilometres we'd do').

'They improved the riders' wages, even if they were still low. And from the first year onwards, they paid for everything – equipment, clothing, suits, the lot,' recalls Perurena – something many teams in Spain were still not prepared to do.

The transport was none too impressive, though – 'we'd travel around the country in an old van which a friend of Matxain's had,' says Otaño, 'and it would take so long to get from one place to another it'd have been quicker to walk! Just two mechanics, two soigneurs and the director. That was it.'

Still, Otaño agrees that the money paid by Fagor 'was good to very good' even if 'the team wasn't as well organised as Margnat', his previous squad. Perurena insists, 'There was no reason for us to be envious of foreign teams, and I know that from personal experience because in 1970 I raced abroad for a year [with Fagor-Mercier].

As for arch-rivals, KAS, 'We beat them into a cocked hat in the one-day races and week-long stage races in Spain,' Perurena says. 'It was only in the Grand Tours where that wasn't the case.' Or, as Otaño puts it more bluntly, 'KAS stuffed us'. But with KAS and Fagor both raising their game, Spain collectively was not weak as a cycling nation – as proved by their taking the 'Best team' classification in the 1968 Tour de France, with five riders in the top 15. What they lacked, though, was a lead figure – and Ocaña seemed destined to fulfil that role.

A first overall stage race win looked increasingly likely for Ocaña, and it finally came in the Setmana Catalana, Catalonia's second biggest race (sadly now defunct), in late March 1969. On the hilly stage two, from Tarragona to Igualada, Ocaña launched an attack that whittled down the front group of contenders to 11. And he then employed a tactic that was to pay dividends in many races: staying within contact of the other favourites on the earlier stages and then gambling it all on the final time trial – in this case a 24-kilometre time trial from Bellvitge to the coastal resort of Castelldefels. He clinched both his first stage win and the overall in one fell swoop. Among those defeated were two former Tour winners, Gimondi and Lucien Aimar, while Poulidor lost over 2'00" in the time trial, and Janssen – who had won the Tour in exactly the same style in the final time trial the previous year – lost over 3'00": in such a short distance, for such a relatively inexperienced pro, a remarkable achievement.

If the Setmana Catalana saw Ocaña punching well above his weight and learning to use a particular race strategy to great effect, more of this was to come at the 1969 Vuelta. It was perhaps not such a major surprise that, after putting Janssen and Poulidor to the sword so effectively in the Setmana Catalana race against the clock just three weeks before, Ocaña scored a victory in the Vuelta's prologue in Badajoz. But as Ocaña began to soar in the Grand Tours, what no one could have expected was that after one Grand Tour abandon and another 34th place overall, only one miscalculation – albeit a major one – prevented him from winning the Vuelta outright.

It is true that for nearly two weeks of racing in which Ocaña remained close to the top of a largely unchanging classification, he remained in the mix more because of the lack of real battles between the main favourites rather than any particular skill of his. However, on what seemed to be a relatively straightforward stage to Moya in Catalonia, the chance was there for a breakthrough overall lead and almost certain victory. Ocaña failed to take it. The race came within his reach as a result of poor weather and a relentless series of short, punchy climbs over which he single-handedly reduced the front group to just himself and Roger Pingeon. Having revealed himself as the strongest in the race, had things continued to go Ocaña's way, even by just staying in contact with the 1967 Tour winner he would have all but sealed the overall lead. Instead, in the last 15 kilometres Ocaña cracked badly and lost 4'00" to the Frenchman.

Ocaña responded positively, pulling back time on Pingeon in two of the three remaining time trial stages to eventually halve that overall disadvantage. But he later claimed that he had 'lost the Vuelta because I had made the mistake' – when the two had broken away on the climb to Moya in Catalonia – 'of telling Pingeon I was not in good shape. And Pingeon immediately realised that, in my one moment of weakness, this was the point to attack.'

Others disagree, saying Ocaña self-destructed on that stage through his own miscalculations. 'It was a hilly stage to Moya, cold and rainy,' says Mendiburu. 'Ocaña had Pingeon on his wheel for about 30 kilometres, and he didn't even take one turn at the front. So when it came to the final climb, which was a really insignificant one, Luis cracked completely. He lost so much time that it didn't matter how much he pulled back.'

Shades of the 1967 Vuelta all over again: Ocaña's impulsiveness and strength drove him forward – and then over the edge. There was a colossal difference, though: in 1967, Ocaña's refusal to insist that the two KAS riders at the tail end of a Vuelta stage help him meant he abandoned. In 1968, by doing all the work again, he actually lost the race outright.

The root of the problem was that Ocaña was not actually racing to win the Vuelta when he attacked with Pingeon on his wheel: all he wanted to do was prove a point to his squad. 'The thing was that Luis was really pissed off with his team-mates,' recalls Aranzabal. 'He'd had a blazing row with everybody the night before at the team hotel in Barcelona. He thought they weren't pulling their weight … so he decided he'd ride everybody off his wheel. He broke the race apart single-handedly.' Had Ocaña appreciated that he was doing that, his day at Moya could have been a masterpiece of an attack, the kind that wins Grand Tours in a single stroke – as memorable as Merckx's first overall Giro victory the year before. Unfortunately, Ocaña had other fish to fry and either did not realise, or did not care (hard to believe, but possible), that he was in the process of making a winning move in the Vuelta and needed to race accordingly. And, as Ocaña's bad luck would have it, the one rider who survived the Ocaña storm – Pingeon – was the one rider who could also hold the Spaniard at a reasonable distance in a time trial.

And Pingeon rode exceptionally well. Despite having just one team-mate, Belgian Willy Monty, after the rest of the Peugeot team abandoned, the Frenchman managed to fend off the combined might of the Spanish, as well as an exceptionally strong BIC team headed by Britain's Michael Wright.

As was to happen so often in Ocaña's career, once he had made a single error, events seemed to start to conspire against him with unnerving speed, ensuring that he failed almost as disastrously as possible. Wright, for example, had been lying second overall until well into the final week and third up until the final time trial and could have helped Ocaña break the race apart. Instead, he blames BIC's inactivity on his manager, Raphael Geminiani, 'for being unable to decide whom the real leader was in our squad, me, Rolf Wolfshohl, or Gilbert Bellone, and working for him and him alone'. Pingeon was also helped towards what seemed to be a most improbable win by the huge rivalry between KAS and Fagor – or, to be more precise, between their managers, Dalmacio Langarica and Matxain.

Mendiburu recalls that he and Matxain went to the KAS hotel for a secret meeting with Langarica and his lead rider, Vicente López Carril – third in the 1974 Tour – to try to form an anti-Pingeon alliance or, as Mendiburu puts it, 'to try and unblock the huge deadlock there was between the two directors'.

'So we told them "hey, Pingeon's going to win the Vuelta, we're fighting each other, let's ..." and his voice trails off, but it is clear he is referring to an unspoken agreement. 'But there was no way it was going to happen,' he concludes. 'There was a very good relationship between the riders on each team, but there was a real problem between the two directors,' says Perurena.

On top of that, Perurena is scathing when asked what strategy Fagor had for the race. 'Tactics? What tactics?' he says sarcastically. Mendiburu confirms that Matxain's contribution was minimal: 'he just told me "stay close to him [Ocaña]," because he wasn't good in echelons.'

So Ocaña had to settle for a very disgruntled second place. It would have been scant consolation to Ocaña that, while losing his first overall Grand Tour, he secured his first and only King of the Mountains win in a Grand Tour in the 1969 Vuelta, given that it came to him by default after two riders technically ahead of him were 'declassified' and a third, Pingeon, dropped behind at the last moment.

'I was going to win the King of the Mountains title,' recalls Balagué, 'but I wasn't allowed to because at the time according to the rules the best climber had to finish in the top 15 overall.' Balagué had finished 32nd, and Mariano Díaz (Fagor) also ahead of Ocaña in the KOM classification, was also out of the top 15 spots. Amusingly, Balagué says his team were indirectly to blame for his defeat, purely because they were French. 'On the mountains when I needed help I didn't receive pushes from fans because they saw the BIC jersey' and therefore thought he was French and not worthy of support. 'I would be yelling away in Spanish "*Soy Balagué*" [I'm Balagué] but it didn't do any good. They gave their support to Ocaña even though he was a huge way behind.'

That Ocaña took the KOM jersey though, was more thanks to the organisers than his own prowess. With France's Pingeon also ahead of him up to the final stage in the KOM classification, the competition was nonetheless awarded to Ocaña on the slightly dubious basis that he had clocked the fastest time up the final climb of the last time trial, the third-category Alto de Castrejana. With Díaz and Balagué out of the running, the extra points awarded in the KOM competition for his fast ascent of the Castrejana allowed Ocaña to rack up a total of 33 points in the KOM classification and inch ahead of Pingeon, on 30. For a rider who believed in winning spectacularly or not winning at all, this was hardly a great triumph even if it was a sign of how his climbing was improving.

But if the organisers adapted the rules a little to ensure a top Spanish 'name' from a Spanish team won at least one major award outright in the 1969 Vuelta, the biggest prize, the overall, remained in foreign hands and out of reach of Ocaña. Mendiburu says that Matxain's ineptitude was only partly responsible for Ocaña's failure to take his first Grand Tour. The most important factor was that 'Had Ocaña not lost those three minutes in Moya, with the two and a half he pulled back on Pingeon in the final time trial, he could have won it riding backwards.' The broad brushstrokes of Ocaña's capabilities and limitations in general were therefore amply exemplified in the 1969 Vuelta: almost unmatchable time trialling and devastating attacks, but also an impulsiveness and inability to see the broader picture that left him vulnerable to more astute riders. And in the 1969 Tour, the third key element in his racing – an inability to admit defeat, sometimes for better but all too often for worse – would become painfully obvious.

But, even so, Ocaña's talent could not help but push him upwards, despite his faults. Shortly afterwards there was another significant breakthrough for him, when he clinched his first major triumph outside Spain – the overall of the Midi Libre in France.

In a four-day race with two split stages, Ocaña's third place behind Belgium's Ferdinand Bracke in a 31-kilometre time trial along the Mediterranean coast at Valras-Plage moved him close to the lead. Then, on a hillier 82-kilometre stage to Font-Romeu, Ocaña made it into a four-man break with Briton Derek Harrison. Harrison claimed the win while Ocaña, second, gained access to the bigger prize. With just the second sector of the stage (a 112-kilometre leg down to Perpignan) left to race, victory should have been a virtual formality, but Ocaña failed to see it like that, and his team-mates had to ensure he did not panic.

'When there were four or five kilometres to go on the last sector [to Perpignan] he was getting really nervous, particularly as there were lots of crosswinds. I told him to ease back and calm down,' says Mendiburu. The team developed an unwritten policy to try to keep Ocaña from risking what he had gained up to that point in the race: 'Rather than allow him to take part in the sprint' – never his strong point – 'we'd always try to get him to sit at the back to make sure he didn't crash.' Just as in the Vuelta, in fact, Ocaña's need for extremely close guidance in order to safeguard any advantage his huge talent might enable him to secure became painfully evident. Without such assistance, as happened in the Vuelta, he risked losing at least part of his gains, and quite possibly without ever knowing either why he had first succeeded or subsequently lost.

***

The 1969 Tour de France started reasonably well for Ocaña, whose second place in the Vuelta ensured his leader status for the biggest cycling race on the planet. Although losing 34" in the ten-kilometre opening prologue at Roubaix to winner Rudy Altig was about the most any contender could be expected to lose without his form being questioned, Fagor's 11th place in the team time trial later that first week kept Ocaña in the picture – just.

After staying out of trouble as the race moved east to Maastricht in Holland and then south through the Ardennes at Charleville-Mézières, Ocaña's first real breakthrough came when he made it into the break of 20 riders tracking Portugal's greatest ever stage racer, Joaquim Agostinho, into the eastern city of Mulhouse. All the big hitters were in that move chasing down Agostinho – Merckx had sparked the counter-attack, followed by Janssen, Gimondi, Pingeon and Poulidor – but Ocaña and Fagor teammate Joaquim Galera were the only Spaniards.

Ocaña, in fact, was the only option left for Spain overall, after Pérez Francés, third in the 1963 Tour, was penalised 5'00" for fighting with Dutchman René Pijnen, and Aurelio González, winner of the King of the Mountains prize in 1968, was struggling with an injured foot.

'When Merckx attacked we knew it would blow apart,' said Galera, clearly proud to have made it into the break. 'We followed Pingeon and Gimondi and we've been in the thick of it.'

The young Ocaña seemed to relish the attention his strong racing was attracting – photographs early on in the Tour show him grinning from ear to ear as he signs a helmet for a Dutch policeman (the policeman still wearing it!) – but he was more cautious than Galera.

'So far it's just been skirmishing,' he warned. 'Tomorrow's stage has three major climbs and the battle will be a lot harder.' 'We'll all be with Luis,' added Galera – words which were to be grimly prescient.

On the morning of stage six Ocaña was lying 12th overall, less than 1'00" back and just behind his old ally in the Midi Libre, Derek Harrison, on the general classification. Footage from the first part of the stage shows him speeding along in the main pack with a nasty open wound in his left elbow – evidence of an early crash and which could have dulled his reactions prior to his falling again. Tension rose in the peloton as this was the Tour's first serious mountain stage and heavy rainfall 24 hours earlier had rendered the descents more dangerous, so stage six was a day on which it paid to be extremely alert.

Instead, almost as soon as the pack started the descent of the second climb of the day, the Grosse Pierre (Mendiburu recalls 'we were racing hell for leather, we were already at 70 kilometres an hour' when the road had just begun to head downhill), a huge crash left Ocaña slumped unconscious on the ground. 'I saw the first corner and that was all I can remember,' Ocaña said later. 'After that, nothing.'

The team only realised their leader was missing and unable to continue by himself when most of them were a third of the way down the climb. Although Joaquim Galera, again in the break, was allowed to continue, the rest gathered on the side of the road to wait for instructions.

'Matxain had told us to try to get him through. He said "He's just round the corner, he's just coming." *Just coming!* Perurena says with heavy irony and rolls his eyes skywards. 'So we waited.'

Eventually they rode back up the hill against the flow of race traffic to look for Ocaña. They found him still lying, senseless, in the middle of the tarmac, face down, stretched out full length. His bike was nowhere to be seen.

'He was bleeding, but the real problem was the impact of the crash, he was so shaken up. He'd forgotten to eat and he'd ended up cracking so badly he had been barely able to see,' Perurena added. Matxain – perhaps all too aware that this was the last card Spain had to play in the Tour – insisted Ocaña continue. So eventually the Fagor riders retrieved Ocaña's bike and slung him over it. There were still 80 kilometres left to race.

What few remaining images there are on the walls of Perurena's mother's bar of the two-hour odyssey – of grim-faced, sweating riders with their hands on the bars of Ocaña's bike, on his lower back and his shoulders, as the blood pours out of several wounds – are painfully mesmerising. With just a small leap of the imagination, this might be the aftermath of some terrible battle, with Ocaña the dying general and his defeated troops now in flight. Not for the last time, Ocaña seems – unwittingly – to embody an individual trying to continue in sport beyond what is humanly possible, one last effort that has exacted a terrible penalty.

Although the hospital check-up ensured that no bones were broken, the injuries and open wounds were bad enough, the correspondent of *ABC* later reported, that 'the entire bike was covered in blood. The frame, the logo, the bidon, were stained in it.'

'What Luis Ocaña did today was greater, greater than Merckx, an act of singular bravery,' said the *ABC* correspondent. 'It's just a pity that it doesn't reflect on the classification. Luis Ocaña, another time you will do it.' But in fact it was his five team-mates, Manuel Galera (the brother of Joaquim, also racing for Fagor in the Tour that year), Perurena, José Manuel López Rodriguez, Luis Pedro Santamarina and Patxi Gabica who – given that Ocaña was at best semi-conscious for the entire two hours it took to guide their fallen leader to the line and the stage's summit finish – made that day's racing by Fagor a chillingly memorable collective performance.

'It was actually harder to help him on the last few hundred metres that we had to do on the last part of the Ballon over the summit and down to the finish, than on all the uphill. Uphill we could steer him, but downhill it was virtually impossible to brake,' Perurena recalls.

Ocaña, unable to feed himself, struggled on for another two days. But as soon as the next Tour stage with a fast start came – the 136-kilometre run north of Lake Geneva to the spa town of Thonon-les-Bains – Ocaña, with no time to get into the pace of the day's racing, was out the back and into the broom wagon. 'Our only question,' reported *ABC*'s correspondent, 'is how he'd even managed to survive for so long.'

The answer was … courage, in part and, as had already been the case at the Giro, a refusal to accept the facts as they stood and that he was in no fit condition to continue. Instead, Ocaña once again raced on, no matter what the long-term cost to his health. As ever, calculation and self-analysis formed no part of the plan.

The Tour might not have done Ocaña any favours in terms of results but, bizarrely enough, his refusal to surrender and futile insistence on continuing when clearly out for the count only increased the expectations around him. Rather than suffer a direct defeat at the hands of Merckx, instead his crash allowed him to remain an unknown quantity when it came to facing the Belgian. Their first, direct, full-scale face-off in a Grand Tour would have to wait until the 1970 Tour de France.

Ocaña seemed suddenly more in favour with the Spanish than ever, with the Federation President Luis Puig proclaiming after his defeat by Pingeon, 'we have lost the Vuelta but found a new champion'. Unfortunately, that spirit of bonhomie between Spain and their next star in the cycling firmament collapsed almost as quickly as it had flourished, when Ocaña announced he was changing his allegiance. To a French team.

6

'DISTURBANCES, SURPRISES AND UNREST'

The news broke in early September, first in the Spanish state news agency Alfil and then in *La Gaceta del Norte*. Ocaña's decision to change to French squad BIC was partly down to the persuasive skills of its notoriously silver-tongued director Raphael Geminiani who, as Ocaña said, 'was famous for his ability to handle a star like Jacques Anquetil with huge success', and partly to a breakdown in his relationship with Pedro Matxain, the director of Fagor.

'Ocaña didn't want to be with him any more,' Mendiburu said, 'and Fagor, because Matxain was a guy who took his responsibilities very seriously, didn't want to let Matxain go. BIC got wind of this and started talking to Luis. But Luis had told Fagor already, if Matxain continued, he would quit.'

Mendiburu says that Ocaña's temperament did him no favours when it came to deciding if he would stay with Fagor. 'I don't know if he was really fed up with Matxain, but he didn't like the way he ran the team. And Luis had a very special character. He was also the big name, and he was getting bigger: it's never easy to be with the stars when that happens. Luis had a bee in his bonnet about Matxain.'

'It was Luis or Matxain,' Aranzabal recalls. 'He told them without Matxain he'd continue. They said [Matxain] had to stay. So Luis went.'

The BIC signing, albeit relatively briefly, almost completely destroyed Ocaña's excellent relationship with his Spanish fan base.

'I think it has earned me a great deal of enmity,' Ocaña said, before publicly threatening to go ahead with his and Cescutti's plan and try to change nationality.

In terms of Ocaña's character, the move to BIC was all but inevitable once he had fallen out with Matxain. As Josiane, Cescutti and countless others have pointed out, once Ocaña had an idea in his head it was almost impossible to dislodge it. But the team transfer was not the last thing to overshadow his end of season, as Ocaña received a seemingly interminable series of suspensions from his Federation. The ensuing scandal was the perfect opportunity for the Spanish press to ramp up the controversy over his move to BIC. A more cautious man than Ocaña might have realised this was the moment to stay out of trouble: instead, he ploughed on regardless.

The first offence that earned him a two-month spell off the bike was for a punch-up in stage five of the Volta a Catalunya in September with another rider, Ramón Sáez – a sprinter who had claimed the National Championships jersey that year (as well as bronze in the 1967 Worlds) and who was nicknamed 'Tarzan' for his strapping physique.

'Disturbances, surprises and unrest' read the headline of *El Mundo Deportivo* in its report of the stage. Things had started calmly enough in the warm weather in Tortosa but, as Balagué recalls, that soon changed.

'We were up near Lleida somewhere and the two started to argue over something.' According to later reports, Ocaña had been 'wound up' by other riders in the peloton over a breakaway the previous day in which he unwittingly helped Sáez. Whatever the reason, 'Luis aimed a kick at Sáez's handlebars, he went flying and hit the road really hard. [1965 Tour winner Felice] Gimondi saw what happened and told his riders to go like hell so they wouldn't have a chance of going on fighting and we were all pissed off because everybody was going so fast.

'Then maybe an hour or two had gone past and things calmed down, then Sáez comes charging up and grabs him by the neck so hard his eyes were sticking out.' The two fell to the ground, going hammer and tongs, with the Civil Guard 'using their rifle butts to try and split the two of them apart'.

Sáez died in 2013, but in an interview with the Spanish magazine *Meta 2Mil* in 2011, he denied hitting Ocaña, saying that he 'only wanted him to be more careful. Ocaña had been badly spoiled in France, where they thought he was the next Anquetil, and sometimes he did things like that.'

Even the Civil Guards' attempts to break them up didn't work, though, with Perurena also intervening. 'I hurt myself so badly in the elbow from trying to stop them I had to abandon,' he recalls. 'But it was a lucky break because thanks to that I was able to get to my home in Madrid and see my child being born!'

Sáez apparently knew that he would be expelled and so voluntarily handed over his race number to the officials before they even asked for it, while Ocaña was given a 5'00" penalty. Then, as the two teams were in the same hotel that evening in Barcelona's central Plaza Catalunya, Balagué recalls, 'they were all sitting around in the lobby. And Ocaña goes up to Sáez and starts telling him he's a "cowardly son of a bitch, now if you've got balls come on over here", and Sáez shouts back "you've caused me enough problems, leave me in peace".' Fortunately, for once Ocaña decided to listen.

Indirectly, the outcome of the race was decided by the punch-up. 'Luis was so pissed off by all of this that he went off to see a friend of his in Barcelona and he stayed there nearly all night,' Mendiburu says, 'and then he was still so angry the next morning he got [Fagor team-mate] Mariano Díaz to win the race instead, too.

'That stage' – 199 kilometres long, from Barcelona to Sant Hilari and with six climbs, the last two first category – 'Luis blasted off at the start with Mariano on his wheel. Mariano didn't have to do a single turn for a whole stage and, because Mariano was high up overall already, thanks to Luis, he took the lead and eventually the outright win. But what Luis did was one of the greatest feats I've ever seen anybody produce on a bike.' It was ironic, but typical of Ocaña, that such a feat of single-handed strength – as in the 1969 Vuelta stage to Moya with Pingeon getting a 'free tow' behind, or when the two KAS riders allowed him to burn himself out in the 1968 race – should come at a point when the fans' main interest in the Volta a Catalunya probably now centred on what would happen to Spain's rising star after his violent outburst rather than his racing ability. Certainly, neither the fight nor what was effectively a 200-kilometre solo break features in any of the accounts of Ocaña's life consulted for this book. But that Ocaña's impulsive off-race and on-race behaviour should manage to cast a shadow over his own brilliance was more than just a regular occurrence: it was something he could not help avoiding.

With the sport in Spain smarting from Ocaña's decision to head for France, for the Spanish Federation a 5'00" penalty was not punishment enough for the Catalunya incidents: in the autumn, Ocaña was suspended for a month. But he paid very little attention to this and continued to race, first in France in October in the Roue d'Or and again in the A Travers Lausanne one-day race in Switzerland, where he took eighth. He even tried to race inside Spain at a criterium in Madrid but the organiser, perhaps realising the chances of falling out with the Federation were high if he let a banned rider take part, told Ocaña he could not do so. A second suspension was duly meted out, this time for ignoring the first.

A third 30-day suspension then followed that autumn – and this time it was for the complete opposite of the other two: for Ocaña's refusal to race! Ocaña had been given a special 'permit' from his ban (rather like a prisoner getting parole) to race for a regional squad, Guipúzkoa, at a team time trial inter-regional competition organised by the Federation on 28 September. But if he had already ignored them when it came to racing abroad, now he further enraged the Federation by refusing to race when told to do so inside Spain.

This final suspension begs the question why Ocaña, living in France, had a Spanish licence – and one from Guipúzkoa to boot. 'The whole idea of giving him the Guipúzkoa licence was Matxain's fault. He put down Ocaña as living at his address as some kind of fiddle. But it backfired,' explains Perurena – particularly as, according to Federation regulations, Ocaña had to take part in races when required to represent his region at National Championships. He did race for Guipúzkoa in 1968 but in 1969 it seems he opted not to – and, as a result, his initial two-month double suspension grew into three.

The bans from racing because of the Sáez fight caused major shockwaves in the media in Spain because they were so rare: Perurena, for one, is blessed with an excellent memory but cannot recall any other rider throughout his entire career, spanning more than a decade, getting any kind of suspension that was not for doping. (And it was not just in Spain that suspensions for non-doping offences were rare: Merckx never got one, for example. At most, riders would be kicked out of a race for fighting.) For Ocaña to get three suspensions in such quick succession put him in a class of his own: it also points to his tendency to make the same mistake repeatedly – in this case, crossing swords with the Federation.

It is possible to suggest that the Federation insisted on this obligation simply to pull rank on Ocaña. But whatever the reason, he continued to ignore the suspensions as they mounted up.

Three penalties on the trot would have daunted many other bike riders, but not Ocaña, who continued to race regardless. That earned him a second 10,000-peseta fine and a public reprimand from the Spanish Federation. Just to rub salt in the wound, the third and final suspension was shifted from 1969 to spring 1970 – seemingly to try to wreck his start with BIC.

The Federation's final reprimand of Ocaña as the whole sorry saga drew to an end is worth reviewing, if only because of its staggeringly high level of pomposity. The Federation claimed: 'We have taken Mr Ocaña into our fold with the greatest of warmth, and at Fagor and in the Spanish races he has become a real champion, something that might not have happened had he not raced on our sacred nation's soil, and we have never been tough with said rider. We could have doubled the financial penalty but we have actually been considerate with him.

'We regret that, despite our understanding attitude, said rider has expressed himself in the way he has.'

It was clear that bubbling under these comments, particularly those about Fagor, was a degree of resentment at Ocaña signing for a French team. And it was surely no coincidence that, at the same time, Ocaña came in for some severe attacks in the Spanish press for failing to stay with Fagor, a decision which they said was responsible for its demise as a team at the end of the 1969 season.

'Ocaña changes to BIC for just 100,000 pesetas more than he would earn with the Spanish team and causes Fagor to collapse,' thundered *El Mundo Deportivo*. They insisted that Ocaña had been 'irresponsible' and 'spineless', had let himself be swayed by 'certain newspapers [i.e. French ones] that consider him more French than Spanish and for that reason heap the most praise they ever have done on a Spanish rider.

'In Spain and Fagor his subjective injuries would have been taken in good faith [sic] and people would have gone down on their knees to help him.

'In France it will be different. He may well have to pay for those 100,000 pesetas with tears of blood.' (Not everybody complained about the money side of Fagor's collapse: 'I got a pay-off cheque from them in November and then signed for

Werner so I made double my money,' Balagué recalls with a grin. 'Nine hundred thousand pesetas in a single year!')

The newspaper then went on to make dire predictions of how Ocaña would be given short shrift by BIC for any alleged injuries in comparison with the way Fagor would behave, described him as a 'limited' rider and in a parting shot argued that he preferred to be a small fish in a big pond, rather than vice versa. 'And this is the man who has killed off Fagor?' the article concluded.

In the end Fagor did not quite collapse: instead the team fused with the Mercier squad, but the entire Spanish side was shown the door 'with the exception', as Mendiburu recalls, of 'two riders, [José María] Errandonea and Txomin'. After continuing sponsorship for just one more year, Fagor then pulled out and only returned to cycling in 1985 with – ironically – Ocaña as one of the directors.

Together with the Federation's barely concealed anger with Ocaña, the line taken by *El Mundo Deportivo* indicates the degree of resentment caused by Ocaña's decision to, as they saw it in Spain, return to his French roots. In the short term, the combination of the triple suspension and the transfer scandal highlighted both his lack of respect for any kind of authority and his inability to think through the consequences of his actions, a tendency that as the result of these repeated run-ins gradually became chronic; the errors, like those he made in the 1969 Vuelta, became fault lines. In the long term, the fallout over Fagor simply reinforced the already painfully complex nature of the Spanish champion's love–hate relationship with his parents' country.

'In Spain he was French, and in France he was Spanish,' argues Perurena, 'and that was a problem', while Mendiburu claims that former Spanish Federation President Luis Puig 'got so worried about the whole question of Ocaña's nationality that he went to a World Championships with the sole intention of asking Luis whether it was true' – that Ocaña was handing in his Spanish passport.

It wasn't, but 'As he lived in France, Luis didn't impact here as much,' recalls Spain's five-times Tour de France winner Miguel Indurain. 'He was really charismatic but it is the same story as [recently retired triple World Champion] Oscar Freire. He was a superb rider but, as Oscar lives in Switzerland, he doesn't have so much appeal as he would do if he lived here.'

Growing up in the 1960s and 1970s, Indurain's own childhood heroes were the French rider Bernard Hinault and KAS. It didn't help that Ocaña also raced for foreign teams, Indurain says, which was at least true in the Spaniard's most spectacularly successful years, riding for BIC when his battle with Merckx was at its height.

Others go even further. Ocaña is 'the great unknown figure of Spanish sport' says the country's longest standing cycling reporter, Benito Urraburu of *El Diario Vasco*. 'Living in France, he didn't have half the impact that other riders of his era had. He was Spanish, sure, and people really liked him and admired his attacking style, but people didn't identify with him as much as other Spaniards.'

Even today, the debate over which nation has the right to claim him for its own seems unresolved: back in 1969, the only certainty was that Ocaña, regardless of which flag he was flying, was set for greatness.

His arch-rival, meanwhile, had already achieved greatness, with its pinnacle at that point a Tour de France breakaway to the town of Mourenx. 'To understand Mourenx is to understand Merckx,' William Fotheringham wrote in his biography of the Belgian star. By extension, to understand Merckx's single greatest stage win in the Tour (taken while Ocaña was recovering from his crash on the Ballon d'Alsace) is to understand the scale of the challenge in trying to beat him. Because, as Bernard Thévenet points out, Mourenx did not just contain the key to Merckx's racing style; it also indicated, more than any list of victories, the level of Merckx's superiority. (That it should also indicate the strength of Merckx's team and why his team-mates were so much more loyal to him than anything Ocaña was going to find at BIC, merely reinforces the comparison.)

At a point in the Tour where Merckx already led by 8'00" – and had two mountain stages and a time trial remaining – rather than race defensively, as textbook wisdom has it, Merckx attacked over the Tourmalet and doubled his advantage over the rest of the field at the finish of Mourenx at the foot of the Pyrenees to 16'00". That he should suffer from 'the bonk' – as cyclists called the sudden slump in glycogen levels that makes you feel as if your leg muscles have turned to jelly – with 20 kilometres to go, lose 2'00" and still win by 8'00" makes it an even more jaw-dropping achievement. By Paris, where the lead was up to 18'00", he had the mountains, points, most aggressive rider and combined competition jerseys in his power, while Molteni had the teams' prize. No rider has ever come close to achieving this, even less so in his Tour debut.

And yet probably the most unnerving thing for his rivals was that Merckx had not broken away because he felt he had to. He had broken away – and teetered along the tightrope of collapsing from the effort for four hours alone in blazing sunshine and over three major Pyrenean cols – simply because he *could*.

Merckx set off because a disloyal team-mate, Martin Van Den Bossche, had tried to get over the summit of the Tourmalet alone and, as Thévenet describes it, 'Merckx went for him, passed him and got there first. The other rivals let him do what he wanted – this was [a case of] the yellow jersey settling his accounts ... then Merckx got 200 metres, decided to do the descent, does the descent and then at the bottom of the climb he had a minute, so he wasn't going all out. But then the rest were dithering and then, little by little, the gap rose to eight minutes by the finish. And all because he was pissed off.' Thévenet's voice trails off and he lapses into silence. Forty years on, he is still amazed at the scale of

Merckx's victory – in a race where every scrap of energy is saved ('don't stand if you can sit down, don't sit if you can sleep', as Robert Millar once put it) – at such a display of force, purely for its own sake.

Merckx's ride to Mourenx sent another unintentional message to his rivals: to try to beat the Cannibal or to pull off a stunt similar to Mourenx, automatically became all but inconceivable. All but.

7

FAST CARS AND LITTLE FIRECAPS

In an era so utterly dominated by cycling's greatest ever racer, Eddy Merckx, for many bike riders there was little they could do but bow to the inevitable. What could possibly be done against a rider who won almost one out of three races he took part in, who was so dedicated to his sport he spent, as Merckx himself admitted, 'a third of my life on the bike, a third at the wheel of my car, eating and getting [post-race] massages, and a third sleeping'?

'We were racing to finish second' is how Lucien Van Impe, the 1976 Tour de France winner put it. Such was the state of general demoralisation that many settled for comparatively minor targets – like Van Impe, who won the King of the Mountains in the Tour six times. Others like Dutchman Joop Zoetemelk, who holds the record number of completed Tours de France (from 1970 to 1986), but who was seemingly condemned always to finish one spot behind Merckx every summer, stayed so blond and pale-skinned, the cruellest critics said, because all he would do, or could do, was race in Merckx's shadow.

Ocaña, though, was the exception to the unwritten rule of the Merckx era. Time and again he tackled Merckx head-on: 'he was the only one to try,' as Van Impe put it. 'He was a total idealist,' says Bernard Thévenet, 'unable to accept the reality of Merckx's winning regime.' 'If Luis got it into his head that he wanted something' – like beating Merckx – says Zoetemelk, 'he would try for it again and again.'

Talk to anybody who knew Ocaña in that era and the same words are almost invariably used to describe his feelings about Merckx: 'It was always Merckx–Ocaña, Ocaña–Merckx. The duel,' says Van Impe, 'Luis was obsessed, really obsessed.' And Merckx reciprocated in kind: 'Eddy wouldn't let him get away, not even by a single metre. When riding for the overall, he'd let everybody else get away. But not Luis. Never Luis.'

'He used to sit there and say, day after day, I'm going to break him, I'm crack him, I'm going to beat that big b—' says Jean-Marie Leblanc, ex-director of the Tour de France and a former team-mate of Ocaña. 'Hate is too strong a word, but he'd think about nothing else apart from beating Merckx. And because [BIC director] Maurice De Muer knew that Luis worked best on motivation, he'd stir that up as much as he could.' So successfully in fact, as another team-mate, Michael Wright, puts it: 'Luis couldn't get Merckx out of his head.' Or to quote De Muer himself, 'Just catching sight of Merckx was more of a stimulant for Luis by far than any drug. He wanted to devour him.'

The press themselves tried to drum up the rivalry as far as they could, churning out books with titles that made their rivalry sound like a no-holds-barred Mafia vendetta, or between gunslingers in bad Westerns – *Merckx–Ocana: Duel at the Summit* is a personal favourite.

And while bike riders and sports directors alike say that Ocaña could not have been more different from Merckx, the press took Ocaña's obsession with Merckx one step further and said that he was a kind of Merckx-lite, a new version of the Cannibal himself.

'He is so often like Merckx in his personality, his winner's mentality, his audacious racing style and his natural ability to be in the right place at the right time in the peloton that we had to have room to be optimistic about the future Merckx–Ocaña duel in the Tour,' gushed French paper *Le Dauphiné Libéré* in 1970.

This was a mixture of half truths and exaggerations: Ocaña's ability to 'be in the right place at the right time' was more than debatable, for example. Yet as any journalist who has lived through an era of domination by a single athlete will tell you, claiming Ocaña was Eddy Merckx mark II was probably the only way to 'sell' the idea of a rival: as somebody who had the same characteristics. You couldn't remove Merckx from the equation when it came to a competition, so you 'created' someone whose similarity to Merckx was such that he had to be able to beat him, on paper at least. That they were so close in age – Merckx was just eight days younger – made the contrast an easier one.

In fact they could hardly have been more different as racers. 'They had a completely opposite mentality,' says Bernard Thévenet. 'Merckx raced after everything, he wanted to win everything. *Tout, tout, tout.* Merckx in a race was there to win it, apart from two or three times when he went mad in the Tour like at Mourenx in 1969, but if Luis wanted to win a race, it had to be with an hour's advance, that was what counted. It was all panache. The way of doing it. He was a real torero. And until he'd killed the bull and it was good and dead, he wasn't happy.'

'Ocaña was an attacker but he was more relaxed than Eddy,' adds Zoetemelk. 'On the other hand, unlike Eddy you never knew what Luis was thinking, then boom-boom-boom, he'd attack. He'd be gone.'

Given Merckx's superiority – and Ocaña would recognise that, even if it infuriated him – the Belgian's margin of victories is ridiculously high. In five and a half years from when Ocaña turned pro to the sporting high-water mark of his career – his Tour win in 1973, in tens of thousands of kilometres of racing and hundreds of races, Ocaña only succeeded at beating Merckx on five occasions. Three times it was in a time trial, all of them less than 15 kilometres long – Ocaña's key speciality were short, intense races against the clock – and, Ocaña only once took an outright stage race win over Merckx, in the relatively low-key

1973 Setmana Catalana in Spain. The fifth victory, however, was another story: it alone would be enough to earn Ocaña a place in cycling's history books.

The greater the rivalry in any case, the worse the relationship between the two riders, which made for a vicious circle that the media kept on trying to spin remorselessly. 'It was all the bloody press' fault,' says Merckx these days. 'They said Ocaña said so many bad things about me we didn't talk for years.' But Ocaña himself had no doubt that racing against Merckx, or anybody else for that matter, was far more than mere competition – and that, rather than any desperate journalist trying to breathe life into Merckx's domination, was at the root of their conflict.

'I knew that the metier I dreamed of could be the most beautiful in the world,' Ocaña wrote in his autobiography in the early 1970s, 'but only on condition that you turned love of doing battle into a religion.' 'Luis was only interested in attacking, not in winning,' observes Josiane, 'and that's why his palmarès is so much smaller than it could have been.' It also made him the ideal rival for a winning machine like Merckx, the ultimate inspiration for those who want to believe that in the teeth of the greatest sporting supremacy the world has ever known, sometimes a normal human being stands a chance, before he or she, like Ocaña so many times against Merckx, is overwhelmed.

***

There's hardly a professional cyclist out there who hasn't kept a file of old photos and newspaper cuttings from his career. And as a strong January wind rattles door frames and the first gobbets of rain patter down high above the River Meuse a few miles outside Liège, Michael Wright sits down heavily at his kitchen table, flicks over a few pages of an album and pulls out a picture. It is a snap of himself and Ocaña in the 1969 Vuelta – Ocaña in the red and yellow stripes of the reigning Spanish national champion, Wright in the yellow of race leader.

Like Ocaña, Wright – now a tall, kindly 70-year-old who still gets out on his bike when a hip injury permits – is an exile, to the point where he can barely string two words of English together. Born to British parents, his father was killed in the Second World War when he was a toddler. His mother remarried a Belgian, in whose country they settled and where a teenage Wright discovered, on a bike he rented from a friend, that he could ride well enough to turn pro.

After racing in 1967 for the improbably named Tibetan-Pullover Centrale team, then signing for BIC in 1968, Wright first ran into Ocaña in the 1968 Vuelta a España, where he became the first Briton ever to lead the race. In 1969, he repeated the feat, wearing the *maillot amarillo* of leader again, taking another two stages and finishing fifth overall – at the time the best ever Grand Tour finish for a British rider. And in 1970, during Ocaña's first year in BIC, they were team-mates.

Wright says it was clear from the moment he met him that Ocaña was very talented, but what instantly struck him as a team-mate – as it did so many people – was that Ocaña had a hugely reckless streak, too.

'You could always tell that Luis was a bit special. But the first thing I remember about him at our first training camp, some-where down in the south of Spain, was what happened on this four-kilometre straight section of road nearby that Luis decided was ideal for trying out his new [Jaguar sports] car.'

'So he invited [team-mate] Johny Schleck' – father of Andy and Frank, who still race today – 'and somebody else to get in for a test drive. And ahhhhhhhh!' Wright says, indicating how fast the Jaguar had got up to speed, 'they came out with their faces white as sheets! He'd taken them up to 300, 320 kilometres an hour! When he was driving, Luis was a bit nuts.'

The tales of Ocaña's willingness to dice with death in cars are, in fact, legion: former team-mate Jesús Aranzabal tells of the time

Ocaña started showing off at doing 180-degree handbrake turns in the middle of an A road – across both lanes; Luis Otaño the same on a narrow cliff-road leading to a castle; Ocaña's soigneur, Emilio Cruz, recalls his driving so fast and close to a lorry that Ocaña's 'shark-fin' Citröen DS ended up minus the fins; and 15 years later, Ocaña was up to it again, driving across a vineyard (roads being for wimps, presumably) with a journalist, *El Mundo Deportivo*'s Javier De Dalmases at 180 kilometres an hour. 'I have never,' says De Dalmases, 'been so close to dying.'

If Ocaña was keen to show off his driving prowess to his new team-mates, perhaps it was not surprising: unlike at Fagor, Ocaña no longer automatically stood out at BIC. Scaring his co-workers was the new kid on the block's obvious, if slightly childish, way of making his presence known. But perhaps even Ocaña was a shade nervous because signing for BIC was the equivalent of moving from what would be a good Pro Continental or second division team today into a squad at the very top end of today's highest division of cycling, the UCI World Tour league.

The difference between the two squads wasn't just that BIC had twice as many riders as Fagor (31 against 16); or that the French team's budget was said to be three times as big; or even that, rather than an all-Spanish rider set-up like Fagor, BIC had riders from as far afield as Denmark, men like Olympic time triallist and future Worlds silver medallist Leif Mortensen. Above all, the contrast for Ocaña would have been in the quality of the line-up, with riders like former Vuelta and Tour de France winner and World Champion Jan Janssen sitting on the other side of the hotel dinner table every evening at races. At Fagor, apart from Ocaña nobody else had finished on the podium of – let alone won – a Grand Tour.

'He was a good rider, but I wasn't so sure about him as a person,' says Janssen about his first impressions when he came across his new team-mate. 'Quite apart from the driving, Luis had a hell of a temper and he was always impatient. I can remember him waiting for his food at supper and if it was even a few minutes late – 10 or 15 – he'd be straight into the kitchens, yelling at the chef and asking where his pasta was.'

(Perhaps it was no surprise that, given his status, Janssen – like Johny Schleck– was also treated by Ocaña to a fast car ride early on. According to Ramón Mendiburu, 'They took Luis' car to go shopping down in Saint Raphaël that first spring. Jan came out of the car shaking like a leaf, saying "*Il est fou!*"')

There were other differences from Fagor, indicating this was a big step up. Having recently partly merged with the former northern French squad Pelforth, BIC also had an extremely solid Classics contingent. In the spring of 1971, for example, while Ocaña was focused on building the Tour de France, his BIC teammate Roger Rosiers won one of the top one-day races on the calendar, Paris–Roubaix.

Reflecting the team's higher international profile, the money was certainly far better than at Fagor: at BIC Ocaña was paid 1.1 million pesetas a year for a two-season contract – the highest wage a bike rider had ever been paid in Spain. (Spain's previous top rider, Bahamontes, was paid a maximum of 475,000 pesetas per annum by his French team, Margnat, in 1961.)

And Ocaña quickly decided what he would be spending a large percentage of his new wage on: cars. Aranzabal, another BIC teammate, recounts that, having found out that a factory in Italy was making special super-wide tyres for his Jaguar, Ocaña 'drove right the way to Milan and back from Spain, just to buy these tyres.

'There was only one problem: the tyres were so big they wouldn't fit into the wheel wells, so he ended up smashing round the wheel arches to try and get them in.' It was a frighteningly expensive error – the special wheels cost 100,000 pesetas each, a price tag 'that would have easily bought you a small flat in Spain at the time'.

One of just three Spanish riders, all signed from Fagor, in the squad, Ocaña was hired to beef up the stage racing side of things after Janssen had failed to deliver more than a tenth place in the 1969 Tour, a race the Dutchman had won outright in 1968. But BIC was patchy in its organisation and – as still happens in major squads sometimes – too apt to concentrate on satisfying its top names.

Part of the problem was that it was simply too big for its own good. 'BIC was a huge team for the time. Thirty riders was a lot,' explains Jean-Marie Leblanc, racing with BIC in 1970. 'Also, 1969 was the last year of Jacques Anquetil in the squad, plus [1966 Tour de France winner Lucien] Aimar, plus you had the Pelforth riders, Janssen, Schleck.' Using a term that can be ambiguous, Leblanc says 'It was a *grande équipe*.' And in 1970 BIC still very much retained the feeling of unwieldiness a team with so many heavyweights can have, even if Aimar and Anquetil had gone. For all a year had gone by, too, the two teams – Pelforth, the northern Classics outfit, and BIC, the Grand Tours squad – had not melded well and in 1970 the power struggles and upsets continued behind closed doors.

'It was a difficult process bringing the two teams together,' says Leblanc. 'There weren't the same kind of customs, the same way of managing things in the two squads.

'[Former Pelforth team manager] Maurice De Muer was well organised, and [long-standing BIC manager Raphael] Geminiani was serious in some ways, but a lot more *ole-ole* in others. Janssen was a very serious, rigorous minded kind of guy from the north of Holland, while Aimar and the rest, well … there were two different kinds of rider. And in 1970 BIC was still an overly big team, only slightly smaller than in 1969. It was tricky.'

At the time, Wright says, 'we were good, but we weren't that special. The Italian squads, like [Merckx's] Molteni, had better technology than almost everybody, they were on another level. We were close to the top, but that was all.

'I can remember our soigneurs weren't up to much. You'd see the soigneurs in other teams preparing the race food really carefully, all nicely wrapped up, and at BIC sometimes they weren't so careful with what we ate.'

As for BIC's big budget, it didn't always trickle down to the team workers like Wright. 'One guy we had called Mario was really mean with everything, he'd give us a massage with a cream called Algipan. But he used to jam the tube of Algipan right up against your leg so nothing would come out of it. We used to take the mickey out of him and say "isn't that the same tube as last year?"'

'BIC was good for its leaders, and they'd tell everybody their race programme at the start of the year,' adds Jesús Aranzabal, whereas 'At Fagor' for whom he had ridden previously – 'you never had any idea what you'd be doing all season. I once got as far as Murcia to start in the Vuelta there before they told me on the morning of the first stage I wouldn't be doing it.

'But in terms of support for any of the team workers BIC was absolutely useless. I lost one Tour of the Basque Country by 15 seconds because they refused to change the tyres on my wheels because "it was the last day and everybody was going home". At Fagor, on the other hand, from the first rider to the last, whatever you asked for, you got.' The only two drawbacks of the Spanish team, he says, were 'poor planning and Matxain'.

Those keen to defend BIC would say its excessive preferential treatment for its leaders was pretty much par for the course at the time, but they could not deny that the team management was unusually unstable in 1969 and for the first half of 1970 because it had more than one main sports director. It was jointly run by Maurice De Muer and Raphael Geminiani, and for a while there was even a third, Raymond Louviot, who was only removed from the power struggle in the most brutal of ways when he was killed in a head-on collision with another car while driving to the start of the Four Days of Dunkirk race in May 1969. Of the two remaining, Geminiani was the longer-standing, well-established figure at BIC, but in the short term the most crucial question for the team's new stage racing project with Ocaña was how the Spaniard would work with the management. It was a slow process but De Muer did better than Geminiani at handling Ocaña, which meant Geminiani was in a less favourable position when it was finally decided by the management which one of the two should be 'let go'.

'De Muer learned to handle Luis with time,' says Mendiburu. 'He started off at the team training camp by getting hold of riders like me after supper, sitting them down and asking them what Luis was like. I told him a lot about Ocaña, as well as predicting that he would finish second behind Merckx in Paris–Nice, which is what happened!

'Luis needed someone who would treat him kindly, not just give him a bollocking. And at the same time, when he found himself in a team with a director like De Muer, who'd got a pretty strong reputation, and with riders as well known as Janssen and [Giro and Tour prologue winner Charly] Grosskost, Luis realised he'd have to raise his game, too.'

Leblanc says, 'Luis and De Muer really got on at the Tour. De Muer loved Luis' panache, the way he'd shoot his mouth off – in a positive way, I mean his honesty, saying what he thought.

'And De Muer liked the fact that as soon as he'd got a little bit of energy, even if he'd not got enough strength to win the Tour, he'd still attack. Raphael is and was a great figure in cycling, and a great director, but he wasn't adapted to modern cycling. Maurice De Muer was the complete opposite – always organising things – but, curiously enough, he was really taken with Ocaña, who wasn't anything like him, either. Maurice liked attacking riders, guys that went from the gun, and they had a great deal of mutual appreciation.'

With a practically minded director – as well as one who knew when to let Ocaña take control – but with a romantic streak to him, Ocaña (whose ability to organise anything tended only to manifest itself sporadically and in short, intense bursts) could live for the bike 'and for the bike alone', something that stretched right back to his adolescence and his rides through the woods to get away from his family. And when it came to running the show during the race itself, Leblanc – who has observed dozens of team leaders in his time as Tour director – says that in that respect Ocaña, even when he and the team were on the back foot, was a natural at inspiring the troops.

'We'd always have a team briefing, just before dinner, about the next day's stage. And Luis, even if he was difficult to work for as a person at times – sometimes angry, sometimes kind, sometimes in form, sometimes not – was always good to work for as a rider. If he was on a good day, he was formidable, he attacked, he rode with panache, he'd be off the front for 100 kilometres, even if he didn't win.'

At breakfast on such mornings, Leblanc recalls, the atmosphere in the team would be electric. 'He'd be shouting, yelling "you're going to see, boys, I'm going out there to give them hell", slamming his fist down. We'd be really galvanised by that. And *allez!* Off we'd go.

'It was the complete opposite to Jan Janssen. Jan's a guy I really like a lot, but he wasn't like that. Same goes for Zoetemelk. But Luis, if he'd been a Napoléon, a general in a war, he'd have been the first guy out of the trench and over the top. He'd have been a hero.'

As a leader, Leblanc says he was 'more Anquetil' – with whom Leblanc also rode – 'than Merckx. I've heard [long-standing Merckx domestique Jos] Bruyère say stuff about [Merckx]. Luis, no. He didn't use the riders in a way that would piss us off. A good *patron*.'

To describe his character, Leblanc uses a French word that is hard to translate: *bordelique* – which is somewhere between anarchic, spontaneous and hot-blooded. 'He was really nervous, hyperactive, sometimes not kind – no, it wasn't that. It was more he had a big mouth and that I didn't like. But he wasn't unpleasant, on the contrary, he would be generous to us small-fry riders.

'When he was pissed off, though, he'd blame absolutely everything and everybody: the riders, the doctors, the team, the organisers.' And also, let it be said, himself.

***

Ocaña's signing for BIC as a top-stage race rider confirmed to the rest of cycling's elite that they had a new member in their 'club'. It remained to be seen what he could achieve, but they already knew that with Ocaña there would never be any middle ground. 'He was either right at the back of the bunch, because he was not going well and was as miserable as hell, or was on the front, feeling great and wanting to attack,' observes 1980 Tour winner and long-standing rival Joop Zoetemelk.

Thévenet describes him – and he is aware that there is a contradiction – as being 'straight as a die but bizarre. When he had it in his head that he was going for somebody' – like, for example, Merckx – 'the blinkers went on. He didn't see anything else.'

However, if things did not work out and Ocaña did not get his own way, as Zoetemelk experienced, woe betide those who had opposed him: 'I remember him at the Nice–Seillans [race] in 1973, and there were just the four of us away: me, [Alain] Vasseur – BIC, Roger Rosiers – BIC, and Luis – BIC. Luis attacked and attacked, then it was one or the other who went away and I chased them down.

'Then Luis started shouting, insisting that he was going to win, and when I said "no, it's going to be a straight race", he shouted even more. Finally it was me that won, and he was so pissed off. He was that adamant it would be him. It always had to be him.' Thévenet corroborates this, recalling that, as an amateur, when Ocaña miscalculated and Thévenet beat him on placings on the very last stage of a race, Ocaña was so furious he came looking for him behind the winner's podium to bawl him out. Essentially, as both anecdotes illustrate, Ocaña was determined to wrench events his way, come what may. Accepting fate just didn't form part of his mental equation: hence his refusal to accept being beaten by Merckx, whom most riders viewed as the man who would shape their destiny, whether they liked it or not.

Ocaña was a 'lone wolf' in other ways, too, his rivals found. 'He was enigmatic, a bit solitary, he didn't go out of his way to socialise,' Thévenet says. And Zoetemelk agrees, adding though that when conversation finally did take place, he found that Ocaña was 'easy to talk to, not a complicated sort of bloke, but he'd get angry very easily, too'.

Ocaña could not be taken for granted in any way, it turns out. 'He was very changeable,' adds Thévenet, 'One day he'd be fine, the next not, one day in a good mood, the next in a foul one. Even he himself had problems explaining why he would be in one mindset one day and another the next.' The only thing you knew for sure, Thévenet emphasises, 'was that he would attack'.

'He came across as a hero out of a Scott Fitzgerald novel,' says Jean-Marie Leblanc, 'with that self-destructive, slightly crazy edge to him. And proud, too, in a very Spanish, good sense. Not to crush the rest. He wasn't necessarily mysterious' – as Lucien Van Impe described him to me – 'he was just not like anybody else. Different.' 'A bit nuts,' says Leblanc. 'But that's always the case with the geniuses. If you want to break the rules, you always have to be a bit mad.' And that unpredictability, he agrees, 'must really have pissed off Eddy'.

The peloton was also quick to notice – again, unlike the eminently hard-headed Merckx – a lack of practicality about Ocaña. During my interviews I lost count of the number of times I was told about a sports car he had bought after one Tour (there are different opinions as to which one) – ideal for whizzing from one post-Tour criterium to another, but which had one major disadvantage: Ocaña had failed to realise it was too small to fit a bike frame into. As Zoetemelk observed sardonically, 'Not very practical.'

Journalists and race organisers appreciated Ocaña's courage, and his gung-ho attitude, which guaranteed both good copy and rarely a dull moment in the racing. And when Ocaña was feeling good, it was total war: 'He used to say he would only brake if a rider was on the ground,' adds Benito Urraburu of *El Diario Vasco* newspaper, a cycling journalist who knew Ocaña well, 'otherwise he'd attack whenever and wherever he could. None of this pissing about they do these days if a rider has a mechanical problem. Once in the Vuelta he dropped everybody when they'd eased up at a feeding station, blew the race apart.'

Remembering Ocaña off the bike as warm-hearted and personally charming, Urraburu adds: 'He was a huge, huge character. Frighteningly dynamic. Like somebody that's escaped from another time in history. Luis was never happy with just living life, as they say: he downed it, in one gulp.'

Ocaña's strong character was one reason why he stood out so much, his willingness to dice with danger was another. 'I can remember him going round one bend on the descent of the Porte,' adds Thierry Cazeneuve, the former race director of the Dauphiné Libéré race and friend of Ocaña's, 'and it was incredible, there was no barrier, his back wheel was right on the edge of the road, like that' – and he makes chopping gestures with the edges of his hands to indicate that the wheel was on a knife edge.

That sort of risk-taking was not so appreciated by his teammates, who saw it as overly rash and typical of a rider who had no sense of his own limitations: 'He wasn't good on the downhills, he took too many risks,' says Wright. 'To follow Merckx, he had to ride beyond his natural limits.

'I lost count of the number of times I saw Luis at a finish with his face all covered in blood from having crashed somewhere along the way.'

***

It is perhaps surprising in somebody as reckless and impulsive as Ocaña to find that he was devastatingly self-critical, too. 'He'd get angry,' as one team-mate recalls, 'but always with himself, rarely with anybody else for more than about half an hour. He would break himself. He was complicated, he lacked self-confidence.'

Part of the reason for that, almost certainly, was Ocaña's bad luck, which became legendary in the peloton. The dog that ran under Ocaña's front wheel in the first stage of the 1973 Tour and which caused him to crash is the best-known incident, but as Thévenet puts it, 'If something was going to happen, you knew it had to happen to Luis. It got to the point that if there was some kind of crash, you didn't have to ask who had been affected.' His bad luck, it seemed, pursued him wherever he went: 'I can remember going to the Carribean with him once for a criterium and we went boating. Guess which guy had the bad luck to step on some rock, slip and all but cut his tendons? Luis, of course.'

Wright has his own recollection of Ocaña's repeated tendency to be singled out by misfortune: 'It was in one of those training camps down at Seillans, where Maurice De Muer lived the last year of his life, and that evening we were having one of those nice fondue savoyarde at the start of the season with lots of cheese.

'Ocaña picked up a huge lump of bread and cheese, swallowed it, but as luck would have it he could only eat half of it and the other half got stuck in his throat. So there we were, pulling this great big long string of cheese out of Luis' mouth for ages. The poor bloke almost suffocated.' It was, he agrees, 'the typical bad luck of Ocaña. He was almost cursed.'

***

Inside BIC, meanwhile, the combination of Ocaña and De Muer made for an atmosphere that varied radically, not least because De Muer, like Ocaña, was not inclined to play a waiting game in a race.

'Maurice had one fault: he didn't know how to save his riders' energy,' says Bernard Thévenet, who had De Muer as a sports director at Peugeot in 1975. 'Everything he did was always flat out, we had to make things happen in the race, and we never got any respite.'

'A good manager for the logistics but tactically, he was not so hot,' Janssen told the magazine *ProCycling*, 'above all for the [domestique] team-mates. He would shout and shout at the riders, "you're shit, go home, no good, 95th again!", it was like he thought he had a dozen Ocañas and a dozen Janssens in the team.' (Indeed, the resentment against De Muer got so bad at times that once in the early 1980s some of his riders in the Peugeot team fed his wife's dog, Scotty, an amphetamine-filled sandwich which sent it to an early grave.)

Thévenet also says that, with time, Luis and De Muer provided fuel for each other's naturally overaggressive approach – which sometimes produced amazing results and sometimes total disasters.

'There must have been quite a lot of friction because they both had strong characters,' he says, and he recalls riders telling him that both would hit the roof if they failed to succeed in their plans at BIC. But it was a question of getting used to it rather than worrying too much. 'Regularly, Maurice would go absolutely livid for 15 minutes,' Thévenet said, 'but then he would calm down again for a long period of time.'

Thévenet concedes that, even if De Muer was overly keen on cracking the whip at times, he also knew how to motivate his riders. And being so well organised was something that Ocaña's anarchic style of racing definitely needed. Unlike Geminiani – whose presence was the original reason why Ocaña had felt drawn to BIC after deciding to leaving Fagor – De Muer, the newcomer, was never happier than when he was drawing up plans. Rather than just sending off riders at training camps, for example, as most sports directors did at the time, De Muer would assemble them round the bonnet of his car, unfurl a map and pencil in a route for them to follow 'like a general directing an army,' says Leblanc.

However, like Ocaña, when De Muer was in a laid-back mood it was hard to believe it was the same person. 'Our race used to be one of the very few where two team cars were allowed to form part of the convoy,' recalls Thierry Cazeneuve. 'And Maurice would do the first few kilometres, make sure every rider had a spare wheel and enough food in the second car, then go off with his packet of fags and find a tree to sleep under for the rest of the afternoon.' But in the early days in particular, and at the critical moments of any race, De Muer ensured Ocaña had the guiding hand he needed. He made a huge effort to understand Ocaña, and discovered a kindred spirit when it came to 'winning with style'. Ocaña, in turn, found a director who both shared his obsession with panache, but who had the thoroughness to make it happen. And in BIC, even if it lacked the firepower to go against Merckx's Molteni man-to-man, at the very least, as a better funded, more well-rounded squad than Fagor it was close enough to give them a run for their money.

***

That closer attention to racing strategy, and a more professional approach from Ocaña all round, proved to be vital in the 1970 Vuelta, which was to be a game of cat and mouse from beginning to end. That was particuarly important in the Vuelta, Wright recalls. After years of political and financial isolation, Spain's top race had an infrastructure that was so miserable in comparison with richer events in richer countries like the Giro and Tour, that it was easy to lose everything at a moment's notice.

'The Vuelta was all a bit *ole-ole*. I remember they had this mobile wooden velodrome, which they'd erect in most cities, and they'd have the finish on that. The only problem was that it was only about three metres wide and it didn't have any fencing at the top side. So if you went too high up you'd fall off. It was incredibly noisy', and Wright suddenly all but shouts: '*tackatackatackatacka* every lap. But it was so narrow it meant only the first three riders into the "velodrome" ever had any chance of winning, you couldn't get past' – something that Wright, as a gifted sprinter with four Vuelta stages in his palmarès by the time Ocaña appeared, found rather annoying.

Get into the mountains and 'the riders would be ten kilometres ahead of the commissaires because all that they had were these really tiny, underpowered cars that couldn't get up climbs quick enough to follow the bunch,' Wright recalls with a chuckle.

'The roads weren't so bad, but when it rained they were like glass. On the descents of the cols, maybe it hadn't rained for ages and then you crashed all over the place.' As for accommodation, he says, the hotels on the coast were fine given they were directed towards the tourist market, 'but if you went 30 kilometres inland, it was almost like they were living in huts. I saw Merckx eating biscuits for supper in one hotel because they didn't have any other food.'

For the second year running in the Vuelta, in 1970, Ocaña took the leader's jersey on the first day in the prologue. It was a close-run thing, though: Dutchman, Olympic track gold medallist and giant of the Six-Day scene René Pijnen, crashed some 30 metres from the line and had to run to the finish, his bike on his shoulder. Without that crash, given he still came within four tenths of 1" of Ocaña's time, he, not Ocaña, would have been in yellow.

Pijnen grabbed a couple of time bonuses on stage one that put him in the top spot in any case, then held on to the lead for another eight days, before Ocaña and another Spaniard, Agustín Tamames, shed Pijnen on the Montserrat climb and began the process of reducing the race to a two-man duel.

With only a handful of seconds between the top riders, bonuses became crucial. Ocaña first regained the lead after the

Montserrat climb thanks to crossing the summit first, but then a sneak attack by Tamames on the Somosierra pass placed the ball back in the Salamanca rider's court.

After an entire week in which the difference between Tamames and Ocaña remained at 1", come the final time trial in Bilbao, Ocaña was only 9" behind: far too little, in Tamames' own opinion when talking to the press, for him to have any chance of retaining the yellow against a specialist like Ocaña.

Sure enough, Ocaña delivered the goods, putting 67" into Belgian Herman Van Springel (who had already lost the 1968 Tour de France to Janssen in the final time trial) and 75" into Tamames. In his very first year with BIC, his first Grand Tour was in the bag. 'Ocaña needed this triumph, which satisfies all the hopes put in him by the international media, and the Vuelta needed the triumph of a Spaniard,' wrote *ABC*'s columnist, 'because it suited it after the lengthy series of foreign triumphs, which started after the win by [Francisco] Gabica in 1966.

'Ocaña can be pleased, the Vuelta can be too, and so, too, is this particular writer, who was nervous about how Ocaña gambled it all on the final time trial – I dared to compare him to [French star and time trial expert Jacques] Anquetil on similar occasions. But now I have to admit how cleverly the rider from Priego kept his options open. And yesterday he played the card he had kept back for the finale with convincing authority.'

***

For Ocaña, victory in his first Grand Tour in his first year in a team as prestigious as BIC, using the tactic he had refined in the Setmana Catalana two years before of gambling it all on the final time trial, was confirmation that he had made it into the club of top Tour contenders and, albeit temporarily, made up for his bungling of the 1969 Vuelta. (The Spanish media even 'forgot' his signing for a French squad, too.) It also gave a huge boost to his status within the new squad that no amount of high-speed driving could have done. But for the BIC riders, such a close-fought race meant a huge amount of responsibility for them.

Wright recalls Ocaña's understandable nerves about the racing and the prospect of winning his first Grand Tour: 'He was constantly waving us to the front to drive after breaks, even if it was a rider who was three-quarters of an hour behind who'd got in the breakaway.

'It got to the point where we got so fed up with it, we told the soigneur to massage his right arm first one evening, before his legs or anything. When Ocaña asked the soigneur why, we told him to say it was "because that was the part of his body he'd used the most during the day!"

'But he took it well. He was antsy, sure. Who wouldn't be in their first Grand Tour they had a chance of winning? But he was a good guy to work for.'

As a regular rank-and-file worker, rather than results, rides in flash cars or how his leaders got on, Wright was more impressed with the way Ocaña would be 'fighting the bosses to make sure there were *primes* [pay bonuses] for us team-mates. He was definitely a good guy that way.' This ensured his popularity remained on a level that, for example, Spain's previous big-hitter, the far less generous Bahamontes, had never achieved.

Another reason why Ocaña appealed, Wright says, was because 'He liked playing jokes. I remember one night there was one rider who'd always go to sleep early so we sneaked into their room and Luis pulled the sheets away. The poor guy rolled out of bed and he didn't really know where he was.'

Nor was Ocaña averse to chasing the opposite sex: 'I've been on an eighth-floor room with Luis and maybe there would be some women in the next room along. Luis was capable of jumping from one balcony to the next just to get a better look!'

BIC could, he says, see that Ocaña had an excellent possibility of victory, 'given he was a great time trialler and wasn't a bad climber. It was weird that he was so good at time trialling because if you look at his muscles he didn't seem to have the capacity to move those big gears. And in those days' – rather than spinning smaller gears as both Bahamontes and, nearly half a century later, Lance Armstrong also did to such great effect on the climbs – 'it was all about using huge gears.

'He was clearly a coming talent, and there weren't many other stars in Spain. There was a gap to fill.'

'Luis was so nervous it was impossible to keep him sitting calm in the bunch. If you didn't keep a very close eye on him, he'd chase down everything that moved,' recalls Grenoble's Anatole Novak, who retired in 1971 after racing with Ocaña for his last year in BIC as one of his top team-mates. 'He was so confident on the bike, too, as proud as a bullfighter.

'At the same time, he was a lovely guy, so kind, that I had only one regret at the end of my career, that I was going to retire and couldn't keep on working with him for any longer.'

Like many others, Wright observed that Ocaña was an exceptionally voluble talker, except when he was angry or had had a bad day. But overall Ocaña was in no way as difficult a star to look after as his Spanish predecessor Bahamontes: Ocaña was skilful at moving in the bunch and capable of looking after himself.

Certainly at the 1970 Vuelta, De Muer felt confident enough of his protégé to let 'some bloke from a cycling club in Bayonne, who in fact organised the team's contracts', work as the team's main sports director. While De Muer was rarely present, it was up to Geminiani to put in brief appearances – and Wright says his practicality and his ability to restore order was much appreciated.

'Luis was okay most of the time, but sometimes he needed a guiding hand, someone to calm him down', something at which Geminiani was more than experienced. He also had the contacts necessary to resolve at least minor emergencies.

'Geminani once sorted out getting me a pair of shoes from an Italian team' – no easy task on a bike race, given that most riders will only take one pair of shoes to races – 'when I'd put mine up against the radiator to dry and in the middle of the night the heat came on and they almost burned out,' he recalls. '"Gem" got me some new ones, sorted it out right away.'

***

Yet one area remained the riders' responsibility – their 'medical assistance', the contemporary euphemism for drugs. Amphetamines were the (banned) drug of choice at the time, as well as being the one most familiar to the public. In two of the most notorious deaths at the time that had at least partly been caused by doping – Tom Simpson, who died on the Ventoux in 1968, and Dane Knud Jensen, who died in the 1960 Olympics – traces of amphetamines were found in both bodies. But Simpson and Jensen were far from being alone in using them.

Nicknamed 'the little firecaps' by the German riders of time – as opposed to *Die Bombe*, a much bigger cocktail of drugs – between 1940 and 1959, 16 out of the 20 doping positives in cycling were for amphetamines. In 1968, Ocaña's first year as a pro, drug tests were becoming more sophisticated, and 12 out of the 14 positive dope tests in cycling were still for the same substance, with six of those tests in the Giro d'Italia alone.

On the lower levels of the racing circuits, the use of substances banned on the Continent was equally widespread. Michael Wright recalls, 'the kermesses would be ridden by riders stuffed up to their eyeballs on gear. It actually got pretty dangerous and pretty strange. I remember one guy was so high every time he started to lead you out in a sprint that he'd start yodelling. In the middle of the bunch going flat out, he'd be yodelling at the top of his voice!'

Until 1977, Ocaña never admitted to the use of any drugs, never mind amphetamines. However, Wright is adamant that Ocaña was a very heavy consumer of 'medication', as he calls it. It reached the point, he says, where the Spaniard pumped him for information about who was the best Belgian soigneur – reputed to be the top dealers in banned substances at the time – to get his 'medication' from.

'He was always very interested in the Belgians. The year he won the Vuelta he got medicines and all that from a Belgian soigneur called X. When we met up at Madrid airport after he'd won and we were on our way back to Belgium, he gave me a wad of notes this big' – his hands form the size of a brick – 'and said, "That's for X." And me and this other team-mate looked at the money and said, "Are you mad? Not so much!"'

'We had to slow him down, otherwise he'd have given [the soigneur] way too much money.' When asked what the 'medicaments' provided by the soigneur were likely to have been, Wright says, 'I don't know, but they must have been pretty good, he did pretty well with it!'

Wright does not seem able to overstate his case about Ocaña's rate of use of 'medicaments': 'It was too much. Way, way, way too much. He was well cared for, but there was too much medication. It was,' he concludes, '*trop exagéré* [well over the top].'

Curiously, this does not sound like a criticism, merely an observation. As Daniel Friebe points out when discussing Merckx's positive for the substance pemoline in his biography of the Belgian, 'it was hard for riders in Merckx's era to take doping seriously, or even get upset about one rider being more medically enhanced than another, when officialdom did not …

'The Merckx generation's ambivalence about doping is mainly as a result of the fact that they were never truly held to account and had been steeped in a culture too old and established to revolutionise its view of doping just because it had become actionable.' Friebe also points out that almost nobody would argue that Merckx's superiority was purely a product of the laboratory. And, equally, Ocaña's performances remain unquestioned.

'I don't know what they gave him, I'm not a doctor,' Ocaña's personal soigneur for much of his career, Emilio Cruz, tells me.

'But I do know the doctors didn't know what they were giving them and the riders didn't know what they were taking.' Asked about what Ocaña would or would not take, Cruz says he was 'daring. He was one of those who didn't hang back.' He pooh-poohs the idea that Ocaña might have had reservations on health grounds, saying 'when you're young, you don't care about that'. And he agrees when asked if he believed the common theory of the time – still current in some quarters – that champions cannot be constructed 'in the laboratory' or, as the cliché in cycling circles has it, 'you can't turn a donkey [via banned substances or otherwise] into a racehorse'.

Apart from further direct claims that Ocaña used 'medications', there are some strong, indirect indications, too. For one thing, Ocaña's one positive test, in 1977, was also for pemoline, a stimulant similar to amphetamines and which causes damage to the liver, Ocaña's perennial weak point.

But what is perhaps an even stronger, if more subjective, indication of his 'riding under the influence' was Ocaña's all-or-nothing style of racing, highly reminiscent of how Willy Voet, the Belgian soigneur who was at the heart of the Festina scandal 30 years later, says he felt when using amphetamines as an amateur in 1962.

'The second the flag dropped I was off like a bullet from a gun, I was spitting fire … the high lasted until about two laps from the finish and then all of a sudden, it was as if I was knocked out,' Voet recounted. 'I hit the wall, I couldn't see or hear anything.'

Ocaña's tendency to surge out of the pack from the word go, and his sudden, absolute losses of strength, have parallels with Voet's account. Then there were other indirect symptoms of possible amphetamine use: the violent mood swings, the insomnia, and above all Ocaña's supreme self-confidence when on the attack. As former Tour rider Paul Kimmage once wrote about his own experience of the same drug: 'My mind has been stimulated. Stimulated by amphetamines. I believe I am invincible, therefore I am.'

Whether or not he was powered by the same substance, Ocaña's determination to sweep the opposition off the field rather than just come first by the bare minimum had that same kind of megalomanic feel to it. If he had taken amphetamines, which seems likely, it would only have emphasised that trait even further.

***

If the Vuelta 1970 was a breakthrough race for Luis Ocaña in terms of the way he was considered by his team, his first victory in the Dauphiné Libéré raised his profile as Merckx's most serious challenger even higher.

Known at the time as the Criterium des Six Provences but run by the *Dauphiné Libéré* newspaper, the week-long event was – and still is – considered to be France's third most important stage race after the Tour and Paris–Nice. Held in the second half of May at the time and featuring a huge menu of Alpine climbs, it was also the less gruelling alternative to the Giro as a build-up to the Tour de France. For a French sponsor like BIC, the Dauphiné represented a major target in its own right.

The newspaper as organiser gave the race huge amounts of coverage, with front-page photos every day. But the images of cyclists were more homely than awe-inspiring or dramatic. A 'guess the cyclist from his legs' competition sponsored by a local photographer's shop featured on one page every day, while early on Dutchman Marinus Wagtmans donned the pink jersey of King of the Mountains flanked by a singularly unthreatening publicity duo of a beaming woman with a towering beehive hairdo and a man with a garishly chequered flat cap.

There were other indications that, although a major international event, the Criterium had not lost its roots in *la France profonde*. While 450 arrests in one day of student riots in Paris gained just a couple of paragraphs in *Le Dauphiné Libéré*, for example, much more space was given to a debate on the wisdom of introducing a 110-kilometre speed limit for the first time on

French roads: 'I drive at 110 kmh through my village and it's never a problem,' one reader commented in a French version of 'Disgusted of Tunbridge Wells'. And in keeping with the paper's small-town, provincial feel, a fifth of its 30 daily pages was dedicated to the bike race – clearly showing it was the event of the year for the region.

Inside BIC, the Dauphiné was seen by Maurice De Muer as 'the opportunity for [co-leader] Jan Janssen to wake up' after a disappointing first half to the season. The same went for Ocaña's old Vuelta sparring partner, Peugeot-Michelin's Roger Pingeon, who was the top favourite. However, it says a lot for De Muer's confidence in Ocaña and the Vuelta squad that, barring the addition of Janssen, BIC fielded an identical team to the one sent to Spain.

Nor did De Muer play down the comparisons between Ocaña and the Cannibal after the Vuelta: quite the contrary, this upped Ocaña's marketability. 'Luis is like Merckx,' De Muer asserted. 'He exploits the slightest weakness in his rivals, he's constantly calling up his team-mates to drive on the front. I prefer riders whom we have to tell to brake to riders that we have to worry about not being aggressive enough.'

The opening prologue, essentially a five-kilometre climb from Terrenoire to the Côte de Rochetaillée near the grimy industrial city of St-Etienne, was won by French national champion Raymond Deslisle. Despite his impressive achievement of overtaking German national champion Pitt Glemser, who started 1'00" before him, Ocaña could only take second, 3" back. But his chance to strike a major blow came soon enough.

After two sprint stages, the first big shift in Ocaña's favour came on a hilly stage four to Sallanches. After a long breakaway by team-mate Anatole Novak – 'I wish he could have won' were Ocaña's first words after crossing the line – Ocaña broke away with Belgian Classics star Roger De Vlaeminck on the Col de

Cordon, the last climb of the day, and, in the time-honoured fashion for two-man breaks, De Vlaeminck, worse placed overall, took the stage win, while Ocaña moved into the lead.

'Was his pride touched by the fact that Roger Pingeon had told us he regarded [Herman] Van Springel' – multiple winner of Paris–Tours and runner-up in the Giro 1971 and Tour 1968 – 'as his worst enemy?' mused *Le Dauphiné*'s cycling correspondent. Whatever the reason, De Vlaeminck and Ocaña's attack came on a fearsomely difficult day, 237 kilometres long and which saw no fewer than 11 abandons. Yet, with six riders in a 59" bracket on general classification, Ocaña was still only barely ahead in the game.

Ocaña had even more reason to be worried after an uneven performance on a stage through the Chartreuse left him trailing behind his young team-mate Jean-Claude Genty, who moved into the overall lead. However, just as in the Vuelta, Ocaña had the trump card of a 34-kilometre time trial on the penultimate stage up his sleeve – and he exploited it to the full.

The race against the clock between Privas and Vals-les-Bains was unusual in that, after the initial four-kilometre climb of Escrinet, around 22 kilometres – almost two-thirds of the full distance – were downhill. Thus, although Ocaña was 10" down on Pingeon at the summit of the Escrinet, he could then open the throttle on the long descent using a huge gear to devastating effect.

Averaging nearly 60 kilometres an hour, overtaking two earlier starters – De Vlaeminck and Genty – before the halfway point he was, *Le Dauphiné* reported, 'riding so smoothly he could have been on a railway track. His judicious reconnaissance helped, of course, but the way he was riding could only underline his supremacy.' By the time trial's second checkpoint, he was 42" up on Van Springel and when he reached the finish the gap was up to 1'05".

As impressive as the result was the style with which Ocaña took the lead and the stage. One journalist following Ocaña in a car said: 'He took the corner on each descent at 80 kmh, his back wheel churning up the gravel of the very edge of the road as he cut through the apexes. De Muer yelled onomatopoeic words from behind, short, sharp shouts and' – in the time-honoured style of sports directors following riders close to a triumph – 'thumping his hand against the outside of the car door. With each corner we feared a crash but instead one kilometre flowed into another. At an average of 60 kmh, we could barely keep up with him on some points of the course.'

'I go from one surprise to another,' said De Muer afterwards, 'before that fantastic descent, he was very consistent on the first part of the climb, despite using a record-size gear of 55x18', which gained him a little over six metres in each complete turn of the pedals. 'Then, unlike in the Vuelta, where he made all the difference on the climbs, he went all out on the descent. Either way, it worked perfectly. Luis knows what he wants in this *metier* and he always likes a good, clean fight.'

It was game over – to the point where, even with two stages to go, De Muer called up BIC general manager Christian Darras and Cescutti (who turned up with the Stade Montois' treasurer and secretary for good measure) to come and see their star receive the final victor's bouquet.

'Van Springel tried to surprise me on the last stage but I had him under control,' Ocaña told *Le Dauphiné*. 'I feel my team-mates' confidence in me growing for the future. This is a good sign for the Tour de France.'

If there was any doubt about Ocaña's ability to bond with his team-mates, or indeed any resentment on Genty's part after Ocaña regained the lead, *Le Dauphiné* claimed that the huge hug the two gave each other at the finish proved that they were true 'brothers in arms'. (Genty was hardly in a position to complain, though: seventh after the time trial, he ended up 24th after he crashed into a tree during the last stage and could barely stay upright on the bike to the finish.)

Just as Ocaña's superb time trial eliminated all lingering doubts about who was the rightful team leader, it also gave him the upper hand in the battle for leadership against Janssen in the Tour. 'There is even talk that he will be Eddy Merckx's successor,' gushed *Le Dauphiné*.

In a big interview on the following day with the paper, Ocaña was adamant that the Tour 'will be decided between Merckx and me'. (He also, touchingly, asked race organiser Thierry Cazeneuve to excuse him 'for having taken so long to decide on whether I would do the Dauphiné or not'.)

'I'm going better than I was in the Vuelta, no mistakes, just one or two hesitations.' He dodged questions about his condition on the Chartreuse climbs, saying that an untimely puncture on the descent of the Col de Porte had been a much riskier moment. 'To avoid a gap of one or two minutes opening, I had to go to the limits of my abilities and I think I risked falling off maybe ten times. Just once would have been enough to blow my chances. I think we are looking better and better for the Tour in our team, with' – spot the putdown – 'Janssen as team captain' – not leader.

'Luis will be our number one rider for the Tour, he knows that now,' confirmed De Muer. 'It's open war against Merckx.'

Asked if he was at all scared at the prospect of taking on Merckx, Ocaña responded, 'Why should I be? If I was scared I would get off the bike right now. My only fear is bad luck.'

Meanwhile, though, there was some ominous news for Ocaña: on the page opposite his interview in *Le Dauphiné*, a short news story reported that Merckx had consolidated his overall advantage in the Giro d'Italia's time trial. And a few days later, he won it outright.

***

On 17 June, Merckx flew down to the Alps for a reconnaissance of the Col du Granier, a climb due to feature in that year's Tour

– for once without his bike, which he had not been allowed to take on the plane because Belgian security control thought the bag in which it was travelling looked suspiciously like a bomb.

Having found himself a replacement, he did the climb in the company of a *Dauphiné Libéré* reporter in a following car: it is indicative of his fame that the *DL* then published a schedule of his training rides through the Alps for the next two days, clearly feeling that Merckx generated enough interest for them and the public to follow him. But between biting on a cherry tart and drinking a beer – 'he asked for one that was not too cold [to avoid a possible stomach upset], you can never be too careful', the reporter said, keen to highlight Merckx's attention to detail – Merckx's sole interest lay, he claimed, in grilling him about Ocaña's form.

Three days later, Merckx won the Belgian National Championships – the only time he took the title – with a 55-kilometre lone break. With such a devastating display of good form the BIC rider Anatole Novak made a sombre prediction: Ocaña can be first in the Tour, he said, 'first, that is, behind Merckx'. In fact, Ocaña finished 31st, over an hour down on Merckx – and, to complete his humiliation, Janssen, theoretically his second-in-command, finished in 26th spot, 5'00" ahead.

***

'It was a lousy Tour for us,' says Leblanc. 'We could see that Luis wasn't going well right from the start, and it was clear he wasn't going to win the Tour. Janssen got dropped early on, too. The atmosphere inside the team was pretty bad, to be honest.

'Luis was a strong rider with a lot of personality, but with the Spanish it was a little bit like a team within a team.'

To make matters worse, Leblanc recalls there were things Ocaña did whenever he wasn't going well that would increase the tension. 'Each evening I remember him going into his room, slamming the door and turning the Spanish music up to deafening levels. There was lot of that in that race.

'The relationship between the riders from the south – Ocaña, and the rest – and with the guys from the north, Schleck and so on, wasn't ideal either. It jarred a bit.

'In the evenings, us northerners – Schleck, Wright and so on, we'd have our massage and then we'd ease back. The other Spanish riders, like Mendiburu, would ease back at least a bit. But Luis would never relax, always talking, always with his music up loud. In the hotel it was like having an electric battery buzzing around that was never switched off.'

In 1970, Ocaña did not blame his team-mates. 'If good luck was not on my side ... the only thing to blame was [my liver],' wrote Ocaña in his autobiography. And, he argues, its condition was one of the key ingredients to success – or otherwise.

Indirect evidence confirms this. Pre-1971, he received treatment for his liver by a doctor in Bilbao that worked so well that he was in perfect shape, while Josiane recalls that another doctor in San Sebastián sorted out his lung problems, and Ocaña recounted that his strong early season in 1972 was partly due to medical treatment by 'a kinotherapist that was so spectacularly effective we thought of bringing him on the Tour'. But if that treatment ultimately failed him at the crucial moment, in July 1972, in 1970 he went to the Tour with no such back-up whatsoever and paid an almost equally high price.

Indirectly his difficulty with racing under pressure – which was, by some accounts, to play such a crucial part in his losing the 1971 Tour – was also a factor. By his own admission, having climbed so high in everybody's estimation prior to the Tour, he could not handle the increased expectations, and he took some time out after the Dauphiné to try to avoid media scrutiny. But when he tried to regain the form of previous months and ramp up for the Tour, it was no longer possible to do so.

'Making a definitive analysis, I have to blame myself for negligence,' Ocaña says. 'I needed a break right after the Dauphiné, it was indispensable. But my physical condition wasn't able to adapt to this excessive spell of relaxation and then trying to get back into form.'

Having first gone down with bronchitis, his liver problems kicked in, too, and, when a bad case of haemorrhoids made the act of riding a bike even more painful, his morale was all but broken. Ocaña's Tour prologue performance was not too bad, losing 15" to Merckx – 'already first' he bitterly observed – but he admitted he was in damage-limitation mode.

At Divonne-les-Bains, after a hard-fought 241-kilometre stage across the Jura, both Janssen and Ocaña crossed the line more than 12 minutes down on Merckx, while Novak – BIC's self-appointed prophet of doom – was eliminated on time difference. 'Our house is wrecked,' was De Muer's graphic description of BIC's collective disaster.

While Ocaña, previously ninth overall, dropped out of the top 20, Merckx's overall advantage was now nearly 3'00" on Zoetemelk. Less than 24 hours after taking a second straight win in a time trial held on Divonne-les-Bain's horse race course, Merckx's stranglehold on the 1970 Tour was complete.

Meanwhile, three days later, on the stage to Gap, Ocaña reached crisis point. Dropped on the first classified climb of five, he regained contact before the second, only to be dropped again. On a narrow goat track-like road that crawled up the side of a sunblasted Col de Noyer, Ocaña, now down with a fever, and the one team-mate the team were prepared to sacrifice to support him, an equally sick Charly Grosskost, were both faced with the choice of abandoning or struggling on despite their terrible physical condition.

Only the fact that Grosskost had worked so hard to defend his chances kept Ocaña from joining him in the *voiture-balai*, he later said. De Muer and Gerárd Morin, egging him on from the team car, also encouraged him to remain in the race, but the look on his face, Ocaña said later, 'must have resembled that of Christ's on the Cross'. That day, he lost nearly 25'00" on the leaders – while Merckx's advantage overall on second-placed Joop Zoetemelk had now stretched to nearly 6'00". A survey among directors published next day in *L'Equipe* produced the verdict that Ocaña should abandon and, as one Spanish journalist wrote, 'not prolong this ridiculous show'.

Ocaña, to everyone's surprise, bounced back. 'Was the survey saying he should do quite the opposite just the injection of morale-boosting doping he needed?' speculated *El Mundo Deportivo*. Ocaña recovered sufficently to take a stage win, his first ever in the Tour, at Saint-Gaudens after a lengthy grind from Toulouse to the town at the foot of the Pyrenees. It was taken in style, with 2'00" advantage over the rider who would become one of France's best-known managers, Cyrille Guimard, but in terms of the bigger picture it was a face-saving exercise that had no impact on the overall classification whatsoever.

'He has saved his prestige and finally he could overcome all the pressure he had created for himself,' wrote *El Mundo Deportivo*'s correspondent before adding drily, 'he's been as strong as he should have been at the start at Limoges.

'His [sporting] reputation was in tatters before this break. Was it actually more respectable for him to have dragged himself around France more than an hour down on the man he was supposed to have put into difficulty?

'This was an *échappée bidon*, as the French call a breakaway which will have no effect on the overall. If he had been in the top ten overall, this would have been another story.'

Harsh words, perhaps, and a second place in the final time trial in Versailles did little to dispel the sensation of overall failure. In fact, for Ocaña 1970 was ultimately a repetition of the same old story that he had experienced since turning professional: a spell of success and heightened expectations, in this case raised to a maximum by his Vuelta success, that suddenly disintegrated with a crash or sickness. And if the pressure and what *El Mundo Deportivo* insisted was a combination of 'poor form followed by subjective illnesses' didn't get to him, then his constant, sapping run of bad luck would do the trick instead.

That said, Pierre Cescutti, the man who was the main influence on his career, believes that there was one vital breakthrough for Ocaña in 1970: he had won his first Grand Tour, the Vuelta, and 'that was when he really started to believe he could win the Tour, too. I had always believed it, ever since he was young. But now Luis did, too.' And at BIC and with De Muer, for all their failings, he had a team and a director that were really in a position to help him do it.

8

1971: HUNTING THE CANNIBAL

Stage four of the Midi Libre, Montpellier, 6 June 1971. Eddy Merckx crosses the race's final finish line safe in the knowledge that the leader's jersey, which he has taken on the first stage, is his for keeps. It should be a moment for celebration, but it is not. Merckx's left knee is giving him such grief that he has to ask spectators to hold him up – he cannot put weight on it. 'Worry, tiredness and suffering are etched on his face,' writes one reporter, who also points out that there is 'only' a 9" gap between Merckx and runner-up Joop Zoetemelk overall: a near-defeat, rather than another near-automatic victory for the unstoppable Cannibal.

Merckx has already had to abandon one top race, Paris–Nice in 1968, because of the same knee injury. Rather than face a long drive north, he therefore opts to fly back to Paris in a private jet belonging to a rival team's director, Jean de Gribaldy, with wife Claudine and a young Molteni team-mate, Jos De Schoenmaecker, who has broken his leg and will no longer be able to support Merckx in the mountains.

'My left knee is giving me real trouble, I've been in serious trouble since kilometre five, when the attacks started going all the time. Things got so bad that I thought about abandoning at least ten times. I have to see a specialist, the Tour is very close,' Merckx says as the drizzle turns to rain in Montpellier and he heads for the airport.

The Midi-Libre, Merckx tells me 40-odd years later, rather than when he had dropped back briefly on the Col du Granier in the 1971 Dauphiné Libéré a fortnight earlier – as is popularly believed – was when he realised he would have serious trouble in the Tour, the moment his rivals had been waiting for for so long.

'The Granier was just a mechanical issue,' Merckx says. 'It was the Midi Libre that had me worried. I was bound to have a bad year sooner or later.' Even the Cannibal, it turns out, could be hunted down.

***

It might be the most unlikely of surroundings, but Eddy Merckx has no problem recalling the man responsible for his greatest ever defeat.

Merckx is in Qatar, as he has been every year for the last 12 years, as the organiser of the country's title stage race. Having left the five-star, 23-storey hotel with figurines of gold-plated camels at reception and suites costing north of €1,000 a night that serves as the Tour of Qatar's race headquarters, this morning we are spinning along pancake-flat, featureless desert roads in a large Land Rover. This is all a far cry from the Tour de France: rather than tens of thousands of cheering fans, when it comes to spectators much of the time all we can see are occasional herds of camels plodding along the horizon. But the finer details of Merckx's career are as fresh in his memory as if he were back in Europe and it had all happened yesterday.

The first surprise that Merckx produces is that he *does* remember Ocaña from the first major Tour they rode together, the 1968 Giro. This says a great deal about yet another of Merckx's talents, his prodigious ability to keep tabs on all his rivals, potential or otherwise, given Ocaña made little impact on the race and Merckx presumably had a lot on his mind at the time – such as winning overall. The second surprise is that he sees Ocaña as 'impulsive, but he wanted to win, not just because he liked attacking. Otherwise he would not have won the Tour de France. He was a fighter, and had a lot of character, but' – as Merckx sees it, and this comment probably says a lot more about Merckx than Ocaña – 'if you race it's to win.'

Merckx recognises, as he always has done, that Ocaña was his most dangerous rival, but then qualifies this by adding 'he had a lot of ups and downs. High days and low days. Gimondi wasn't so spectacular, but he was more consistent.' A lot of the time, Merckx seems to suggest, when it came to beating Ocaña it was only a question of waiting for the Spaniard to hit a low point, rather than actually doing anything specific himself. As for the thorny question of how he saw Ocaña's nationality, Merckx believes that from the French fans' point of view at least it was dependent on his success rate: 'when he was winning he was French, and when he lost he was Spanish'.

Although Ocaña's defeat of Merckx in the 1971 Tour was widely, and perhaps wrongly, put down to his climbing ability, Merckx is well aware that the Spaniard had plenty of other strings to his bow.

'He was good at everything. Fuente was a better climber, particularly in the Giro. But there were nine summit finishes in one year in the Giro, and Fuente could only put me in trouble in the Giro because the average speed was slower on the flat', meaning Fuente, even more erratic than Ocaña, was more likely to be caught out. 'When Luis was good, though, he was a real all-rounder.'

Merckx says that Ocaña was no quicker than any other rider to notice if he was suffering. But then he casually reveals again the acuteness of his own powers of observation when he debunks the myth that Ocaña was so devil-may-care and uncalculating that he never checked on his rivals when he attacked.

'Oh, he looked back all right, but not directly, he looked under his arm', through the crook of his elbow, where he would not be observed by anyone but the rider right behind him.

Merckx vividly remembers one of the occasions when he was that man, struggling to stay on Ocaña's wheel. 'The way he got rid of me on one [Vuelta 1973] climb in particular, the Orduña, that was when he most impressed me. I thought, "Hmm, this is going to be hard in July." In 1971 I wasn't good, but in 1973 I was good and he still dropped me. I went on to win the Vuelta, the Giro and the Tour de Suisse. If I had raced the Tour that year, it would have been a great battle.'

But if Ocaña was superior to him on a very few occasions, Merckx is still keen to point out that after his terrible crash in the Blois velodrome in September 1969, 'I was never like I was before in the climbs, because of my back problems from that accident.'

Although he realises that his knee issues in the Midi Libre were what gave his rivals hope they could beat him in the Tour that year, he says that in fact 'my back injuries were the really big problem. I had had problems with my knees, but it was that 1969 crash that really did it. That was why I was constantly changing my position on the bike: both my hips had been dislocated and I wasn't so good on the climbs.' Indeed, 25 years later he was still having physiotherapy for his injuries.

He adds in another factor: not doing the Giro. 'I was never so strong if I hadn't done the Giro first. In 1975, too, I lost the Tour after not doing it. The same in 1971. I was always better after the Giro than if I did the Dauphiné, like in 1971 and 1975.'

Yet even then, Ocaña could not beat him – most of the time. 'The thing was the press and the people, they wanted him to beat me,' he says. 'That's why when we got to the GP Nations [race]' – at the end of what had been Ocaña's best season – 'I made sure I beat him by two or three minutes.' But Merckx barks 'No', repeatedly, when asked if there was any chance of the two of them racing on the same squad: their rivalry went too deep for that. He is equally dismissive about the idea of Ocaña working in a break if the two of them happened to go clear together.

In fact, the conversation – and the sense of the intensity of their rivalry – gains an edge of surreal humour when I suggest that Ocaña might have been such a fighter because of his poor upbringing. Perhaps without realising he is mimicking the celebrated 'we lived in a cardboard box in the middle of the road' *Monty Python* sketch, Merckx immediately retorts rather pugnaciously, 'My parents were not rich either. There were three kids in my family, myself, my brother and my sister.' It is as if, even now, he cannot face the idea that Ocaña might have had the edge on him at anything – even having had it tougher as a child. Traces of the old rivalry, it seems, still linger.

From 1971 to 1973, the low point in their relationship, there was no communication whatsoever between the two. 'No. The newspaper would say "Ocaña has said this" and then I would go and do that and he didn't speak to me and I didn't speak to him. Why should I if I read what he's been saying?'

'Luis rode for a French team, De Muer was French as well,' Merckx points out, as if those facts alone were enough to add another layer of separation between the two of them.

'Everybody has to make their own choices,' he concludes somewhat cryptically before suddenly adding, 'but he was a good guy, a correct guy, with a good sense of humour, too.' In the criteriums, for example, widely viewed as fixed in their results, he says they never had any problems coming to agreement.

It was after the 1973 GP Nations (a defeat that must have stung the Spaniard given the number of wins Ocaña racked up that season) that they had their first reconciliation – as it happened, at 30,000 feet. 'The day after, we had to ride in Lausanne, and on the plane' – he draws a rectangle in the air and indicates the top left-hand corner and the bottom right to illustrate his point – 'I was sitting there and he was over there.

'Then he comes up to me and says, "Hey, we shouldn't go on fighting. It's the newspapers and you make comments about me …" So we had a drink together, and then things were better. But we didn't have so much contact. We'd talk a bit in the peloton and just a few calls after he retired.' Certainly, according to Josiane, things were not as rosy as the press liked to suggest until the latter years of Ocaña's life and Merckx's offer to assist in selling the Spaniard's Armagnac, when, as Merckx recalls, 'I put him in touch with the biggest drinks distributor in Belgium to try and help him.'

There were some areas, Merckx says, where Ocaña could not complain. 'He had a good director and his team at BIC weren't bad. [Johny] Schleck, [Alain] Vasseur, they were good riders.' As an afterthought, he then adds 'Roger Rosiers' – which is a bit of a double-edged compliment, given Rosiers was so good that he 'poached' the Paris–Roubaix winner for Molteni from BIC in 1974!

As ever, a strong top name causes everybody to raise their game, Merckx points out, and enables a leader to focus on keeping the same group of riders around him rather than testing out new talent – which, again, strengthens the collective performance. 'That's what happened with me, I had the same group of core riders for eight or nine years. They asked me at KAS in 1973 and 1974 if I wanted to go there, for double the money Molteni were offering, but they would only let me take three or four riders with me and I wanted to stay with my team-mates.'

As for Ocaña's constant battling with misfortune, Merckx feels it was compounded by other factors. 'He had a lot of bad luck, but he crashed a lot because he took a lot of risks. That was his character. You could see that with what happened with his car accidents after the Tour.' Like everybody else, Merckx got in a car once with Ocaña, but was not keen to repeat the experience. 'We were running late for a plane to get to a criterium. Ai! Ai! He drove like a lunatic.'

Just as the rivalry and comparisons with Ocaña must have gone from motivating – as it did when he beat Ocaña in the GP Nations – to tediously repetitive, so Merckx said that the constant studying for cracks in the carapace of his invincibility also eventually became wearisome. 'The French people wanted me to have problems,' he says bluntly. He cites one French TV commentator as being overly keen to say, '"Merckx at two minutes, Merckx *en difficulté, Merckx c'est fini*". They *hoped* it was finished for me.'

For that reason, perhaps, even if Merckx was clearly superior to Ocaña for the bulk of the four years that their rivalry was at its peak (1970–73), for many fans (particularly the French, if Eddy is to be believed) the open-ended nature of the 1971 Tour defined their relationship. And Merckx unconsciously confirms that appeal of uncertainty when he is asked who could conquer the upcoming Tour. 'I don't know,' he replies, 'but it's nice when you don't know who's going to win.' Coming from Merckx, that is quite an admission. But when it came to Ocaña, it is clear that element of doubt was something he would never have willingly permitted.

***

If there was one high point in the 1971 Vuelta – Ocaña's only other Grand Tour of the season – in what proved to be a singularly dull race, it was Luis Ocaña's attack on the stage to Vitoria. 'An earthquake in the pedals of Luis Ocaña', according to *ABC*, and, heaven knows, the race needed one.

The route had a lot to do with the tedium: there was virtually no real terrain for the riders to try to establish any differences. As for time trials, where Ocaña had effectively won in 1970, there were three: a prologue, one in Bilbao and one on the final day in Madrid. But they came to a grand total of 10.5 kilometres.

The mountains didn't offer any real opportunities either: there were no Pyrenean stages whatsoever, and summit finishes, while featuring in the Tour and Giro d'Italia, were still a thing of the future in the Vuelta – the first appeared in 1972. The organisers had trebled the number of classified climbs, from 12 in 1970 to 33, but they were invariably a long way from the finish and so would give the peloton the chance to regroup. When a Classics specialist like Walter Godefroot won the 'toughest mountain stage' into Manresa – with René Pijnen, the track specialist who had been beaten by Ocaña in the 1970 Vuelta prologue, remaining the leader – the race's singular lack of appealing high points was clear.

Ocaña's lack of motivation was, he said, only partly due to the absence of terrain: it was also partly financial. The organisers had refused to pay him a decent start fee, and on top of that there was no Merckx to spur him on to greatness. As if that was not enough, Ocaña's new team-mate at BIC, Pijnen, had been in the lead ever since the race had started in the Spaghetti Western town of Tabernas in Almería (where the journalists raved more about accidentally crossing paths with Ursula Andress than the race). With no room for manoeuvre given Pijnen's surprisingly strong hold on the lead, the previous year's winner seemed to be making up the numbers.

That impression was reinforced on stage ten to Pamplona, a seemingly innocuous stage where 20 riders (among them future race winner Ferdinand Bracke, Raymond Poulidor and Agustín Tamames) went clear on a small climb after some 60 kilometres. When the penny collectively dropped later that Ocaña was missing – as well as race leader Pijnen and Godefroot – the group of 20 picked up the pace. By the time they reached Pamplona, Ocaña and the main pack were at more than 5'00", and Tamames, only in the move initially because he was working for Werner team-mate Luis Balagué, took both stage and lead. It seemed that Ocaña had been eliminated from the running, almost by a fluke.

But rather than give up completely, losing time in such an unexpected way proved to be just the kick up the backside that Ocaña needed. According to Lucy Fallon and Adrian Bell's history of the Vuelta, Ocaña criticised himself for 'losing the Vuelta because I haven't been intelligent enough to be in the right place at the right time'. But he vowed to put the record straight on those who had stolen a march on him. 'I'll make them sweat blood,' he claimed.

A brief truce then followed, with the only interest a switch of lead to young Basque rider Mikel Lasa thanks to the Bilbao 'time trial'. But it was very brief: on stage 12's twin climbs of the Orduña and Herrera in the Basque region of Alava, Ocaña took the Vuelta by the scruff of its neck. In blazing heat, he attacked at the foot of the Orduña, breasting the summit alone. Caught by a small group of riders on the descent, he repeated the operation on the Herrera. And this time, no one could follow him.

With 30 kilometres left to race to the finish in Vitoria, Ocaña might have been doomed to failure. But instead he went into time trial mode, doubling his advantage of 1'00" to 2'00" by the time he reached the Basque capital. Bracke, himself no poor time trialler who cleverly limited his losses by keeping to a steady pace, moved into first place overall. But given that Ocaña gained 22 spots and was now in third place, just 2'19" back on the Belgian, the BIC leader looked very much to be the coming man. In stark contrast, Tamames and Zoetemelk, as well as Lasa, were all out for the count.

Yet for all Ocaña's brave words, as the race wended its way southwards through Burgos and Avila to Madrid, the terrain (steady, long climbs perfectly suited to Bracke), the heavy rainfall and the absence of time trials all combined to make it impossible for him to turn the tables. On top of that, on the stage to Burgos, Bracke's team-mate Wilfried David combined forces with Lasa, smarting from his defeat in Vitoria, and moved into third overall. David, playing a clever strategic game, let Lasa – in theory with more to gain, and briefly yellow jersey on the road – do the bulk of the work as the rain pelted down, and then dropped him ten kilometres from the finish in Burgos. The result was that while Bracke, greatly helped by Godefroot on the climb of Las Mazorras, considerably reinforced his lead, Ocaña and Lasa each lost a place overall.

Ocaña's protests at Burgos – 'I've worn myself out for nothing, why does it have to end like this?' – smacked of a man throwing in the towel. But instead it was Bracke who hogged the limelight after the judges first insisted he had received an illegal tow and penalised him with 30", which would have caused him to lose the lead, and then reinstated him when they 'realised', after some vigorous protests from the Peugeot sports director, that the guilty party was another rider.

Hope still remained that Ocaña might yet do battle on the stage from Segovia to Avila, but even the ultra-partisan *ABC* seemed to harbour a few doubts given Ocaña's mercurial nature: 'Can Ocaña dislodge Bracke? Excuse me from answering [that question] because Ocaña is a man from whom we can expect everything. But he is a man capable of disappointing whoever expects anything from him at all.'

Yet all the speculation that Ocaña could turn in a second stage like the one in Vitoria evaporated as Bracke was dropped early on, but Ocaña seemed incapable of shedding David in the sierras of Avila. Over the Guadarrama climb Ocaña's repeated charges helped form a ten-man group ahead. But if David's shadowing him was not discouraging enough for Ocaña, as the rain turned to sleet, Bracke – a far less explosive rider than Ocaña but equally tenacious – slowly caught up with the front group again. The race was effectively settled, and if Ocaña moved up to third overall again, it was only thanks to Schepers testing positive for a banned substance on the last day.

For Bracke, in the twilight of his career, the Vuelta lead was a wholly unexpected bonus. The former World Hour Record holder's only other outstanding Grand Tour performance, third overall in the 1968 Tour, had left him wondering what might have been given that both he and the outright winner, Janssen, had moved on to the podium thanks to blistering time trials on the last day. A victory in the Vuelta provided confirmation for him, at last, that Paris 1968 had not been a fluke.

As for Ocaña, his third podium in a Grand Tour in three years – all in the Vuelta – might have felt disappointing in the short term, but his lone flight in Vitoria marked an important breakthrough. Apart from underlining his strong form, it was also the first time he had tried a long-range attack in a major Tour, establishing the difference in the final major climb and then increasing it on the run-in to the finish. But it would not be the last.

***

Ocaña had already felt that this season might be a different one for other reasons: he had already been to a liver specialist over the winter in Bilbao who had provided him with new treatment that was proving very effective. An initial duel at Paris–Nice had seen him suffer from more bad luck – a black cat running into the road that had caused both him and several team-mates to fall – but still hold on to third place overall. Ocaña attributed his failure to make any more of an impact to not being fully in form and to making some mistakes with his gearing on the Col d'Eze.

Then, in the Vuelta al País Vasco, Ocaña made it clear he had yet to reach an upper limit in time trialling. In one of his greatest ever displays of strength, in 30 kilometres between Tolosa and San Sebastián, Ocaña opened up a gap of 1'50" on closest rival Raymond Poulidor that netted him his first overall victory in Spain's third biggest bike race. That an international star and gifted time triallist of the calibre of Poulidor should be unable to squeeze the gap any closer is one indication of Ocaña's superiority. Another is that the following eight riders on the stage were all timed within 1'00" of each other.

A third indication of the increasingly yawning gap between Ocaña and his rivals was that in a victory in the Setmana Catalana's opening prologue of ten kilometres a month earlier, the gap between Ocaña and Poulidor, also second in the Catalan race, had been just 7". In the Vuelta al País Vasco in a stage just three times the distance, the time gap was ten times that of Catalonia.

Barely 48 hours after the curtain had fallen on the Vuelta, Ocaña found himself facing Eddy Merckx in the Dauphiné Libéré. Merckx had had an odd spring: victories in Het Volk, Paris–Nice, a fourth Milan–San Remo and the GP Frankfurt all

121

suggested business as usual. Losing Paris–Roubaix after five punctures was hardly his fault, but a stunning long-distance breakaway in Liège–Bastogne–Liège through the snow and sleet that ended with him cracking in the last 30 kilometres then coming round his most tenacious rival, Georges Pintens, in the finale was an unusually last-ditch victory for Merckx. It was as if he had sorely overestimated his own strength.

Then Molteni announced that Merckx would be making his debut in the Dauphiné, not the Giro, because of 'intense activity in the spring'. Given that it had never bothered Merckx in the past, his rivals must have pricked up their ears. 'He will be going to the Dauphiné with a 100 per cent Belgian team,' the communiqué added as if that somehow explained it all. But it didn't.

On the plus side for Merckx fans were his 13 victories in 1971, even before he reached the race's start line in Avignon. If Merckx's rivals needed discouragement, they need only have opened the sports pages of *Le Dauphiné Libéré*, still the race's main backer. Of the 32 major stage races he had taken part in since turning pro in 1966, the *DL* reported, Merckx had won half of them. Of cycling's 30 major competitions, only eight remained out of his clutches, and given he had not tackled five of them yet – Bordeaux–Paris, the Tour de Suisse, the Vuelta, the Dauphiné Libéré and the Hour Record – that was hardly his fault.

Writing in the paper, top French cycling journalist Roger Cornet said of Merckx that year: 'His attention to detail, his well-finished work, his unwillingness to take part in races except for winning, his meticulousness about his bike material to the point of obsession, his rigorous self-discipline in all walks of life, not to mention the calm brought about by an excellent marriage, have made Merckx what he is.

'Contrary to what his amazing palmarès might suggest, he leaves nothing to pure chance and he uses all his courage, maintains his single-mindedness, reacts as a man and triumphs.'

However, as was also typical of Merckx, given that he had gone an entire 17 days without racing, prior to the Dauphiné he expressed concern about a possible weakening of form. As if to prove he was not going to allow himself the slightest concession to weakness, he refused the deluxe suite of rooms (including a round bed) the Hôtel Davico in Avignon had specially reserved for him prior to the opening stage, saying it was 'more suitable for a Hollywood star'. This was no mere posing: he went along the corridor with his suitcase, knocked on his team manager Guillaume Driessens' door and told him to pack his bags because they were swapping rooms.

In honour of Merckx, Molteni were given last place-off in the opening team time trial, with BIC and defending champion Ocaña finishing second behind them at 5". De Muer said afterwards that they had made a sluggish start, and, indeed, on the first of the five laps of the city centre circuit, BIC lost 6" to their Italian arch-rivals. Ocaña, using a huge gear as was his custom, tried to spark some life into his squad and on the fifth lap BIC scraped back 2". But it was too late, and Merckx, first across the line, earned himself the race lead. For the last three years, since winning the Paris–Nice team time trial in 1968, Molteni had been undefeated in this particular speciality: in Avignon, as implacable as Victorian railway engineers laying down another section of track on a new line, the Italian team pushed out the record a little further.

Stage one was a collective effort: stage two was all about the individual. A bunch sprint victory by Eric Leman forced Merckx briefly to lose the lead in the stage's morning sector and change into his Belgian National Champion's jersey for the afternoon's racing. But after making a spellbinding ascent of the Col de la République, Merckx then won the sprint into St-Etienne. 'I didn't trust the others so decided to go as hard as possible' was his laconic explanation at the finish.

Merckx's devastating start made it clear he would – as usual – be the man to beat, and *Le Dauphiné* was so delighted cycling's number one had more than lived up to expectations that it devoted the front page to Merckx's win. (News that the Russians were sending the world's first ever rocket to Mars earned just a paragraph in comparison: *Le Dauphiné* knew what its readers cared about.)

The first big mountain challenge, the Col de Montaud on stage three, saw Merckx come through unscathed. But he warned that 'the opposition are massing, with Ocaña, Poulidor, Aimar, [Joaquim] Agostinho and all of the Peugeots waiting for their chance. And Agostinho is the big challenger now.'

Worryingly, of all his Molteni team-mates, only De Schoenmaecker had stayed with him in the mountains, and Ocaña – albeit cursing the maladroitness of his team-mate Désiré Letort on one of the descents that had, he said, cost him a few seconds – was up to second overall.

The next stage to Annecy was the toughest mountain challenge of the race, featuring four cols: the Granier, Revard, Leschaux and Forclaz. Faced by a blizzard of attacks on the Granier, Merckx briefly lost contact. At most there were 300 yards, no more, between Merckx and his chief attackers, and on the descent of the Granier he bridged back across. But for all that he blamed mechanical problems rather than a moment of weakness, the press instantly smelled blood and claimed Merckx was beginning to buckle. Rather than look at the results – which saw Merckx claim second behind Letort on the finish on Annecy's lakefront – this was a sign of vulnerability badly needed by the media given that Merckx seemed permanently head and shoulders above the rest.

Ocaña helped boost the plethora of 'what if?' articles by saying that only the weather had stopped him from deposing Merckx. 'After the [Col de] Revard, the rain let me down and when it wasn't so hot, Merckx was less vulnerable on the Forclaz. If it had been as cold as it had been on the Granier, he would have been a lot more vulnerable.'

'It was a mechanical problem,' Merckx retorted, 'I had to stay calm, that was all. A quick bike change on the descent sorted it all out.' Indeed, although Ocaña had tried to drop Merckx five times on the ascent of the Forclaz, on each occasion the Belgian romped back up to the Spaniard's back wheel.

Le Dauphiné's columnists preached caution, criticising what they called the *anti-Merckxistes* who had dominated a lively local TV post-race debate with claims that Merckx's brief problems on the Granier were 'the beginning of his decline, his first drop in power'.

The newspaper instead posed ironic questions, saying, 'It is so simple to doubt ... Merckx should surely be unhappy – shouldn't he? After such hard work and failing to lose any time whatsoever, he kept total control on what was a defensively fought out race.

'Too many questions are being asked about Merckx after his slight problem on the Granier, and his eighth place across the summit ... this is just seizing on the slightest sign of weakness to try and question his status as a super-champion. Even if it's the wrong sign.'

That, the paper added, should not detract from Ocaña's performance 'always bouncing around, a born attacker, persisting with his one charge off the front after another, he has fired off some *banderillos* [small lances used in a bullfight] with accuracy and authority'. But the implication was clear: by no means had Ocaña killed the bull.

This was proved conclusively in the final time trial, from Creusot to Montceau-les-Mines, where Ocaña lost 24" to Merckx over 30 kilometres. Eight seconds ahead of Ocaña after nine kilometres, Merckx steadily inched ahead, doubling his advantage by the second checkpoint despite what he called a 'strong headwind, so strong I reckoned I'd need 40 minutes for the course'. In fact he took 36'17": not permitted to know the time gaps, he relied on his sports director Driessens using a pre-established code of car horn hoots to let him know how he was going.

Overall the Belgian took what he called 'a great win because it shows how well my preparation is going for the Tour'. Ocaña, on the other hand, was forced to claim again that he 'had started too slowly' but that he had regained 1" on Merckx in the second half of the course. It was a risibly small claim to fame on Ocaña's part, but it perfectly indicates how even Merckx's greatest challenger was sometimes forced to clutch at the tiniest of straws if he did not want to lose all hope completely of beating him.

And even Merckx was not averse to mind games. Well aware how important a role the Dauphiné played – and still plays – in the battle for the psychological upper hand in July, Merckx said, 'I was basing everything on how I'd go for the Tour, but I wouldn't let a victory go by just like that.

'The race was really demanding on each level, and I had to progress rapidly, keep going to be sure of my level and watch out for the guys who'd come out of the Vuelta with good form.' This was a not so oblique reference to Ocaña, whom he singled out as the main challenger, in cycling a time-honoured way of piling the pressure onto your rival. (Thirty years later Lance Armstrong used to win the Tour every year – before being stripped of his titles for doping – but he would insist each June that Jan Ullrich was the big favourite.)

'Since 1 May when I won in the GP Frankfurt, I haven't ridden any big races and I've only been training for fun,' Merckx said. 'I've been coming and going in the car and by plane, to Portugal, Brittany, Italy for the Coppa Bernocchi on 12 May before going back to Milan again last Sunday for another criterium, having just ridden a race in France in between. I knew I was going to have real problems getting into the top level of race here,' he added – although given that he nonetheless won, the subliminal message to his rivals was plain: they still couldn't beat him.

'But as I felt in good shape, I decided to take the initiative on the first day to see who my rivals would be.'

Le Dauphiné, meanwhile, conceded that Ocaña – who won the Mountains prize and the 'fair play prize' for a slew of good qualities including 'friendliness, charm, good looks and good mood', had put up a '*belle resistance*'. But they immediately pointed out that Merckx had beaten him by the equivalent of 297 metres – almost exactly the same distance the Belgian had lost on the Granier before returning to the pack. (If *Le Dauphiné* had wanted to emphasise that there was no chance of any major upheavals in the cycling or, indeed, any other world in the near future, it could not have done better than the story it put on the same page as the Merckx article: a highly dramatic local court case centring on a family of rabbits discovered nesting in the engine compartment of a car.)

The received wisdom among Merckx biographers is that the Dauphiné Libéré marked a turning point in the Belgian's fortunes in 1971. Yet Merckx himself indicates it was the Midi Libre that had him the most worried, and, given the extent of his nagging knee injuries there, it is understandable why he felt vulnerable. The Dauphiné, in fact, revealed that, if anything was off the boil, it was Merckx's squad in the mountains. BIC claimed the team prize in the Dauphiné by more than a quarter of an hour on Molteni, with Mann-Grundig and Mars-Flandria far closer than the Italian outfit, and Ocaña's team-mate Letort was strong enough to win at Annecy with a lone late attack.

'I made more of a clear-out on the République than I expected, but I also saw that my own team was weak. So I opted to take things as calmly as possible, race on the defensive and in that sense I felt restless rather than disappointed [with my performance],' Merckx explained. Indeed, his one solid climbing team-mate, De Schoenmaecker, who had performed well on the République and the Montaud, was soon to be hospitalised after crashing in the Midi Libre.

'Apart from Ocaña,' Merckx said, 'most of the teams were trying to make me lose rather than win themselves. On the Revard, for example, nobody moved even though I was down to just one team-mate.'

Ultimately, though, the Dauphiné – particularly when it was held six weeks before the Tour, rather than finishing less than three weeks before the Tour starts, as it does now – only functioned up to a point as a form guide for July. The key favourite remained the same; what was different was that the key pretender to his throne was aware that he could come closer and – after the Vuelta – had already seen that one of his strategies for turning the overall classification upside down could work to devastating effect.

On an individual level, after all the speculation, the claims and counter-claims over who knew, with the glorious benefit of hindsight, that Merckx was going to have a hard time of it in the Tour, perhaps it is wisest to leave the summing-up to the one protagonist who is still alive: 'The difference between other years and 1971,' Merckx says, 'is that I wasn't going really badly but I wasn't going that well either. It wasn't a good year. Ocaña, though – he had got a lot better, he was super-strong.'

With the omens, if not positive, at least looking less negative than they had been, Ocaña's way of 'easing back' before the Tour itself was to buy himself a powerful new motorbike, a 750cc, added to his collection of motor vehicles 'to help me relax and go faster than ever before'. Only someone as mercurial as Ocaña could fail to notice the contradiction in that – or wonder where his restless fixation with Merckx would finally take him.

***

North of the Pyrenees, Ocaña was ranked number one rival to Merckx in the 1971 Tour de France. 'Scared? Why should I be scared?' Ocaña spat out when asked if he was worried about that particular label. 'If I were scared I'd stop racing and run away home.'

De Muer insisted that Ocaña was in great shape and that only a crass error by his leader (while De Muer wasn't there, of course) had wrecked his Vuelta: 'My only regret about the Tour of Spain is that I arrived there too late, the day after Ocaña and Pijnen, both of whom had been riding well, were stupidly dropped [on the way to Pamplona],' De Muer said later. 'Luis is going just as well as in 1970, I think Eddy will be surprised at the level of the riders who've done the Vuelta.'

Others who knew Ocaña well were not so optimistic. 'I think it will be Eddy first, Ocaña second,' said BIC's gloom merchant Anatole Novak for the second year running, a rider almost as well known for trying (and failing) to get journalists to call him 'Roger' instead of his slightly archaic Christian name as he was for his cheerful predictions. That said, Novak warned, rather ominously, 'but Merckx will have to be sure he doesn't have a single bad day, because Luis will take advantage of that in a flash. The problem I have is trying to work out who will be third on the podium in Paris.'

In Spain, they were none too upbeat about their chances in the 1971 Tour with Ocaña, with *MARCA*, the country's leading sports newspaper, saying in its preview, 'the times of [climbing aces] Bahamontes, Julio Jiménez and [Basque 1950s cycling star] Jesús Loroño are behind us and we don't have, for the moment, anybody capable of getting away on the climbs and staying away'. There was barely a mention of Ocaña, with the paper naming Francisco Galdos (fourth in the 1971 Giro but with only ninth in the Tour as his best result) as the one rider likely to cause Merckx any trouble.

'Ocaña could be a rival,' *MARCA* argued, 'but the fight will be an unequal one … Merckx with his superiority has wiped out all possibility of a contest.' It then promptly changed the subject. Its one prediction that actually proved accurate concerned the stage to Orcières-Merlette: 'With three climbs – Laffrey, the Noyer and

Merlette itself – if the riders make the most of it or try to do so, then it will be a spectacular stage.'

Only KAS director Dalmacio Langarica was in any way optimistic, saying, 'if somebody's going to finish off Merckx, it could be now'. Given he had been behind the driving wheel when Bahamontes had taken the country's first Tour back in 1959, perhaps the Spanish papers should have paid a little more attention. Or for those believing in fortunate coincidences, they might have taken it as a good sign that for the first time since 1959 the Tour finished on the same date on which Spain won its first Tour – 18 July.

***

The Tour, the shortest since 1905, could not have started better for Ocaña. On stage two to Strasbourg, he formed part of an elite breakaway group of 15, headed by Eddy Merckx, that claimed nearly 9'30" on the rest of the field.

It was a massive gap for so early in the race, even if Merckx was the stage winner, squeaking ahead of Roger De Vlaeminck at the last moment to claim the day's victory by a quarter of a wheel, as well as reinforcing his lead. But what truly mattered was that the break of 15 had an emphatic enough margin and contained enough prestigious names, to ensure that they, and they alone, would be fighting for the right to wear the leader's jersey in Paris.

'The hierarchies became stabilised in the teams as a result, in favour of those in that break,' comments specialist cycling history website *memoire du cyclisme*. Aimar had to work for Van Impe and Ferdinand Bracke lost his position of leader in favour of Bernard Thévenet.'

Ocaña, in BIC, did not have these leadership issues: but at the very least it was clear who he was up against – Merckx, Zoetemelk, Van Impe, Mortensen – and when it came to designated Tour contenders, the Spaniard was very much on the right side of the divide.

'We were expecting that,' said Merckx's sports director, Driessens, 'we have seen from the start of the season Luis is not half as nervous as he used to be, and with that added confidence, he's got it in him to be a great rider.' The implication being that he still had some catching up to do on Merckx.

Driessens' doubled-edged compliments notwithstanding, Ocaña was also the only Spaniard in the Strasbourg move, which rather put paid to *MARCA's* theory about Galdos being the man to follow. For now, at least, they were not facing a repeat of 1970.

'Last year I went through the Alps on my hands and knees,' Ocaña said, 'and I hope that won't be the same this year. Others want to have the honour of runners-up spot to Merckx. I don't think he's invincible, nobody is. So we have to know who would be the most powerful person if that was the case and Merckx cracks.'

'We can tire him out ... he's a surefire candidate for the overall win, and that's why we have to attack him every day.' Others like José Antonio Momeñe, a top five finisher for Spain in the Vuelta and the Tour, preferred to take the usual defeatist line with Merckx: 'He's the number one rider. We'll just have to leave him to it.'

***

For Merckx the start of the Tour had been like the rest of his season: odd. After the organisers forgot to bring the yellow jersey to the beginning of the race so that he could wear it as defending champion, he nonetheless took the lead on the Mulhouse team time trial prologue thanks to Molteni's repetition of their Dauphiné victory. However, Merckx then lost it again to his team-mate Marinus Wagtmans on the first sector of three on stage one because Wagtmans had finished ahead of him in the bunch sprint. Less than 15'00" into the second sector of the stage, though, Merckx took a time bonus and was back in yellow.

As if all this 'pass the parcel' with the leader's jersey was not strange enough, on the first sector for the first hour there was a riders' strike – over the prize money remaining the same since

1963. Classics specialist Eric Leman amused the photographers on the back of motorbikes by pretending to be asleep on his bike as the race covered a grand total of one kilometre in 10'00". And then Merckx, presumably annoyed at this frivolity, went on the attack and the bunch lined out: back to business as usual.

But even if the first week gave little indication of later developments, as he was just 52" down on Merckx by the time the race reached its first rest day at the Channel resort of Le Touquet, Ocaña could nonetheless continue to be optimistic. He had not been squeezed out of the mix when the race tackled the *murs* (short, ultra-steep, usually cobbled climbs) and *monts* (short, ultra-steep, usually wooded climbs) of Belgium, nor had Merckx, apparently discouraged from attacks by strong headwinds, managed to increase his lead.

In fact, little of note at all had happened since Strasbourg, other than Merckx clocking up his 50th day in yellow when the race reached Roubaix, more than any other rider in the history of the Tour. 'You can say what you like about all the others, but Merckx is superior to the rest. I don't know what I'd do to beat him,' Jacques Anquetil said as the Belgian seemed to be heading inexorably towards his third Tour de France win in as many years.

For once, there had been no crashes or untimely punctures for Ocaña, and if it had rained and been exceptionally cold on some stages, the sunshine that accompanied the Tour as it approached the English Channel eased Ocaña's worries again. But that success came at a price: he was becoming more and more of a favourite. And as the mountains loomed on the Tour's horizon, and the pressure on him to perform became inescapable, Ocaña became deliberately elusive. After sleeping 12 hours solid, from 10 p.m. to 10 a.m., on the rest day he made the most of the enormous, largely empty beachside hotel that housed the team to avoid reporters seeking interviews, hiding in vacant guest rooms and dodging from one empty corridor to another as the journalists asked team-mates of his whereabouts.

The one journalist who did track him down was rewarded with the blandest of predictions: that Merckx would continue to be 'the king' and that on the Puy-de-Dôme, the first mountain-top finish, there would not be enormous time differences between the top names. Ocaña also predicted that, apart from Merckx, Giro winner Gösta Pettersson and Zoetemelk, lying fourth and sixth overall, could cause him problems.

'The [upcoming] Puy-de-Dôme [summit finish] will be the point that confirms if Merckx is as good a climber as last year and if Zoetemelk has progressed,' he said, 'and I think both are true.' He remained as gung-ho as ever: 'I'll go all out, give it everything. If you sink as a result, what does it matter?'

Apart from avoiding the press pack, Ocaña did make one visit, however – to see his bike in the hotel garage. 'It glistened and shone,' he claimed. 'It seemed as if it was as impatient as its owner to break away from the bunch.'

***

If Merckx was soon to be in serious trouble, the Spaniard's victory on the Puy-de-Dôme over the Belgian provided – finally – the first real indication of the shape of things to come. En route to the extinct volcano and its mist-shrouded summit, Ocaña gained a sliver of his future margin over the Belgian, just 15", and he was not the only one to do so: Zootemelk claimed 8", the Portuguese stage race specialist Joaquim Agostinho 2".

Yet of all the attacks that day, future double Tour winner Bernard Thévenet's and Ocaña's were the most telling. Or, as Ocaña put it, 'We were the ones that broke the belief that nobody would attack the ogre of the Tour into little pieces.'

Former French national champion Raymond Deslisle had been the first one to surprise Merckx on the road that wound round and round the Puy's summit like a helter-skelter slide, jammed between the mountainside and the valley below. And although Deslisle's derailleur gear blocked up, stage-race specialists Enrico Paolini of Italy and Spain's Agustín Tamames continued the Merckx-baiting with a couple of brief digs. However, it was Thévenet's prolonged acceleration that made Merckx really struggle and, after Zootemelk and Agostinho counter-attacked, it was Ocaña who shot away into the fog, this time gone for good.

Albeit a minor setback for Merckx, that left Ocaña still lagging by 37" on the Belgian, the Puy marked a watershed. '[It was] Merckx's first big defeat,' *MARCA* said, rather smugly. Merckx had been seen to hesitate, had failed to take up the challenge when laid down not by one, but half a dozen different riders. He had beaten back numerous attacks on the 210 kilometres that preceded the Puy-de-Dôme, Ocaña said. But when the crunch came, Merckx could not respond – and at the finish, as his rivals watched him with barely disguised delight, Merckx wandered around 'like a man who'd been stunned', Ocaña recalled, 'unable to explain to himself what had happened. His pride wouldn't let him.'

'I felt delighted at winning the stage, I didn't think I was a good enough climber to do that. Last year on stage eight, I lost 20 minutes to Merckx and was just thinking about getting from one team hotel to the next. What a difference one year makes!'

'It was a severe defeat for Merckx,' *MARCA* wrote. 'Ocaña has "killed" Merckx and the Tour is reborn,' added *L'Equipe*, while Goddet himself named Ocaña and Zoetemelk as 'the real rivals of Eddy Merckx, his most permanent threat'. It seemed like a lot to make of 15" loss, but making even the slightest inroad on Merckx was always important: just a month before, Ocaña had been crowing about regaining a second on the Belgian in the Dauphiné time trial (which Merckx nonetheless still won). 'Now,' Paris–Nice organiser Jean Leulliot, present at the race as a journalist, said, 'Ocaña should sit tight and wait for the [stage 15] time trial to Super-Bagnères.'

Instead, two days later, en route from St-Etienne to Grenoble, the knives came out again. Rather than a knockout blow at the finish, though, this time Maurice De Muer ordered the Spaniard's team-mate Désiré Letort to stage an early attack on the Col du Cucheron in order to wear out Merckx's Molteni troops.

It went even better than planned. When Letort came within sight of the group of favourites on the descent of the Cucheron, only five riders remained alongside Merckx – and none of them were the Belgian's team-mates. Then as the six shot past Letort, who raised his drinking bottle in a mocking acknowledgement of his 'defeat', Merckx punctured.

Ocaña seized this chance with both hands. Rather than wait for the Belgian, as might have been considered more in the spirit of fair play, he stormed away from Merckx – who was zigzagging from one side of the road to the other as he fought to keep control of his bike, and none too concerned with what was going on around him.

'It was Luis who drove the hardest,' recalls Thévenet. 'I saw Merckx puncture and I was a bit dumbfounded because I'd never seen Luis attack somebody in those circumstances. Attacking somebody when they puncture, that's not good behaviour.'

There were no real options on the table for the riders with Ocaña at that point – Thévenet, Zoetemelk and Gösta Pettersson. 'Luis didn't let us have the choice.' Thévenet later realised that the decision by Ocaña to drive so hard was explicable in terms of Ocaña's character 'because when he got obsessed with something or somebody like Merckx, the blinkers came on.

'He drove like a madman up the Col de Porte, we were all following him like that,' he says – and makes a graphic gesture of throat-cutting. 'I've still got this image of Pettersson taking a bottle in his hand and Ocaña was going so hard on the front Gösta couldn't even get it to his mouth to drink it. He had the bottle in his hand for 300, 400 metres and then he had to throw it away undrunk.' Merckx, meanwhile, closed the gap to 80 metres, but then crumbled.

Ocaña was so strong that it was all the other four could do to stay close to his back wheel, and Van Impe, one of the best climbers in the world, was dropped. By the summit, with Merckx dropped, Thévenet says that – as is also accepted in cycling – once the damage had been done it was no dishonour to make sure there was no restoring of the previous situation. 'And as it had all got moving, we worked a bit on the descent into Grenoble to make sure the gap stayed open, to keep the gap open.'

'I wasn't cross,' Merckx now says about Grenoble, 'that's bike racing. The day he has a flat tyre I would do the same.' And he laughs drily. 'As we say, "eye for an eye, tooth for a tooth".

'I was not that good on the climbs, normally the Col de Porte was a climb that I liked, but I didn't feel so good. Normally I would have got back onto the guys ahead, but that's life.'

By the finish in the Grenoble velodrome where, after an initial attack by Ocaña 'to try and surprise them, I'm no sprinter' – Thévenet finally spurted ahead to win the stage. The quartet's gap of 96" over Merckx saw the Belgian deposed from his top spot overall, with Zoetemelk taking yellow. It was the first time that Merckx had lost a straight duel with a top contender in the Tour.

Ocaña, ahead of Merckx for the first time in a major Tour, too, made the most of the situation to claim: 'Even before the puncture Merckx was in trouble.' Merckx, clearly on the back foot but by no means out for the count, resorted to clichés to avoid too much close questioning. 'The Tour is long and has only just begun, the important thing is to make an attack at the right time, that's when things will be good. I'm not making a drama out of this.'

Not even Zoetemelk, in yellow for the first time in his career by 1" over Ocaña and 1'00" over Merckx, was that optimistic. 'I got the race lead but I was a second-year pro,' he recalled to me, 'basically [I thought] if I got it, with Ocaña racing the way he was and being so strong, I had struck lucky. We didn't make any calculations, it was just a process of elimination on a route and with climbs we all knew well from the Dauphiné – the Cucheron, the Porte, the Granier. There were five or six of us ahead, and I happened to be the best classified.' But Ocaña, despite the increasingly clear evidence that Merckx was not in a position to dominate and despite being the strongest, was still furious about one thing.

'They [the other breakaways] never worked with me for a single moment and then they can pick up the spoils without the slightest effort. It's not right,' Ocaña said when it became clear that Zoetemelk, not he, would be in yellow, and Thévenet's efforts to calm him, by saying, 'relax, you were the strongest, you'll have the yellow jersey tomorrow', failed to have any effect. On the road to Orcières-Merlette the next day, however, Ocaña would find the ideal way of venting that anger.

9

THE ROUTE NAPOLÉON

Driving the route of stage 11 of the 1971 Tour, from Grenoble to Orcières-Merlette, it is hard to imagine this was the scene of what is repeatedly described as one of the greatest exploits ever of the Tour de France.

There are three cols: the Côte de Laffrey, the Noyer – its summit, at 74 kilometres of the 134 kilometres that make up the route, essentially the watershed for the stage – and the final ascent to the ski resort of Orcières-Merlette.

But all three – even the 14.5-kilometre Noyer – were classed as second-category climbs in 1971. And for the bulk of the stage, the peloton found themselves racing along the Route Napoléon south-east towards Gap, now a busy A road and up which the emperor and his troops marched from Elba and Nice in 1815. The road undulates – quite a lot – but it remains well surfaced and broad. There are no sudden dips or steep gradients to break the pace: it is designed for steady, 20 miles a day marching speed by armies, not vicious accelerations to break a two-wheeled rival.

For the last 40 kilometres of the stage where it swung away from the Route Napoléon, the road is even flatter. Apart from the occasional chicane through a village, its curves are as long and smooth as those of a railway. So, too, are the gentle uphill sweeps towards the beginning of the final climb up to Orcières-Merlette, officially 11 kilometres long but only really challenging in its final seven.

What Ocaña, Merckx, Zoetemelk and Co. would have come across first on that day's stage as they headed towards what was taken to be Merckx's Waterloo was the Côte de Laffrey. Just 7.5 kilometres long and steepest at its foot – up to 18 per cent – again this sounds like good terrain for an ambush. But in fact its long, straight, agonisingly steady upward slope – known locally as 'the Ramp' and the scene of numerous fatal traffic accidents when brakes failed on heavy vehicles in the past – is really too smooth a rise for a sudden surprise change of pace. For a relentlessly high rhythm, though, the Ramp would be perfect, and as an early wake-up call for tired legs from a previous stage it would be brutal.

The Laffrey concludes in a village of the same name, and as the long, high plateau stretches away southwards, a lake gleaming on the left, the point of such a straight climb becomes clear. It is to take the Route Napoléon as quickly as possible from the valley floor in Grenoble to the upland plains that ring the western edge of the Alps.

But the road does not go into the Alps. Instead, as it leaves behind the end of the railway line from Grenoble at the town of La Mure and moves higher away from the denser pockets of civilisation, it winds through fir forests and drops past rough pastureland in a broad valley. On the left is the main mountain mass, on the right is one long, snow-gleaming chain of peaks, ringing the Vercors plateau. Dotted along the route, in fact, are small stone monuments like the one dedicated to Dominique Meunier, who died on 25 June 1944 – one of thousands of members of the French Resistance who perished before and during the battle for the 'Free Republic of Vercors', the first French territory liberated from the Nazis.

Compared to the Laffrey, the Noyer is almost a disappointment, at least in terms of gradient: a mere 4.5 per cent, 5.3 at seven kilometres. Compare that, say, with the 25–28 per cent slopes of Spain's steepest single climb, the Angliru, or the 8.4 per cent of France's best-known ascent, the nearby Alpe d'Huez. The one crucial difference is that, rather than the smooth highway the race has been on since before the Laffrey, the ascent of the Noyer was – is – almost all on narrow, twisting roads with cracked tarmac and switchback curves. At 14.5 kilometres – more than twice the length of the Laffrey – like the previous climb it does not seem designed to produce a sense of sudden suffocation for anyone feeling physically on the back foot. Rather, the pain produced by such a relentless upward grind, particularly on a hot day, might be slower to seep into the muscles. But ultimately it would be far more remorseless and inescapable.

After a fast but not exceptionally tricky descent the stage rejoins the Route Napoléon briefly before swinging left onto a slightly smaller road towards Orcières and into an area known locally as the Haute Plaine. This is a pancake-flat, broad valley floor at roughly 1,000 metres above sea level and perhaps 30 kilometres at its widest point from one outlying Alpine spur to another: in fact, the name, meaning 'High Plain', is spot-on.

Thanks to the Haute Plaine, we are treated to a lengthy, dull interlude of driving through a series of flat, windswept potato fields as featureless as anything the eastern fenlands of England can offer. Finally, the village of Merlette – essentially a series of traditional-looking Alpine houses criss-crossed by external beams and with large handwritten signs advertising juniper gin – looms on the horizon.

Just before it, the final climb of the 1971 stage begins. On reading the history of Orcières-Merlette, it is surprising to find it has rarely been used in the Tour (on four occasions only, the last in 1989). But driving up it, it is easy to see why.

The gradient, albeit a little steeper at the bottom, is once again steady, the road surface good, the hairpin bends open and relatively unchallenging even for the sorest legs. Finally the road snakes across the top of a flat-topped mountain and one last long bend to the right takes you almost past the signs announcing the ski station.

And that is it. Orcières-Merlette's one truly difficult feature is that, like the Laffrey and the Noyer, there are no 'false flats' in which to catch your breath and limit the damage. But truth be told, as Alpine climbs go, it is not at all hard, and compared to the jaw-dropping glaciers that act as a backdrop for the Galibier or the uncanny, vast emptiness of the Casse Deserte on the Izoard, only one word is needed to sum up Orcières-Merlette and its surroundings: bland.

And finally, on the drive back from Orcières, the penny drops. Ocaña's victory, hailed as a mountain masterpiece, was in fact a triumph for one of the world's best time triallists on a route made, as much as it could be in an Alpine foothill region, for what effectively became a lone race against the clock. Having broken Merckx's spirit on the early climbs, the flatness of at least half of the 60 kilometres that Ocaña rode alone would have crushed mountain imps like Marco Pantani: rather, they were designed for what the French call a *rouleur-grimpeur*, a rider able to handle both the flat and the uphill, churning a massive gear rather than spinning the pedals like Pantani 'the Pirate' used to do. And the steadiness of the final climb would still have allowed a time triallist like Ocaña to maintain a ridiculously high pace.

To sum up, the terrain suited Ocaña perfectly. As for Merckx, perhaps steeper, shorter efforts on the stage's three categorised ascents might have been more manageable. Instead what sunk him was not the distance – a mere 134 kilometres – but the unrelenting nature of all three climbs: once he had begun to suffer, in other words, this stage was a smooth-sided bowl of pain, with no footholds to slow or even reverse the pain. The other, even more devastating factor, though, was provided courtesy of Ocaña, more in his time-trialling element on the approach roads to Orcières-Merlette and most of the way up it: speed.

***

A tape recording of a dead man's voice, crackling into my ear for almost two hours first on the freezing platform of Paris' Gare de l'Est and then on an agonisingly slow local train through the city's eastern suburbs. A man aged 87, at that stage near the end of his life but still with his own little ways of talking, who wheezes, makes the occasional harrumphing snort that signifies total disbelief of, or scorn for, the person he is discussing. Maurice De Muer's voice is there in my ear, in a scratchy cassette recording interview from 2008, one of the very last he gave. That was the closest I would ever get to De Muer, aka *Le Petit Napoléon*, the man who guided Ocaña on the Route Napoléon to his greatest ever victory, who directed him for the five, main years of his career. But I could feel his dry humour, his rambling but impassioned sense of involvement even after nearly 30 years away from the sport, his profound, almost despairing affection for Ocaña, even if I could barely put a face to the deep, scarily creaky voice. And his honesty.

Asked what Ocaña thought of Merckx when they were rivals, De Muer gives a voluble, crude answer. Ocaña, it turns out, didn't dislike Merckx: as a rider, if not as a person, he *detested* him and truly did not care who knew it. 'He'd say, "I'm going to beat that fucker of a Cannibal, I'm going to destroy him, I'm going to pay him back,"' De Muer says. 'He even said that right to the Queen of Belgium's face when he met her – "I'm going to make that *con de Cannibale* eat his bloody bike!" To the Queen of Belgium!

'What pissed Luis off was that it didn't matter if it was a big rider or a little rider, Merckx would chase them down. He wanted to win absolutely everything all the time. He couldn't respect a rider like that. They didn't communicate apart from the time they got drunk on whisky together after a criterium. But he was always saying, "Merckx is going to pay for that. *Cet con de Cannibale.*"'

So was Ocaña easy to direct? 'No!' De Muer says almost sharply. 'He would get too nervous about absolutely nothing. I once gave him a few drops of a lotion for an injury before the start of a race and it stung a bit, just a bit. And he got absolutely furious and jumped in a fountain, completely dressed, to try and stop it stinging.

'He made bets, too, with himself, that he could attack at such and such a point. I remember one Tour of Spain, he already had the yellow jersey, but he charged off the front. And I went up to him and said, "Why have you done that? What for?" And he says, "Well, I made a bet with myself, to see if I could get away …"'

'Was he "allumé [lit up]"?' De Muer is asked – a slang word whose meaning quickly becomes clear, when he replies that he has no idea but that he believed it to be a widespread condition in the peloton. 'Due to what?' 'Basically amphetamines.' So did Ocaña take a 'double dose' for Orcières-Merlette? 'No idea, but as one of his friends said, 'I take 20 mil, I race, I do my course, I win. I take more of it and that's it, I go *phhhtttt*. So that's it, the more you take, the less well you go.' And did Ocaña go over the limit with drugs? 'Luis took whatever was going,' De Muer responds. 'It was impossible to discipline him in those matters. He was completely wild.'

Infuriating, uncontrollable and unpredictable as Ocaña was, suddenly the huge affection De Muer feels for him becomes more than apparent – when the interviewer switches subjects, and De Muer is asked about Bernard Thévenet and directing him in the 1975 Tour. 'No comparison, is there?' De Muer says suddenly, 'No comparison is possible …' even though Thévenet won two Tours de France under his direction, his voice traces off in tones of total dejection. Ocaña, it is clear, was one of a kind. And even in 2008, it sounds like De Muer still misses him.

According to De Muer, his voice crackling with excitement now, Ocaña and he began plotting the downfall of Merckx the night before Orcières-Merlette. It was clear, he says, that Merckx was in trouble. 'Anybody who found it impossible to regain contact after having a puncture [like at Grenoble] had to be.' He had attempted to slow Ocaña down, he claims, after Merckx had punctured 'because attacking somebody when they punctured wasn't right'. But for the next stage De Muer was determined to try to speed things up.

'We enlisted Agostinho for support,' he recalls. 'He wasn't in our team but Agostinho was like that – a real star of a rider, one of the nicest guys out there, somebody who became the big forgotten figure of the sport.

'So we talked to Agostinho in the corridor of the hotel we were staying in and he was' – and he imitates the Portuguese rider's somewhat pidgin French – '"me help, me help".' Money did not change hands, he insists, which, given Agostinho is long since dead, killed when a dog ran under his bike in the Tour of the Algarve in 1984, cannot be corroborated. But the quiet insistence with which De Muer says money had nothing to do with it lends credence to his claims.

Agostinho kept his word, too. Indeed, the Portuguese rider went so hard on the Laffrey at the front of the bunch that even Ocaña, caught in a second group, briefly lost contact on the steepest lower slopes. De Muer, stuck in the race convoy, couldn't get in touch with Agostinho to tell him to ease up briefly and was forced to resort to telling a French TV cameraman to drive to the front and pass on the message.

Before the 'string' of riders leading the pack snapped completely, Ocaña bridged across to Agostinho, as did three of the four strongest riders from the previous day: Van Impe, Gösta Pettersson and Zoetemelk. But, crucially, Merckx was missing.

These days, Merckx blames the Laffrey, and not the rest of the stage, for being responsible for his defeat. And, indeed, the steepest part of the single hardest climb came right at the beginning – before his muscles had any time to warm up and a rider who has been feeling rough could have any chance of easing himself into the stage. So as soon as Agostinho drove so hard at the front, Merckx had no time to recover. As he was to prove the case again on the Noyer and again at Orcières-Merlette, on a climb which has no resting points there were no false flats or chances to limit the damage. And nobody to help the Cannibal as the opposition began to make mincemeat of him.

'It was the Col de Laffrey,' Merckx tells me, 'I had two team-mates at 30 seconds, my director didn't tell me, if he had I'd have waited. If there had been a radio and I had good information it would have been different. But nobody helped me, nobody took turns. They all rode to make me lose, not to win it themselves. They wanted me to lose.'

That was certainly the case with Agostinho. Others, like Thévenet, dropped with Merckx on the Laffrey, were neutral observers, although amazed at the power that Ocaña – now leading the quartet ahead, with a 2'00" advantage on Merckx at the summit of the Laffrey – was showing. For the next 40 kilo-metres, as they soared along the Route Napoléon in baking sunshine, the gap stayed at 2'00". But for once Merckx no longer had the whip hand – and when the front four moved on to the narrow roads and lower slopes of the Noyer, the margin between the two groups began to rise fast. At which point, Ocaña – in a little canyon – stepped on the accelerator, to move away alone. There were still 60 kilometres left to race: for once, just once, somebody was out-Merckxing Merckx.

'It was really impressive,' Thévenet recalls. 'I was in Merckx's little group behind and we weren't hanging about. Merckx might have lost some team-mates but he still had [Jos] Huysmans with him who was doing a lot of work. But it was fast and each time the *ardoisier* – the motorbike pillion-riding official carrying a chalkboard that showed the time gaps – 'came down, he took longer and longer to reach us. There would be another minute added on, and another. There comes a moment when you say, "it's just not possible, has he [Ocaña] taken a short cut or what?" Or you think, "how the hell has he taken two minutes like that, how could anybody do it?"'

Even though Merckx gestured with his head to ask for assis-tance, Thévenet says the speed was such that he could not help much: 'We caught Zoetemelk and Agostinho from the break but the thing was I was on the limit myself.' Thévenet insists that he would have given Merckx a hand, but all he could do was give him some water. 'He asked me for a drink – Merckx always drank a lot, not like me, and I gave him my bidon.'

But that Merckx should expect further help (and not get it) was just one indication that, at long last, the Cannibal was not just losing a minor skirmish, he was suffering a full-scale defeat – and so conclusively that it must have felt not just like losing a stage or even the Tour, but the end of an era.

The tide was turning in other ways: Merckx was right, too, about Van Impe; the Belgian had been racing in Merckx's shadow ever since he turned pro in 1970. But now the rivals, cowed for so long, were turning on him. Van Impe freely admits that he wanted to help Ocaña, and the two formed a working alliance – partly because, as he puts it, in terms of the long struggle against Merckx, 'it finally felt like we were getting somewhere. It was a very exciting moment. It was the only time he was in difficulty. This was a very special moment, we had to take advantage of even the smallest moment of weakness.'

Van Impe pulls no punches when it comes to discussing why he was prepared to assist Ocaña. From what he could see in the Orcières-Merlette stage, he thought Ocaña was the 'coming man', and at the same time, having come to that conclusion, he would do everything in his power to ensure that remained the case and that his new-found loyalty was not misplaced.

'He was going to win the Tour, and I did everything I could to help him. I would chase down Merckx so that Ocaña could win. The most important thing was to work against Merckx because we felt he could lose the Tour. We knew [we could] do something about it.

'We wanted to beat Merckx. And Ocaña did it.' His decision, he admits, cost him some home support. 'The Belgians weren't happy.'

As for how Van Impe assisted, Van Impe was the last rider to stay with Ocaña on the Noyer, although he reveals that he chased down Zoetemelk, who had previously attacked, 'because I didn't want Zoetemelk to win the [overall] classification, because he was always sitting on the wheels and never working. So when Ocaña went for it, Zoetemelk thought I was going to follow and he could get on my wheel, but instead I didn't.'

Nor was it so clear, according to Van Impe – finally second on the stage – that Ocaña was going to be the one who got away and eventually become the central figure of one of the Tour's most legendary stages.

'He said to me, "either you or I can win". So we worked together, agreed not to chase each other down. Had Zoetemelk attacked [on the Noyer], then I would have followed him. But instead it was Luis who attacked first.'

The data from that attack is, as Thévenet remarks, jaw-dropping. In three kilometres on the Noyer, Ocaña opened up a gap of 2'40" on Van Impe, Agostinho and Zoetemelk, with Pettersson flailing even further behind.

Such a margin is – just – partly explicable given that Agostinho's bolt was shot after the Laffrey and Van Impe and Zoetemelk could have been changing pace in their bid to shake each other off. But at the summit, that margin had increased, and managing to put Van Impe at 3'55", Agostinho and Zoetemelk at 4'00" and Merckx already at 5'25" did not just mean Ocaña was leader on the road by the time equivalent of a country mile. Simultaneously, the defeat had become a rout of Tour-winning proportions.

'We all wanted to be with Ocaña, but we couldn't, it was impossible,' recalls Zoetemelk. 'I wanted to stay up there, but it just couldn't be.'

That Ocaña knew only too well how much damage he could inflict on the Noyer's twisting switchbacks on a rider who was suffering was born of bitter personal experience. The Noyer had marked a low point in his 1970 Tour, where both he and BIC team-mate Charly Grosskost had come within a whisker of abandoning through illness. Grosskost, after supporting his leader as long as he could, had thrown in the towel; Ocaña – as usual, acting against his team doctor's advice, although De Muer wanted him to continue – had struggled on. 'Opposite a fountain which, thanks to my fever, turned into some sort of oasis, I felt tempted to quit,' Ocaña admitted afterwards. But the fact that he would have had to sit in the broom wagon next to Grosskost, who had worked so hard to keep Ocaña in the race, kept him from doing so.

Fast-forward 12 months and, on the same terrain where he had suffered so badly, Ocaña inflicted a terrible sporting revenge both on the race and the previous year's winner. On the twisting descent from the Noyer, through the blistering heat on the interminable flat of the Haute Plaine, and on the draggy, steady rise to Orcières-Merlette, several things became clear: the scale of destruction that Ocaña was single-handedly wreaking on the Tour peloton, and the scale of his obsession with the *con de Cannibale*. He did not ask for any references, De Muer noted, on any other rider apart from Merckx himself: everybody else was irrelevant.

'When Luis attacked, I'd drive up alongside him and say, "okay, take it steady now, you've got four minutes on him" [Merckx]. And he'd yell back, "well, it's going to be five". And then I'd say, "okay, it's five now, steady" and he'd yell back, "well, it's going to be six". And so on. And so on.'

The images of Ocaña that day as he stages his lone break-through into the heart of Merckx's Tour domination are compellingly simple. In one, alone against a backdrop of Alpine mountains, he is staring fixedly at his handlebars, cap shading his eyes, his head bent over the bars, hands taut on the brakehoods, utterly caught up in his own effort, devoid of doubt.

'Luis was all alone, nobody helped him,' said De Muer. 'He rode for 60 kilometres like that. He never cracked, he never gave up. He actually lost a bit of time at Orcières, he'd gone in so deep.

It was' – and this is praise indeed from a director as prestigious as De Muer – 'the most amazing thing I've ever seen on a bike.'

Or as the Tour's director Jacques Goddet put it after Ocaña crossed the line in Orcières-Merlette, with an 8'42"-margin on Merckx, 'things will never be the same again'.

Goddet was right. In one single stage, the world of cycling had changed. How could it not? Sport's most dominant racer in decades, if not in history, had suffered his most important defeat in a Grand Tour since he began racing them in 1968. Ocaña had not just staged a breakthrough. He had single-handedly stopped the greatest ever race-winning juggernaut in its tracks.

'After so many years, this was payback time. I could accept that. A lot of journalists were happy to see me lose,' Merckx said in an interview in the mid-1990s.

'But I thought the Tour was lost. I didn't think there was anything I could do.

'I'd had a bit of a stomach problem, but that had got better. What Ocaña had done was out of this world.' At the time, he added that he did not think 'that even if I had been in top condition, I would have been able to follow him. He took the risks he had to, and he's still progressing, I could see that at the Dauphiné Libéré.' Asked at the finish if he thought that Ocaña could crack, he said, 'The gap is virtually impossible to overcome, unless I find some new strength and he blows really badly. I don't think so.'

'Nobody could have conceived beforehand what he was capable of doing,' says Thévenet. 'He was riding like a beast. It was the one time in my career that I was beaten by somebody by ten minutes when I was in form. It was on the limit of comprehensibility.'

Ocaña's ride to Orcières-Merlette was of such a calibre that it had even managed to put Eddy Merckx's feat at Mourenx, when he 'only' took 8'00" on his closest pursuers, into the shade. More to the point than mere time, that day Merckx had had nothing to achieve bar reflecting on his own superiority (and squashing an irritating team-mate's attempt at rebellion). Orcières-Merlette, on the other hand, saw Ocaña take the first ever lead of his career in the Tour de France with an advantage that made it seem impossible that he could lose: 8'43" on Zoetemelk, 9'20" on Van Impe … Merckx fifth overall, at 9'46".

There was even praise from Federico Bahamontes – not known for letting anyone take his place in the limelight, but pleased to see someone as anarchic as himself finally tearing up the Merckx-dominated script of previous Tours.

'Merckx is a rider who shapes an era, like Coppi or Bartali, but Ocaña has shown that Merckx is not invincible,' Bahamontes argued. 'Merckx is human like everybody else, and if you attack him tenaciously, he has to give way. That's why this hasn't been a surprise, apart from which Ocaña … knows how to take risks and suffer, he's a giant of a rider.

'The myth of invincibility that surrounded Merckx has been dispelled once and for all, and the reason why that myth existed was that nobody dared attack him, everybody raced in his shadow and he knew how to make the most of that.

'Now the myth has fallen and I'm pleased it's been a Spaniard who's achieved it. Spain was a little bit forgotten in the world of cycling. It was about time that we counted for something again.'

Even Bahamontes, famous for being one of cycling's most erratic and unpredictable attackers, told Ocaña he should take it calmly from here on. With an uncanny degree of accuracy in his predictions, Bahamontes said, 'He has to race calmly, that's all he has to do. They'll try and destabilise him … If he gets through the next four stages okay, without any crashes, he'll have won the Tour. The last four stages nothing will happen, everybody settles for what they have.'

With a keen eye, as ever, on the financial possibilities of any given situation, Bahamontes' scent of the money to be made outweighed any thoughts that he himself might lose out by no longer being Spain's only Tour de France winner.

'For me, it would be ideal that a Spaniard won every year. I've got a [bike] business to think of, those suspicions are absurd,' he retorted.

Had the rules been applied and the time cut in the mountains not been extended, Ocaña would have single-handedly been responsible for sending 61 of the Tour's 109 racers home early, among them Jan Janssen, Ocaña's old team-mate and the 1968 Tour winner, and British sprint ace Barry Hoban. Eight riders, in any case, abandoned, among them two Belgian stars, Classics specialists Walter Godefroot and Roger De Vlaeminck. But not Merckx.

Ocaña said afterwards he had thought of his family, Josiane and his son Jean-Louis, apparently jumping for joy next to his mother and father as he crossed the line on his lone 60-kilometre trek across Orcières' high plateau. He particularly enjoyed the fact, he said, that he had, in a single stage, been converted from 'the Luis Ocaña who limited the gaps in the Tour to the Luis Ocaña who was winning it'. But Ocaña's thoughts were mostly centred on Merckx.

'Was he going to give up and go home?' Ocaña had reflected. 'Anybody who thought that didn't know Merckx.' (Merckx did, as he said, contemplate it briefly, but only briefly.) 'That evening if I had told my team-mates I had been thinking of him, and that would not have been hard to do, they would only have laughed. But there were two races going on here: mine of course, and that of Eddy Merckx, whose morale must have suffered more than he did physically.'

Furthermore, Ocaña, sheafing through the classifications on the rest day that followed, would have noticed then, if not before, that Merckx had placed third on the stage, outsprinting his rivals in a small group of chasers: hardly an act of surrender, more one of defiance. For his part, there were echoes of his nervous, persistent gesturing when leading the 1970 Vuelta in his comments to one reporter that Fausto Coppi had won the 1949 Tour de France after being more than half an hour down: again, hardly the words of a self-confident man, more of one who has hit the jackpot and cannot believe it. As he told *MARCA*, 'I have no right to consider the race is over.' On the other hand, he insisted, there was no way he was prepared to lose the yellow jersey. 'They will have to rip it off my shoulders,' he said – another uncanny prophecy.

'Maybe others in Merckx's place would have been discouraged, but not Eddy. It was unfeasible,' argued Thévenet. 'It just wasn't in his character, and until the last line was crossed, there was always the chance of him doing something.'

***

Sure enough, Merckx did not put his feet up on the rest day, which preceded a 251-kilometre stage south from Orcières-Merlette to Marseilles. Rather than flying home, he went training, looking in particular at the descent from the ski resort back to the Haute Plaine. Then he went hunting for postcards in a local tourist shop – hardly the act of a man trying to forget where he was.

There is a story that Merckx was up at the crack of dawn on the morning of the following stage and riding in a hotel room on the rollers as a way of 'hitting the ground running': 'completely untrue,' he now says. On the other hand 'the evening before the stage, I said, "tomorrow we'll be on the front, and [team-mate Rinus] Wagtmans will go for it on the descent from Orcières".'

Just one opponent dared raise his voice against the plan – Merckx's sports director Guillaume Driessens. 'He said, "look what Ocaña has already done",' the implication being that Ocaña was so strong he was unbeatable. Merckx's opinion was one of utter contempt: 'Driessens was like that, bullshit.'

Merckx's counter-attack, when it came, was as brutal as it was brilliantly timed. Ocaña was at the back of the peloton at

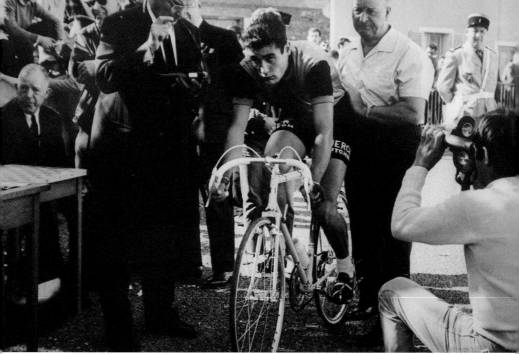

Ocaña at the start of the amateur GP Nations 1967 time trial. France's top amateur event, it was his breakthrough victory prior to turning pro a year later with Spanish team Fagor.

Ocaña with Michael Wright at the 1969 Vuelta where Wright became the first ever British leader of the Spanish Grand Tour and Ocaña claimed second overall, his first Grand Tour podium finish. The two were later team-mates at BIC.

A semi-conscious Ocaña is guided by his Fagor team-mates including Txomin Perurena (l.) towards the Ballon D'Alsace in the 1969 Tour de France after crashing. He quit three days later.

Cescutti's diet plans he gave to the teenage Ocaña to follow. Amongst the many prohibited substances: molluscs, fatty, salty or smoked meats, powdered milk, snails, green bananas, white wine, beer, and overly cold drinks. No fizzy drinks before racing, either. Draconian as they may sound, Cescutti's ideas were surprisingly advanced for his era.

CONS
————

Recommandations général

Manger lentement
Veiller aux soins
fonctionnement de l'estc
Boire peu pendant
Boire environ un
Au petit déjeuner,
chicorée; ou du chocolat;
Tartines de pain s
croissants au beurre). Ta
Avant une course a
sur le plat ou riz au lai

Aliments particulièrement

Bouillons de viande
Lait en poudre - la
Viandes grasses, vi
ou en conserve. Gibiers, e
Ne pas abuser de cha
Tous les crustacés e
Tous les poissons fu
Les légumes suivants
(sauf la racine).

Pierre Cescutti poses in front of Adolf Hitler's bunker at the Berghof in the Berchtesgarten – which he was one of the very first Allied troops to enter – a few days before the end of World War II. On his return to Mont-de-Marsan, Cescutti became the club's trainer, with Ocaña the star pupil of his career.

Pierre Cescutti at home in Mont-de-Marsan with the 1973 Tour de France yellow jersey received and worn by Luis Ocaña in Paris as outright winner. When Ocaña came off the podium, he gave the jersey to Cescutti in recognition of the importance of the trainer's role in his career.

ɪentation du coureur cycliste

•ien les aliments. Parler peu en mangeant.
dentition en bon état étant la base du bon

re à la fin des repas et entre les repas.
e par jour (un litre I/2 à deux litres en été).
t seul ou du lait avec un peu d'extrait de
•viter le mélange café au lait).
sis, ou biscotes (éviter les croissants, surtou
rre, confitures, compotes, miel plus fruits.
tin: ajouter fromage ou jambon blanc ou oeuf

ages en sachets.

ɜ, viandes marinées, viandes salées, fumées
ɪ. Tous les abats, toutes les sauces.
jambon blanc naturel) éviter tous lles patés.

n conserve.

Luis Ocaña climbs to the finish at Orciéres-Merlette in the 1971 Tour and his greatest ever triumph, claiming the yellow jersey and gaining more than eight minutes on arch-rival Eddy Merckx with a long solo breakaway. For many, the crowning moment of Ocaña's career, and Merckx's most severe defeat.

Ocaña with Merckx at the stage finish in Marseilles in the 1971 Tour following the Spaniard's six hour pursuit of the Belgian, finally losing just over two minutes. Merckx described the Spaniard as his 'greatest ever rival' and was obsessed with keeping him under control: as 1976 Tour winner Lucien Van Impe puts it, "Merckx wouldn't let Luis get a single metre's advance."

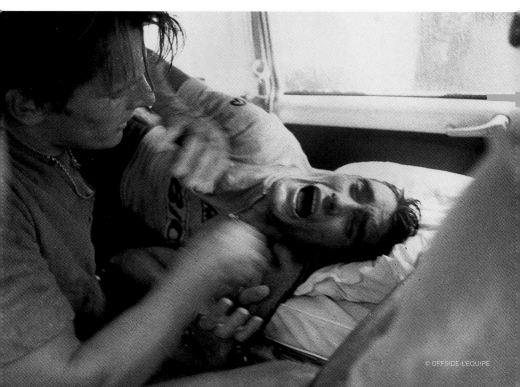

Ocaña after crashing out on the Col de Menté, with race director Jacques Goddet (l.) looking on mournfully at the fallen rider as BIC management attempt to help their star. But there was no chance of him recovering.

Ocaña as he waits to be flown out by helicopter from the Col de Menté.

Ocaña with his wife Josiane [l.] during the 1973 Tour de France first rest-day, 24 hours after he had taken the yellow jersey at Gaillard. It would stay on his shoulders all the way to Paris.

Ocaña ascends the Galibier pass in the Alps with key Spanish rival Jose Manuel Fuente – the day Ocaña delivered the definitive knockout blow in the 1973 Tour.

Ocaña having won the 1973 Tour de France. It was his greatest victory and taken in resounding style with six stage wins, but overshadowed by the absence of Merckx – and severely underrated as a result.

Ocaña in the 1976 Tour on stage 20 to Puy de Dôme. By now a shadow of his former self, Ocaña performed poorly on the same ascent where he had first defeated Merckx in 1971 and crushed his rivals for one last time in 1973 – finishing 27th, nearly five minutes down on winner Joop Zoetemelk.

A 1998 Pellos cartoon in honour of the Bastide D'Armagnac chapel, where Ocaña's marriage and funeral were held. Ocaña, Anquetil and Bobet salute from above, Tour boss Jean-Marie Leblanc drives for Hinault, Merckx and Indurain and local star André Darrigade. One-time French national champion Anglade, who made the chapel's stained glass window portrait of Ocaña, shows the way.

The Col de Menté corner with (inset) a plaque above commemorating, 'Monday, 12th July 1971, tragedy in the Tour de France… yellow jersey Luis Ocana lost all hope when he crashed against this rockface.' More than 40 years on, the sharp corner's technical difficulties remain unchanged, too.

Orcières-Merlette ski resort, doing an interview and waiting for the start, when suddenly it was filtered back to him that the race had actually begun – before the start flag had dropped, according to Ocaña, although this cannot be confirmed.

'There they [the BIC riders] all were, blethering away to some radio journalist, and I had told Luis he had to be at the front, and he was saying, "oh, it doesn't matter",' recalls De Muer. 'But then Merckx got all those riders together who could give it full gas on the downhills, Wagtmans and the rest, and they were away.' 'The beast was not defeated,' as *MARCA*'s headline put it the next day, 'it was only asleep.'

Swinging his leg over his bike, Ocaña powered through the pack – only to be held up by the Spaniard Luis Zubero, who had crashed. By the time he reached the front, Merckx, a handful of low-level riders from rival teams, 1966 Tour de France winner Lucien Aimar, and Merckx's team-mates Wagtmans, Julien Stevens and Jos Huysmans – ten riders in total – were already out of sight.

Even then Ocaña did not panic, Zoetemelk says – which, given there was a five- to six-hour ride ahead, was understandable. 'They [the Merckx break] went for it, got a minute and then it was flat out, Merckx organising ahead, Ocaña charging around behind but telling us to go gently, not too hard. He didn't want to catch them straightaway, he wanted to burn them out,' Zoetemelk says.

As it was, the entire Tour ended up all but self-combusting. For the next 240 kilometres, all the way to Marseilles' old port, a flat-out pursuit between the Merckx-led group of ten – which shrank to nine after Stevens dropped back – and the Ocaña-led peloton ensued. Their advantage wavered between 40" and 2'00", sometimes so low that Ocaña could see the last riders in the group ahead. The average speed was such, though, that riders in the lead group had more than one near miss against oncoming everyday traffic; there had not been time for the gendarme outriders to wave it to the side of the road.

Ocaña and his BIC squad had some assistance from the Fagor-Mercier team, keen to keep their leader Cyrille Guimard's options open overall, all the Spaniards in Werner as well as two from KAS, but others sat firmly on the fence. In fact, this was Ocaña's first nail in his own coffin: Thévenet, also in Ocaña's group, down to 60-odd riders at the finish, says the yellow jersey's attempts to negotiate with others trapped behind for support fell foul of his own personality.

There was no guarantee with Ocaña, Thévenet says, that he would repay the favour because 'that wasn't in his character. He might ask you to do something for him, but he would have forgotten pretty soon afterwards.' On top of that, his director specifically instructed Thévenet to stay 'neutral'.

'There was a moment when I got caught up in it all, but just as I was going to help, [Peugeot director] Gaston Plaud came up and said, "hey, you didn't work with Merckx very much [on the Orcières stage] ... We don't want to get a label stuck on you as being "anti-Merckx".'

'So immediately I dropped back, and Luis came up to me, he wasn't at all happy, he started to wind me up. I explained it all to him ... I wasn't going to win the Tour. Merckx was ahead of me overall and I wasn't going to be able to catch him.'

Thévenet said his explanation went down like a lead balloon with Ocaña, but that was to be expected: 'Luis wasn't that much of a diplomat, rather for him things were just going one way or another, full stop. He didn't try to explain, to turn the situation around to his advantage. He wasn't that good at understanding that somebody could have a different opinion to his.'

All the same, sheer weight of numbers, with the chasing group at least six times the size of Merckx's ten-rider posse, probably helped make up for Ocaña's lack of direct backing. Finally, Merckx only gained 1'59", at the expense of losing more than a few friends – given that, on paper, nearly 50 riders should have been eliminated they finished so far behind the main pack. (Yet again, the race commissaires cast a blind eye on the affair.)

It was the leanest of pickings for what had been a huge investment of energy, by Merckx and two other riders from the Molteni team. Ocaña had not cracked. Merckx himself admits, 'Had I known that we were going to get such a poor return, I would never have gone along with this idea.'

But it could have worked, Merckx insists to me in Qatar. 'If my sports director [Giorgio] Albani hadn't made two or three riders wait for Bruyère when he punctured to make sure he didn't lose time, then for sure we would have taken ten or 15 minutes on the road to Marseilles. For sure.' So much for his claims after Orcières-Merlette that he felt Ocaña's lead was unbeatable!

Merckx's disappointment that the destruction was not as great as it should have been is still palpable. He criticises the decision to reinstate the riders, pointing out that seven or eight KAS riders were among them. (The implication presumably being that, as mainly Spaniards, they would naturally go on to help Ocaña: presumably he'd forgotten about Van Impe at that point.) Then he says that Ocaña 'promised everybody something: Guimard wanted the green [points] jersey but his green jersey is still hanging on a tree somewhere in the Landes,' he sneered, a reference to Merckx's attack to Bordeaux a week later that, after helping Ocaña, ensured the Frenchman did not reap his reward.

'We never panicked, though, we had support like Guimard,' says De Muer, although he recognises that the Tour was at stake that day as much as on any other in the race.

'The gap stayed at about two to three minutes. We were lucky because they had some punctures, considering what could have happened … we could have lost it [the Tour], we could have lost it.'

Ultimately the stage that could, as *MARCA* said, 'have ended in catastrophe' ended in stalemate. But perhaps more than Orcières-Merlette, the 245-kilometre day-long charge from the foothills of the Alps all the way down to the Mediterranean, all at an average speed of 45.351 kilometres an hour and with 155 kilometres covered in the first three hours, revealed the scale of the conflict between the two leading figures of the 1971 Tour: the depth of Merckx's desire to regain the yellow jersey, and the determination of Ocaña to keep it.

'I attacked him every day because he had a lot of doubts' is how Merckx put it, and that was the key to his strategy post-Orcières-Merlette. Knowing the brittleness of Ocaña's personality, coupled with the nervousness Ocaña felt at having ousted Merckx from his throne, the Marseilles stage showed Merckx was as good at fighting a defensive game as he was when the tide was flowing in his favour. Rather than letting Ocaña gain a single shred of self-confidence at being in the lead, he set his teeth into the problem with a ferocity that must have shaken Ocaña enormously. What makes Orcières special was the time that Ocaña managed to gain on Merckx. In Marseilles, what impressed the most was Merckx's tenacity – and Ocaña's refusal to crack. Best of all from a sporting point of view, there was everything to play for.

One person who was completely unimpressed by the potency of the Marseilles stage was Gaston Deferre, the mayor. When the speed of the stage meant it arrived ridiculously early – at least half an hour before the fastest expected schedule, and possibly more, meaning the VIP seats in the finish stands were empty – he refused to welcome the race in Marseilles again during the rest of his time in office.

The Tour did not return to Marseilles until 1989, but Zoetemelk, a man who controls his emotions very carefully and is sparing with praise even when praise is due, gives what must have been one of the tensest days in Tour history a worthy accolade. 'It was,' he says simply, 'a great, great stage.'

***

Two nights later, as the race entered the Pyrenees, Ocaña rang Cescutti in Mont-de-Marsan. 'He was full of confidence,' Cescutti claims, 'he told me that on the road to his old home in Vielha, he was going to stick it in Merckx's mouth.' In other words, on the Portillon, the thickly wooded frontier climb that Ocaña knew so well from his childhood in the Aran Valley, Ocaña would strike the final knockout blow that would be the end of the Cannibal. As Ocaña said later, 'I was going to execute him.'

In Daniel Friebe's biography of Merckx, Wagtmans claims that Ocaña was weakening visibly by this point in the race, saying, 'his face [after Marseilles] was as yellow as his jersey'. Yet beyond these subjective opinions, there is little real proof that physically he was on the back foot. In Merckx's Marseilles ambush he had withstood, albeit with support, a 250-kilometre onslaught. Then, in a time trial at Albi, he lost a mere 11" to Merckx. The narrow gap between the two does suggest that Merckx was getting stronger. But the Belgian's protests that Ocaña had been sheltered by a motorbike in the time trial, not to mention a sympathetic Belgian radio journalist's suggestion that the Belgian navy bombard the French coastline as a reprisal, indicate frustration that Merckx could not close the gap. And with a 7'00" advantage, there was every indication that Ocaña could hold on.

'Luis wasn't going quite so well,' says Thévenet, 'that is to say, he was less impressive than he had been at Orcières.

'But, just because he was less impressive doesn't mean at all to say that he was less strong than the rest of us. I think he had something left in the tank. He closed down every attack by Merckx.'

De Muer, who was closest to Ocaña, says that the problem was not a lack of conditioning. Instead, Ocaña's self-confidence was so high – and after holding Merckx in check in the mountains, on the flat and in a time trial, how could it not be? – that by the time they reached the Pyrenees he was refusing to pay any attention to his director whatsoever. And that included warnings about overreaching, attempting to out-Merckx Merckx on all terrains, not just on one stage in the Alps.

'I warned him that Merckx was going to do that, that Merckx would try and put him under pressure, and Luis was just like "yeah, right, whatever". Ocaña, when he decided to piss about, he pissed about, he was uncontrollable.'

And after he paid a visit to a church in Revel on the morning of stage 14, to pray, Ocaña's morale was lifted dangerously higher. His only worry, he claimed, was a slight, inexplicable sensation of anxiety; his only regret that his father was not alive to see him in yellow.

Just as on the stage to Orcières, stage 14 from Revel to Luchon had three classified climbs: the Portet d'Aspet, ranked third category, then the second-category Menté and Portillon. And when Merckx made a classic early move, by sending two of his team-mates, Roger Swerts and Herman Van Springel, up the road, Ocaña responded in identical fashion: BIC's Désiré Letort and Alain Vasseur went with them. Once again, stalemate. Then, after a long 100-kilometre grind across the Pyrenean foothills south of Toulouse, with the morning break reeled in and lone attacker José Manuel Fuente away, on the lower slopes of the Portet d'Aspet, the battle began in earnest.

It has been said that in the subsequent events, Ocaña's desire to imitate Merckx, in fact – fuelled by excessive self-confidence and psychological fragility – is what let Ocaña down. But in his defence it has to be said this aping of the Cannibal might have been more logical than it appears, given that since 1968, when Ocaña turned pro, in the Grand Tours there had only been one way of racing that seemed to guarantee success: Merckx's.

Yet by failing to forge his own path, Ocaña was falling into the trap laid for him by the Cannibal, because he was letting Merckx call the shots. As Merckx tells me, 'I knew that Ocaña would have problems if I kept him under pressure.'

Merckx accordingly tried to force the pace on the first ascent of the day, the Portet d'Aspet, as much as possible to try to shred the field. But instead he discovered that Ocaña, Zoetemelk, Thévenet and Van Impe were on his tail.

History repeated itself on the race's second ascent, the Col de Menté. After Cyrille Guimard made a brief dig over the summit, behind him Merckx attacked again and again as they went over the top; Ocaña followed, the two passing Guimard. 'Luis was doing fine,' Thévenet recalls, 'every time Merckx went out of the saddle, Luis was with him.'

But then the conditions changed, brutally, and with them the whole race. Shortly before they began the long drop down towards the Portillon and Spain – on roads that Ocaña, having grown up a stone's throw away from, knew well and which may have increased his confidence even further – the heavens opened, with a vengeance.

Hail and torrential rain suddenly poured down, reducing visibility to the bare minimum. On the early sections of switchbacks on the descent of the Col de Menté, footage shows fans running around on the side of the road, in the midst of what seemed like a tropical rainstorm in the middle of the Pyrenees – underneath umbrellas but in their swimming trunks and laughing wildly at the unexpected change of weather into a virtual monsoon.

'We found ourselves in a sort of unreal night,' Ocaña said later, 'the kind of conditions only an angry mountain could whip up. Voices would shout, warning both themselves and the next person to be careful, but we were caught up in a tornado of madness. It was a route of death.' Nor could they see more than 20 yards ahead. At some points, according to one driver of a media car, Francis Yardin, the rain was so dense that visibility was reduced even further, to five yards. Yet when Merckx tried to open up a gap on the descent, Ocaña unthinkingly, unhesitatingly, opted to follow.

This was, with the considerable benefit of hindsight, Ocaña's single biggest mistake: the error which, indirectly but in one fell swoop, was to cost him both the Tour and the label of the strongest rider in the world, the error that would send him from being the living proof that Merckx could be beaten back into the ranks of the also-rans again. By common consent, Merckx was the greatest descender of his generation. Ocaña's bravery on the same terrain was equally exceptional. Yet in the battle between one rider's technical skill and the other relying on pure emotion to muddle through the most dangerous of weather conditions, there was only ever going to be one outcome.

***

Three kilometres further down, on a sweeping left-hand bend with a small, sloping plateau of flat, open terrain on the outside lip, Merckx skidded and fell. Ocaña, taking a very slightly different line behind him and riding on a flat tyre, fell as well. It was almost predictable, given the weather conditions, and fortunately the crash initially seemed to have little effect on either man. Rather, it was the knock-on effect that proved disastrous.

Just as the two leading Tour riders had got up and reshipped their chains on the bikes, the most arbitrary twist of fate led one rider to continue his reign as world leader, the other to be assigned the role of nearly man.

Another rider, most probably Agostinho but possibly Zoetemelk, hurtled into the corner, lost control of his bike on the poor camber when he was unable to brake because of the mudslicks and rain – a universal complaint that day – and went skidding across the road. Merckx, who was just on the point of leaving the scene of the crash, was missed by Agostinho completely. But Ocaña, having asked Maurice De Muer for a spare wheel, remained in the same spot for a few seconds more and was struck full-on by the Portuguese rider and smashed down onto the tarmac again. Then, as Agostinho got up and moved on, and Ocaña got woozily to his feet, a second rider, most likely Zoetemelk, ploughed into Ocaña as well. This time, lying hunched just a few yards from a tiny stream that had by now turned into a minor torrent, the Spaniard's injuries were such that he did not try to stand up again.

In a few seconds, and thanks to the most inconsequential of decisions – to ask his director for a wheel – Ocaña's Tour, his lead and his four-day reign as cycling's strongest rider with it, was over. While Merckx, it is said, took a quick look at Ocaña then rode away, the grey, grainy photos of the Spaniard, his mouth open, his face a picture of agony as the rain lashes down are some of the most haunting and brutal in cycling. The best-known image, of Ocaña lying almost completely hidden under a soaking wet tarpaulin, his face contorted and with a doctor raising one arm towards him, makes him look like an injured soldier from some distant, terrible battle.

'I felt a terrible pain in my right shoulder, and even though I was half-conscious I wanted to get back into the battle and ride on,' Ocaña said later. 'We were told that Zoetemelk hit me and Agostinho, too, but I can't recall it at all. I just remember that I couldn't breathe, and my fear became panic, I thought I would die.'

De Muer feels that it was an error, pure and simple, on Ocaña's part, and one he puts down to his excessive, almost unnatural, impetuosity. It was that same quality that had led him to beat Merckx in the first place, as *L'Equipe*'s cycling writer Philippe Brunel, a friend of Ocaña's, told Daniel Friebe: 'Luis lived his life at the extremes and that was why he became the only person to challenge Merckx, because you had to be extreme to take on Merckx.' But now that quality had become a two-edged weapon.

'That climb was so hard, there were hailstones, thunder, he was determined to go down it as quickly as Merckx but he had everything to lose,' De Muer points out. 'All right, so Merckx fell off, too, but he fell off well.

'I told Luis beforehand, "don't be an arsehole, don't follow him and he just"' – and he imitates Ocaña responding with the early 1970s equivalent of 'yadayada' – '"blahblahblah". He just wanted to do exactly the same. He knew perfectly that with his bullfighter's spirit he was going to piss about. He knew it.'

One of the first on the scene, De Muer insists that there was no possibility – raised by several Belgian (and therefore possibly partisan) journalists – that Ocaña might have continued. Although a hospital check-up later at Saint-Gaudens, showed he had no broken bones, the scale of the impact had left the Spaniard with severe bruising in his upper body, to the point where he had difficulty breathing and was slipping in and out of consciousness – and howling in agony as he did so. But if part of De Muer felt annoyed with Ocaña, another part felt compassion.

'I just felt it was a shame, that he hadn't understood, that he'd been too impulsive, he'd just wanted to be better than everybody else.

'He couldn't have continued, he was really shaken up, he looked to be hurt all over. He couldn't even speak. My impression was he'd broken his collarbone. But he couldn't have continued.'

After the first crash – when Ocaña skidded behind Merckx and first fell – however, 'he could have gone on. But it was the second one [crash] that did it for him. When Agostinho hit him. Seventy kilos of rider at 60 kilometres an hour.'

When De Muer says Agostinho was the first to hit Ocaña and Zoetemelk second, given the weather conditions, neither sports director, following at a distance in a team car, nor any of the other parties involved, could be sure it was in that order. But it hardly matters. Their combined impact left Ocaña out for the count.

There can be no question, as has been suggested by the most partisan of Ocaña fans, that Merckx himself was to blame. At most – and this is pushing it a bit – he can be accused of having put Ocaña in a position where he had to follow on a dangerous descent. But as De Muer points out, with a 7'00" advantage Ocaña did not have to do that. Rather, he should have played a more cautious game and eased back.

Merckx says that although he fell, it was at a different point on the corner, something the grainy footage seems to confirm.

'I also crashed, you can see from the pictures I have gravel in my wounds, cuts,' Merckx says. He also – 42 years on – even recollects the mini-flash flood that was flowing at the bend, but adds, 'I saw nothing, I was in front, he was behind me, he crashed at the beginning of the corner and I was on the outside, I was coming out of it, the wind blew and whoah! I fell away.'

'I got up, I continued, what was I to do? Stop? It's a pity he crashed, but it wasn't my fault. He was always riding with very thin wheels, so on the descent, it was raining, he attacked, and he crashed. For sure I was a better descender, he was brave, but not as good as me.'

At the time in a newspaper interview shortly afterwards, Merckx pointed out that he, like everybody else, was doing the descent with what were effectively no brakes: 'They didn't work, I thought I heard Ocaña's front tyre blow but either way we were both moving out to the far side of the curve [when we crashed].

'I could hold on to a fencepost, but Ocaña fell. I saw him very briefly, but after that I had to go on descending, braking with one foot on the road. I fell again, hurting my right knee.

'That was when my sports director drove up and told me what had happened to Ocaña. He told me to avoid all risks because there was no possible fight with Luis now.'

Merckx says he couldn't believe that Ocaña had been so badly injured, which makes sense when you remember that he did not see – a matter of seconds later – Zoetemelk and Agostinho's arrival. No records are available of the now deceased Portuguese rider's recollections of events but, according to the Dutchman, Ocaña was initially in the middle of the road, not at the side – which is why he ploughed into him, pushing him back across to the edge with his bike.

'The two of them [Merckx and Ocaña] had gained a few metres over the top of the climb. It had started to rain really hard on the ascent, it was impossible to control your bike going downhill in that storm, not like on the way up.

'He was in the road, he'd fallen, and I hit him, I went right over him with my bike, I couldn't avoid him.' Zoetemelk hit him 'really hard, and I couldn't do anything. Then Agostinho hit him.'

Zoetemelk, understandably given the rainy conditions, perhaps gets the order of events wrong. One witness of all of this was Van Impe, given that – unrecorded by newspaper reports at the time – he was the closest chasing Merckx and Ocaña. According to the Belgian, who also ground to a halt on the same corner, 'Ocaña fell by himself, got up and then Agostinho went into him. Agostinho was right on his chest.' At which point, having fallen, it seems that Zoetemelk – whom Van Impe did not see, because he had already gone – slammed into him.

In Van Impe's opinion weather, as much as Ocaña's poorer descending skills, provided the tipping point for the debacle on the corner. 'It was tough, like a hairpin, but if it had been dry it would have been no problem.' Conditions were exceptionally bad, he recalls. 'A little further down Wagtmans, one of the best descenders, went past me like a rocket and I thought, "what the hell is he doing?" And a little bit further down we saw him climbing up the road with his bike on his shoulder!'

On top of that, if Ocaña's bad luck had always dominated his racing beforehand and was to continue to hold him in its grip afterwards, it could hardly fail to be absent on this occasion even if the original fault was Ocaña's. His first piece of ill fortune was that he punctured as well as crashed, secondly that he asked for a spare wheel, thirdly that others following took the same line as he did, rather than that of the more expert Merckx. And as if that was not enough, as Van Impe recalls, there was a fourth factor that ensured Ocaña, finally, could not recover.

On the edge of the bend 'there were big wooden posts and we could hold on to them, even if we crashed and slipped a bit.'

But it was really unfortunate that where Ocaña fell initially there were no wooden posts, approximately a car's width or enough for a rider and his spinning bike, 'otherwise he would have held on to one'. And like the proverbial horseshoe nail that indirectly caused a kingdom to fall, had he been able to do that, most probably the two massive collisions – first involving Agostinho and then Zoetemelk – that followed in the space of less than a minute would not have taken place.

'I was with Zoetemelk,' said Merckx's green-jersey adversary, Guimard, 'and he braked really hard, but the collision was so brutal that Ocaña couldn't get up again.'

To this day, Zoetemelk cannot explain why Ocaña was still standing where he was, because 'normally you'd get out of the way when you fall. You don't stand in the middle of the road.'

But it was perhaps the shock of the initial crash that was responsible for that, and in any case Zoetemelk, like Merckx, did not hang around to see what was going on. 'I had my own classification to look after, I took my bike and went', although he recalls that Ocaña had lost consciousness as a result of the crash'. Although people were shouting at the Spaniard, 'he wasn't answering any questions'.

Ahead, Zoetemelk says, they neutralised the race, but it soon became clear that Ocaña was not coming, as others like Thévenet, could testify.

'I got there [to the bend], I don't know, maybe 30 or 40 seconds later, none of us could brake, the only way [to do so] was by putting your bike into the grass, that wasn't so bad,' Thévenet recalls. 'Unfortunately there was such heavy rain, I've never seen anything like it before or since, it was like buckets of water being poured over your head. And as you couldn't brake, it was horrible, you felt like you were accelerating.'

'When you got to a corner, you'd all take the same line, and as you couldn't brake, you'd all end up in the same place' – although in Merckx's case, his greater descending ability saved him from the same fate as Ocaña.

Moments before they reached Ocaña, Thévenet was saved from being the third rider to hit the Spaniard in less than a minute. 'Fortunately the BIC car had just overtaken me, and the mechanic got out [to assist Ocaña] and saw straightaway I wasn't going stop, rather I was going to hit Luis, we were all taking the same line', and the mechanic was able to drag Ocaña, now close to the edge, out of the way.

'He was still on the ground, I thought I heard him screaming, but that's a long time ago now; he was there, and De Muer came up, I had no idea that he had done himself so much harm.'

Nor did it seem feasible that in such a short space of time and on one stretch of tarmac, perhaps 50 metres from one end of the corner to the other, so much that Ocaña had achieved could have been so conclusively destroyed. It is a fact of every race that riders crash. But it is also a fact of the 1971 Tour that this was the one race where a giant of the sport had been so thoroughly pole-axed – only to rise from the depths again, in a way that nobody could have predicted, and on a day that he said later, 'was going to see my last attack'.

'If Luis had not cracked that day, barring the final day's time trial into Paris, I was going to leave it.' Even Merckx, it seems, had his limits. But Ocaña reached his first.

The fruitless debate as to what would have happened if Ocaña had not been struck down so conclusively – not just to the Tour, but to the sport – continues to this day. Would others have attempted to follow in his wheel tracks and beat the Cannibal? Would all the races that Merckx then took after his Orcières-Merlette defeat – the three Tours and Giros, the Vuelta and World Championships, the eight 'Monument' Classics – all have gone his way?

Merckx, even now, admits he was having a lousy year. Equally importantly, he has not said whether he could have won the Tour de France outright had Ocaña continued: 'And I won't say that … [but] I would have made his life difficult,' he insists.

'Was it difficult for me to go on?' he asks rhetorically. 'How many stages did I win? Six, seven?' (Actually, it was four, his lowest total for a single Tour, but even so.) We should also remember, Merckx points out, that as for riders like 'Guimard, his green jersey is in the Landes. Okay, I was not good, but everybody else was worse.' Everyone, that is, apart from Ocaña.

For all the speculation and conjectures, there is no way of knowing whether Merckx could have outstripped the Spaniard again. Not even in the 1971 Tour de France. As Thévenet says, Ocaña might have been weaker, but he was still stronger than the rest, and had proved himself able to respond to Merckx on each occasion thus far. And if De Muer, well known to be demanding – 'No, I'm just realistic' is how the Frenchman responds to that criticism in his tape-recorded interview – had seen there was any chance of Ocaña continuing, he would surely, given there was so much at stake, have forced the Spaniard on.

'It was Ocaña's personality that was to blame,' Thévenet says. 'When he had an idea in his head, there were times when he was too impulsive. In 1971, if he hadn't been like that, he would have just taken it easy on the descent. Merckx would have gained time, but he wouldn't have made up seven minutes. But Luis was like that, if he wanted to do something, he had no caution, he went for it and as for the consequences the next day? He just didn't give a fuck about them.'

For those who say that Ocaña 'could have continued' but lacked the mental resilience to do so, they have clearly forgotten this was the same rider who continued for two days after crashing so badly on the Ballon d'Alsace that his bike was covered in blood. This was the rider who rode himself, despite having 14 injections a day and chronic bronchitis, into the ground at the Giro d'Italia in 1968 despite being told by his doctors to stop – and who would do so again in the future. It is too easy to confuse a man who lived on his nerves like Ocaña with someone who cannot take pressure

– as Ocaña did brilliantly, albeit by driving his team-mates up the wall in the 1970 Vuelta. Then, he was 1" away from winning his first Grand Tour for over a week, and he finally won. Ocaña did not handle pressure well, as Cescutti pointed out to me, but that is not the same thing as not being able to handle it at all.

It is also too easy to say that the Col de Menté was where Ocaña, continually being ground down by Merckx, finally lost the plot. It is fairer, perhaps, to see it as a single, potentially minor, error of excessive self-confidence and pride which mushroomed, through no fault of his own, into complete disaster. Ocaña, as the man of passionate, uncontrolled extremes was the right man to stage a successful uprising against Merckx. But he was the wrong man to reap the benefits of it. Therein surely lies his tragedy.

10

HANDLING DEFEAT

For Josiane the central issue on the afternoon of the events on the Col de Menté was not whether her husband might have been able to continue in the Tour de France or finally beat Merckx. It was whether he was still alive.

Listening to the live broadcasts on the Tour de France at her home at Bretagne-de-Marsan, Josiane recollects that of the three or four radio stations she had playing simultaneously at least two said that Ocaña was dead. And given that De Muer and the following team cars were impossible to contact, and TV coverage had dried up completely because of the storm, she had no way of knowing whether or not it was true.

'I had been following the race and when they said the weather was so bad, I was very worried. But I said to myself, "well, so long as he doesn't take any risks ..." and then I kept on listening while they went on about the weather and then when I heard, all of a sudden, "the yellow jersey is down", I thought "well, that's torn it".

'And then suddenly I realised I was all alone in the house and that the radio commentators had practically been saying he was dead. Then twice on the radio, I heard that he had [actually] died, twice I heard that. And I knew I'd have to go to find out for myself.'

Accompanied by Cescutti, she drove off towards the Pyrenees 'not knowing at all what we were going to find'. Further radio broadcasts then said that Ocaña had been taken to hospital in Saint-Gaudens, some 40 kilometres north of the Col de Menté.

But it was only when Josiane actually got there that she discovered Ocaña was in fact alive and with no bones broken – but in a severe state of shock that would have prevented him, she says, from continuing to race. Her first thought in any case 'was that his life was not in danger'.

Ocaña, suffering from severe back pain, remained under observation in Saint-Gaudens for another two or three days, nonetheless, before returning to their new home in Bretagne-de-Marsan. It was painfully ironic that he left hospital the evening before the Tour stage was due to start from Mont-de-Marsan, something the organisers had done as a kind of homage to him. That Ocaña could only have watched it from the sidelines rather than in yellow – in fact he refused to go to the start at all – was, Josiane says, 'something that plunged everybody in Mont-de-Marsan into [collective] gloom'.

Others were not so depressed about Ocaña's crashing out of the Tour. Maurice De Muer, who was 'holed up that night [of the Col de Menté] … in the dormitory of some school … if I remember rightly' – fairly typical accommodation for Tour teams until the 1990s – 'I wasn't too annoyed about it all.' Rather, he says, it was the sponsor who took it badly.

'It was a big blow for the BIC boss. He would ring me up [before the Pyrenees] and say, "so have we won?" I'd told him to get everything ready for the victory celebrations as if BIC had won, to book a swanky restaurant on the [rue de la] Rivière in Paris. There were going to be 150 tables for BIC, loads of champagne …' all of which was written off on a single corner of one descent of the Tour. Or, as Maurice De Muer put it in one final, ultra-expressive snort of annoyance in the interview: 'Hah!'

According to De Muer, Ocaña himself was 'fatalistic about it all. He just said that it was bad luck. He lay there on the [hospital] bed, his head hanging off the pillow at an angle that was so weird that you thought something had to be wrong with him. And he was talking to himself, "it's not possible, it's not possible, *pas possible*". Luis believed that things would happen in such and such a way and when they didn't, he didn't understand.' As De Muer points out, once Ocaña had decided on something or that the result of the race would be *x*, there was no telling him anything else could happen.

As for the Tour, the life had gone out of it completely. The winner was now clear, but it was almost no longer relevant – something Merckx indicated by refusing to accept the jersey at Luchon, although he would wear it from the Pyrenees to Paris.

'Everybody was a little bit down that it happened that way. It would have been a beautiful duel with Eddy right the way until the finish,' observes Van Impe.

'It makes me very sad,' Merckx told reporters there. 'I have the impression that it's me that's lost the Tour in Luchon.' He even briefly considered pulling out himself, but instead concentrated on proving as best he could that he was a worthy winner of the Tour – ousting Guimard from the green jersey on the stage to Bordeaux and taking the time trial into Paris on the last day. Yet for once Merckx faced a battle that he could not win: against the speculation, that remains to this day, as to what would have happened without the Col de Menté.

He did his best to master it, though, and that was obvious from the way he treated Ocaña. Now revealed as his most dangerous, if inconsistent, rival, Merckx kept the pressure on him as best he could. 'Eddy was clearly very acute at finding his rivals' weaknesses,' points out William Fotheringham, and it is clear that the 'psychological war' began as soon as Merckx went to visit Ocaña at home on the morning of the Mont-de-Marsan stage.

With two gestures, Merckx made sure that Ocaña was both reminded of his failure and that the press would maintain high expectations of the Spaniard. According to the correspondent of *Le Dauphiné Libéré* – sitting expectantly in the hallway of Ocaña's

Spanish-style home underneath a huge aerial photograph of Priego and two of his Spanish landscape paintings – Merckx walked through wearing a yellow jersey, a reminder of the trophy Ocaña no longer possessed. On top of that, according to other reports, Merckx told Ocaña – to whom he talked behind closed screen doors in the kitchen while De Muer kept guard outside and munched his way through a bowl of goose confit at the same time – that 'next year you will win the Tour'. He did not have to look far to see who had won the 1971 race.

Yet there was one battle Ocaña had already won: the post-Menté popularity contest. Sympathy for the underdog was such that while the *DL*'s correspondent was waiting for Ocaña to appear, the Bretagne-de-Marsan postman turned up with two kilos of fan mail for Ocaña. 'It's been like that every day since he fell off,' he told the *DL* reporter. Merckx, in comparison, had to face fans throwing stones at him en route to Paris. But it was his name in the history books, not Ocaña's, as Merckx's third Tour in as many years left him only with Anquetil's record to beat.

The problem for Merckx, longer term, was that ever since Orcières-Merlette a jack-in-a-box-like figure now threatened his number one spot. At the Col de Menté, the lid had gone firmly back on Ocaña, but only in terms of the Tour, and for Merckx a large part of 1972 would be dedicated to making sure the lid stayed shut everywhere else.

Paris–Nice next spring was a case in point. After winning the prologue ahead of Ocaña, Merckx took a seemingly definitive lead on stage two and led the race all the way to the foot of the Col d'Eze time trial on the Sunday. On each occasion that he could, at Autun on stage two, at Manosque on stage five, even in a ridiculously short team time trial, just 4.9 kilometres, at Valence, Merckx snatched one handful of seconds after another on Ocaña. The fact that he had cracked a vertebra in a crash at St-Etienne mid-race was a minor distraction in comparison.

Raymond Poulidor, by this point a venerable veteran, played a far more conservative game and ended up clinching the race overall: but for Merckx what was important was staying ahead of Ocaña, which he duly did, finishing second overall to Ocaña's third. That compulsively beating Ocaña while injured probably cost him the race was beside the point. Equally irrelevant in that particular game was the fact that it took Merckx two months to recover from the vertebra injury: Merckx was asserting his authority, come what may.

The pressure applied by Merckx continued for the next five months. In a pattern re-established decades later by Lance Armstrong on Jan Ullrich – raising the stakes by saying he was the favourite, then implying he had not worked hard enough to earn that status – in the first half of June 1972, Merckx stated that Ocaña 'had not raced enough before the Tour'. His point was that while he had by that stage taken a second Giro on the trot, Ocaña had not taken part in the Vuelta a España, or even the Vuelta al País Vasco, where, despite being defending champion, he pulled out at the last minute on De Muer's orders for reasons that remain unclear.

This psychological warfare might have ended up toppling Ocaña mentally. But instead he built steadily towards the summer. Falling out with the Vuelta organisers and refusing to line up over a lack of start money may well have cost him some basic racing condition. But a stunning victory in the Spanish National Championships and a follow-up win in the Dauphiné Libéré in June 1972 strongly suggested that Ocaña was en route for a second battle royal with Merckx in the one race that – then as now – makes or breaks a top stage racer's season: the Tour de France.

Too much, in fact, has been written about Ocaña's inability to handle expectations as being at the heart of what caused him to crack in the 1972 Tour. It is true that the man who knew him the best, his old trainer, Cescutti, says that 'when it came to handling pressure he wasn't so good'. But in 1972 it was the combination of two other factors that did for him: Ocaña's huge desire to win, and his willingness to go way beyond the limits set by his excessively fragile health. Put simply, Ocaña's way of handling defeat was to dig himself an even deeper hole in the ground.

To get an idea of how involved Ocaña would get with pushing himself to the limit, the Trofeo Baracchi race of November 1971 offers an example which – after questioning a range of riders, directors and journalists – it seems is unique in the sport of cycling. Certainly, Emilio Cruz, Ocaña's soigneur from 1970 to 1975, and who then went on to work as a masseur with Teka and finally ONCE before retiring in 2001, says he never saw anything like it in 40 years' work.

As Cruz explains, the Baracchi was a two-up Italian end-of-season time trial, which Ocaña raced that year with Leif Mortensen, his BIC team-mate. Over a distance of 108 kilometres, Ocaña and the Dane managed to average nearly 49 kilometres an hour – a race record which stood for nearly 20 years – and completed the course 2'26" faster than the closest pursuers and previous year's winners, the Pettersson duo, Giro winner Gösta and brother Tomas.

In conjunction with Mortensen, the Baracchi was one of Ocaña's most spectacular wins, as well as direct proof that his time trialling was his strongest suit. After 25 kilometres with an advantage of 1'14" over the Petterssons, as *El Mundo Deportivo* put it, 'the race ceased to exist'. By kilometre 50, the advantage of the leading duo was 90 per cent of their final advantage, 2'12", and for the second half, with Mortensen so tired from such a fast start he was unable to take any further turns on the front, Ocaña almost single-handedly raised the margin even further by a further 14".

'Luis gave it everything,' Cruz tells me, 'he was so into the racing that day that' – and his voice drops – 'he did it all over the bike. From the effort.' When asked what he means by 'did it' – perhaps losing control of his bowels? – he lowers his voice even further and says, 'He came. And after the stage [time trial] he was in bed for three or four hours because his balls hurt so much …'

The explanation is perhaps a bit shocking, but Cruz believes that Ocaña's willpower was such that he could force himself to limits – as at the Baracchi – that others simply could not match. 'In that way he was a *superclase*', a Spanish word that translates rather lamely as 'top champion'. 'And *superclases* can do stuff which for normal people just wouldn't be possible,' he explains.

Apart from the Baracchi, Cruz cites as evidence of Ocaña's *superclase* status his lack of nerves before some big challenges – 'his blood would boil in the races, he could attack and attack, but he could disconnect fast, too'. Cruz also points to Ocaña's digestive system and the fact that, unlike other riders, he would eat normally the night before major challenges. But only, it turns out, what was normal for Ocaña …

'I've seen him do the Subida a Arrate hill climb [in 1971] and get to the hotel the evening before and ask for two *raciones*' – a typical Spanish portion which normally serves at least two to three people – 'of baby eels, a speciality round here. There was a director of another team, Julio San Emeterio, who asked him what he was doing eating so much food the night before a race and Ocaña just answered: "Fuck it, if I want them why am I not going to eat them?"

'Oh, and after the *raciones* of baby eels, he ate a whole steak. And that was at ten o'clock at night. "I'll have an infusion and then I'll be able to sleep," [he said].' After which, almost needless to say, he then won the following day's race – an eight-kilometre uphill time trial on one of the Basque Country's single toughest climbs.

'Other normal people, if they ate that sort of food, would go down with diarrhoea, but these *superclases*, they have got something, they don't even notice it. Luis could spend the night with his wife in the Tour, which isn't recommended, and then be right as rain the next day.'

Quite apart from Ocaña's metabolism, his exceptional physiognomy, Cruz says, was again worthy of a *superclase*. 'His leg muscles were strange, something I'd not come across before – so soft and flexible, you could almost turn his knee right over in a massage.' Being able to relax so totally would have been a huge advantage when it came to recovery on stage races in particular – together with time trials, Ocaña's forte.

Equally exceptional, Cruz says, was 'his not asking for anything in particular. He wasn't fussy. In the Tour you'd maybe give a longer massage for three riders, rather than four, and one of them would be Luis, but that would be about the extent of it.

'You'd never get any funny games with him. No mucking around. If dinner was at eight, he'd be there at eight. And from riders who were not exceptional, they'd be far fussier and more complicated to handle for us soigneurs. But not Luis. He was only demanding with himself.' Yet even if he was a *superclase*, Ocaña had his limits, as the 1972 Tour would show – and his team-mates knew it only too well.

***

Hemmed in on three sides by ultra functional-looking, ageing, grey high-rise blocks of flats, as winter rain darkens its cement the atmosphere in the Plaza Simón Arrieta in Bergara, a murky industrial town in the Basque Country, could hardly be gloomier.

Yet in the well-lit bar in one corner of the plaza, pop classics boom out of the speakers, there is a blast of fresh coffee as you open the door and, if the atmosphere could hardly be friendlier, there are no raised voices, none of the amiable raucousness, so typical of Spanish bars. But given that the bar is run by Jesús Aranzabal, Ocaña's key team-mate, closest ally and confidant at Fagor and his first three years at BIC – it is perhaps hardly surprising: just like his bar, Aranzabal has always made a living out of being both upbeat, and, above all, calm.

Aranzabal's role with Ocaña was essentially that of full-time minder: off the bike, he was the regular hotel room-mate who would put up with the Spaniard's temper tantrums when he lost or messed up a race. On the bike, he was the rider who, thanks to his stocky, solid build, guided Ocaña through the peloton, brought him water bottles or rain capes, chased down breakaways or provided strategic advice. If Ocaña was the genius, Aranzabal was the man who tried to keep his feet on the ground.

It was no easy task, but one which Ocaña knew Aranzabal was the best person to tackle: he was one of just two riders to go with Ocaña from Fagor to BIC, at Ocaña's request. But unlike Ramón Mendiburu, who retired from racing to become Spanish national trainer in May 1970, Aranzabal lasted until the winter of 1972, the year after he had opened his bar in Bergara: ample time to witness Ocaña's strengths and to see the chinks in the armour when he was at the height of his powers.

Then as now – sitting sipping a coffee at one end of the bar, where he can keep an eye on the custom – Aranzabal appreciated Ocaña greatly, but recognises he was a nightmare to direct. He has lost count of the number of times, he says, that Ocaña, having conscientiously reconnoitred the time trials of a race *and* insisted on the most up-to-date material for his bike *and* studied the stage finales would either attack way too early or simply abandon the race … 'because if he was pissed off about something, that would be it, he'd go. Just like that.'

At the other extreme, Ocaña could become so involved in a stage he would be impossible to stop. 'I remember one day in the Volta a Catalunya, it ended on the Alto de Toses, a two-kilometre uphill finale, and Luis said beforehand that we, the team, would do "this, this and this" and he'd do "this, this and this".

'Instead we hadn't even got on our bikes at the start and he had taken 200 metres on everybody. He was away with 90 seconds to a minute advantage the whole day, even though everybody was chasing him, KAS, [Italian star Franco] Bitossi, the whole lot. They caught him with 200 metres to go and [Miguel Marí] Lasa won the stage.

'You should have seen Luis in the hotel afterwards, yelling his head off about "why hadn't we stopped him?" And the director had tried to by driving his car across the middle of the road and Ocaña just ignored him and kept going!'

Aranzabal was an unwilling guinea pig, too, in one of Ocaña's bids to prove that life was only worth living at the extreme. He was the co-driver in a car with Luis in the Aosta Valley in Italy one autumn en route to the Trofeo Baracchi as Ocaña drove at 120 kilometres an hour through very thick fog.

Given that visibility was zero, Ocaña used the white line in the middle of the Italian road for guidance. ('I asked him to slow down and what if we hit somebody and he just said, "*No pasa nada*".') And in Segovia, where Ocaña stormed away from the peloton after Aranzabal had single-handedly reined in every earlier attack, he was another unwilling witness to how Spain's Inland Revenue officers were waiting for Ocaña as he came off the winner's podium, to ask him to hand over the prize money. Dodging taxes was something you'd almost expect Ocaña to do: his umpteenth attempt to outrun fate – and umpteenth failure.

As a reward for his superb ride in Segovia, probably the race in which he had to employ another of his skills – laying the groundwork so that Ocaña could attack most effectively – to the fullest ever, together with Ocaña, Aranzabal was one of just two Spaniards to race in the Tour in 1972. And as Ocaña's regular room-mate at BIC, he was a direct witness to the disintegration of what effectively became Ocaña's last bid to oust Merckx once and for all in the Tour.

First of all in the Tour, Aranzabal recalls, came the post-race fits of anger as Merckx, time and again, managed to peg him back, first in the team time trial in the first week, and again on the Ventoux. Only by a few seconds each time (on the Ventoux Merckx marked Ocaña all the way up the climb before slipping ahead at the last possible moment) but enough to ensure he was always behind the Belgian – and for a rider who had been convinced that Merckx was beatable, Ocaña's frustration grew and grew. On top of that, a crash on a descent of the Pyrenees did not knock him out of the race, but it provided an unwelcome reminder of the Col de Menté, and cost him nearly 2'00" on Merckx.

'He would yell out "I don't want anybody to call me", then go into the hotel room and slam the door. As I knew him well I wouldn't pay him any attention,' Aranzabal recalls. Indeed, as Cruz suggests, once Ocaña had 'got things off his chest', as it were, he would quickly relax.

But if able to switch off, Aranzabal recalls a certain degree of restlessness no massage could cure. 'He always went to bed very late, he'd go out for walks, stay up reading or listen to the radio. And if the stage went really badly, then he'd go out and party.

'His suitcase was always packed, ready to go, at eleven o'clock at night,' adds Cruz. 'Many cyclists I've known just kick all their clothes into the bag half an hour before they have to leave the hotel, but Luis would be ready to go, even in the Tour. First thing.'

In the mornings, no matter the race, Aranzabal would be up first, and after he'd opened the window Ocaña would open a sleepy eye to check on the weather. 'If it was raining, I'd still open it – I liked the rain – but Luis would yell "not the blooming rain again" at the top of his voice.'

And it was the wet weather that July of 1972 that finally forced Ocaña, indirectly, to call time on his Tour bid. The end came, Aranzabal recalls, 'somewhere outside a town [Aix-les-Bains on stage 15] in the Alps. It was raining so much, so hard, for days. I can remember him vomiting blood, when he was coughing he would sick up blood in the phlegm. He was like Indurain, he didn't like the cold either. After three days of rain he'd get bronchitis and he would always be out of it.'

Standing at the roadside with Ocaña, that was not just the end of the Tour for the Spaniard – or so it seemed. Aranzabal recalls that 'the doctors told Luis there and then that his career was over'.

For Ocaña to be told he had to give up was exactly the sort of provocation he would have needed to continue onwards into 1973. But even he could not escape the fact that, thanks to a combination of fragile health and ridiculous amounts of willpower, in 1972 he had ridden himself into a box. The duel – so widely anticipated – between Merckx and the one rider who had managed to have Merckx up against the ropes, had ended in conclusive defeat for the Spaniard. 'He wanted to win so incredibly badly,' says Aranzabal, 'that finally he sank. He had no self-control.'

Merckx's post-1972 analysis of Ocaña, as Daniel Friebe points out, was painfully accurate. 'He's a good rider, he made a big impression on me in the first week of the Tour, but he doesn't cope well with repeated efforts … and to end this debate once and for all, I'll ask all those who maintain that the war of supremacy between Ocaña and Merckx isn't over to examine our palmarès and to remember that he's started four Tours and abandoned three of them.'

This was vintage Merckx when handling his enemies on and off the bike: relentlessly logical, piling on the pressure at all times and seeing where they cracked, keen to ensure that their defeats were so resounding that they would be too demoralised to return to the fray, and reminding them of their failures. For Ocaña, though, rather than overreacting to pressure such as that coming from Merckx, he was a victim of his excessive self-confidence, his fragile health and, above all, his chronic inability to tell himself when enough was enough.

11

THE EMPTY THRONE

Just as Eddy Merckx's 1971 Tour victory will for ever have a 'what if?' element about it, so a question remains about Luis Ocaña's greatest win: the 1973 Tour de France. With no Merckx in the field, there will always be doubts as to whether Ocaña would have been able to put the Cannibal to the sword in the way he did the rest of the opposition that year.

Almost every race until 1973 had revealed the differences between the two. The Tour that year showed up all the similarities. The time gap between Ocaña and second-placed Bernard Thévenet, of over 15'00" in Paris, was worthy of Merckx in 1969, his greatest Tour win. So, too, was the number of stages Ocaña won – six. There was the same need to win for winning's sake, shown at the Puy-de-Dôme or in the Versailles time trial. There was also the same kind of opportunism and versatility. No doubt about it, Ocaña's 1973 Tour win was taken with a degree of domination that Merckx would have been proud of.

All of which makes the issue of what the Tour would have been like with Merckx present even more relevant, and even more difficult to answer. The issue hangs over the race to the point that *L'Equipe*'s final headline over a photo of Ocaña standing triumphantly in his yellow jersey in Paris wasn't even about the 1973 Tour, but, rather, what would happen in 1974: 'Next year, it's Merckx v. Ocaña,' they predicted. All that mattered was the grudge match.

Yet, as Britain's Bradley Wiggins said when asked about whether he regretted not being able to race against cycling's then top stage racer, Alberto Contador, when he won the 2012 Tour de France: 'I can only beat the people who are there.' With or without Merckx, Ocaña's victory was as much a masterpiece as Orcières-Merlette, executed with clinical detachment and a degree of self-sacrifice that went all the way back to the previous winter.

Merckx himself recognises that Ocaña that year was on a level that could have taken their rivalry to new heights: 'When he was on form he was a great all-rounder, and I really wish I had done that Tour,' Merckx now says. 'It would have been a great battle.

'But I'd have been the first foreigner to win it five times in a row and the public and the organisation didn't like me so much because I would have beaten the Anquetil [Tour] record.

'The journalists convinced me not to go. So I decided to do the Vuelta and the Giro instead.' This was not a one-off decision by Merckx. Even two years later, media opinion again swayed him and the public too much. In 1975, he says, when it came to fighting for Tour win number six, '[Félix] Lévitan [Tour organiser] really wanted me to go, after I'd won five times, he wanted me to take part. But the press made the people go crazy on the road, and I received some letters, death threats.' Sometimes, he asserts, 'the press go too far'.

Despite beating Ocaña in the 1973 Vuelta a España, Merckx says his number one rival was 'just as impressive that year as he was in 1971. You could see immediately if he was in good shape, his expression, the way he was riding, something about the way his legs moved if he was going well. When you're a pro you get to know these things.'

For once, he seems to be saying, he would have had a rival who it might have been impossible to match. And as Thévenet, who finished second that year, observes, 'I don't see how Merckx could have beaten him.'

Luis was never so conscientious about training and eating as he was in the winter of 1972, Josiane recalls. 'He had been sick in 1972, and he decided to be far stricter, with a really tough diet and training at incredible levels.' It even got to the point where on New Year's Day and New Year's Eve, 'when we eat really well here in this area, good wine, foie gras … I swear on the heads of my children that he followed his diet, he didn't do what everybody else was doing and stuff himself silly.

'He even said it: "In 1973 I'm going to win the Tour, I have to do everything, not bend the rules at all. And to do that all the way through Christmas and the New Year, not even have a drop of champagne or a drop of [any other] alcohol, that's really hard.'

Merckx himself said he was more impressed by Ocaña in 1973 than he had been in any previous year, including 1971. Having opted to do the Vuelta – which he had never raced before – and the Giro rather than the Tour, the two only crossed swords in Spain.

The Vuelta itself saw Merckx racking up a huge advantage thanks to his ability to sprint and claim time bonuses – something that Ocaña, never at ease in the bunch finishes, could not hope to compete in. But on the one major climb of the race, the Orduña near Vitoria in the Basque Country, Ocaña finally managed to find some terrain where Merckx was at last a little exposed. And he dropped Merckx.

'I remember thinking, "this is a different Luis",' Merckx recalls. 'He was not the same, much stronger. I caught him before the finale, but it did make a difference.'

There were other indications in the spring that Ocaña was functioning on a far better level than usual. In the Vuelta al País Vasco, despite the appallingly cold, snowy weather – in which he would usually be at a disadvantage – Ocaña managed to fend off an exceptionally strong KAS team almost single-handed to claim his second victory there in three years. In the now defunct Setmana Catalana, at the time one of Spain's top five events, Ocaña finally managed, for the first time in his career, to defeat Eddy Merckx in a stage race. 'I am a complete rider again, not like last year when I seriously thought about finishing my career' – when he was told by the doctors in the Tour that he would have to do just that. 'Eddy and me will be running the show this season,' he predicted at the finish, a statement that would have bordered on the outrageous considering their respective track records. But given Ocaña had just managed to put a hefty 28" into Merckx in a 13-kilometre time trial, it didn't cause quite as much controversy as it could have.

The fans of the Setmana Catalana were also witness to an arguably even rarer sight than Ocaña beating Merckx: a Merckx–Ocaña alliance. On a whopping 249-kilometre stage to Castelldefels, Ocaña attacked early on, Merckx responding by bridging across with three of his Molteni team-mates, and when Ocaña began taking turns at the front, the damage inflicted was colossal. In a minor masterpiece, the two giants of stage racing in the early 1970s and ten other riders in the day-long break ensured that Poulidor, Zoetemelk and early leader Raymond Deslisle all lost a staggering 28'00" by the time they reached Castelldefels, and that the Setmana Catalana would be played out between the two top contenders. Sadly, this was the first and only time that Merckx and Ocaña ganged up together – their opponents must have been thanking their lucky stars that the rivalry between the two was so extreme it did not allow them to do so more often.

Merckx had not been in top form throughout the eight-stage, seven-day Setmana. On stage one he had a mechanical problem two kilometres from the line and Ocaña, Leif Mortensen, Zoetemelk and Poulidor instantly went on the attack. 'Freed from the monster, they couldn't hit the pedals hard enough, they fled from him like poisoned rats,' was how *El Mundo Deportivo* described it. The monster then recovered to the point where it was breathing down the quartet's necks by the line. But if reducing a gap of 1'00" to 10" in a couple of kilometres on four of the biggest names of the time was something only Merckx was capable of doing, he paid the price for it the next day. In the final kilometre of the stage to Andorra, Merckx cracked, losing another 10" on Ocaña. 'He was almost delirious and his eyes were coming out of their sockets at the finish,' said *El Mundo Deportivo* in typically B-horror-movie style. 'Could Eddy be paying the price of [his recent Hour Record bid in] Mexico?'

At Castelldefels, though, after ripping the race apart between them, Ocaña said that 'Merckx has recovered completely, I tried to drop him several times today but I couldn't. The [decisive] time trial [the following day] doesn't suit me much, it's too mountainous … and Eddy is the kind of rival that gives you nightmares.'

'Luis is very strong, but he shouldn't doubt that I will give it everything,' Merckx warned. 'The Setmana is a race which I haven't got in my palmarès and I want to set that record straight.'

However, Merckx would have to wait another year. Ocaña managed to defeat him in the time trial and then, despite a late puncture to which Merckx responded with an attack, stayed close enough to the Belgian on the final sector of the last stage to claim the victory.

'Luis was irresistible but I was not performing to the best of my abilities,' Merckx said. 'I'll have time to get my revenge.' Even so, the psychological importance of a definitive defeat of Merckx, even once, is clear from Ocaña's statements on the line. 'It's going to spur me on and it gives me a sense of obligation,' he said. 'Eddy's not unbeatable, but I needed a victory like this to convince myself of the fact. I've shown what I can do, and I will show it again.'

While warning that the early season races like the Setmana were not always reliable omens for the rest of the year, Ocaña pointed out that his health – always a major issue – had not let him down so far.

'I've had a perfect winter's preparation, my breathing problems have stopped, my morale's back up and I'm going very well. All I can hope for is that this will continue.

'My whole year is focused on the Tour de France. I don't want to burn myself out before then. I have a debt there with the Spanish fans that I can't forget. It's a big gap in my palmarès and I can't fail this time.'

***

Thursday 31 May 1973. Stage three of the Dauphiné Libéré: a monster Alpine stage including – appropriately enough for that year's Ascension Day – climbs of the Croix de Fer, Télégraphe and Galibier. Bernard Thévenet recalls that, as the race starts off, Luis Ocaña – whom he'd met and chatted with the night before as their teams shared hotels – comes up and says, "Do you realise we're both in the Dauphiné and nobody [in the media] has mentioned us yet?"

'And with his funny accent, he says, "*Bordel* [Dammit], all those sprinters, have you seen how they make us suffer? Right, come on, let's do the same to them." And I said to him, "well, if you're going to make them hurt, then I'll come with you".' (There are also unconfirmed stories that Ocaña's attack was specifically aimed at Cyrille Guimard, with whom he had fallen out.)

Either way, after the two of them attacked on the Croix de Fer, there was no question as to who would be doing the lion's share of the work. It got to the point where, Thévenet recalls, 'It was all I could do to come up by his side from time to time to pretend I was going all right and so he wouldn't accelerate … God, the way that guy was climbing!'

And even so, the gap kept increasing, to the point that when the duo reached Briançon the race was effectively theirs for the taking – 'we had the next guys at nine minutes, the third group at a quarter of an hour, the bunch [including expert climbers like Van Impe] at 45 minutes'.

As Thévenet says, 'the margins sum up Luis completely. It was never worthwhile winning with just two minutes on the bunch. He had to do it with panache and, fucking hell, when it got to six or seven minutes, I wanted to say, "hey, isn't that enough [of an advantage] now?" and I realised that if I did, all he would do was accelerate.'

The 1973 Dauphiné Libéré had come down to a two-horse race, with just the time trial from Creusot to Montceau-les-Mines as a decider. Thévenet says he was inspired by racing on roads he knew well from his childhood, and as leader he also had the advantage of knowing Ocaña's times. But it did him little good. Ocaña put a minute into him and had his third Dauphiné in four years in the bag. 'At least,' Thévenet now reflects. 'I wasn't beaten by a "nobody".'

***

Merckx's decision not to take part in the Tour de France that year, and instead opt for the Vuelta–Giro 'double' was due in large part to what he felt was antipathy from the French. You name it – the organisers, the fans, the media were all, he believed, fed up with his presence in the race.

That his absence was noted was unquestionable. On the first day of the Tour, *L'Equipe* published a cartoon of an empty throne with the name Merckx written on it, and various riders – Ocaña among them – edging their way towards it.

Asked about the consequences of Merckx creating a huge power vacuum by deliberately opting out, Ocaña played them down. 'Not everybody's in the Vuelta or in the Giro, nor is everybody here,' he reasoned simply.

Just as Wiggins felt about Contador's absence in 2012, Ocaña could hardly argue anything else. But even if Merckx had not been commentating on the Tour for a Luxembourg radio station – and his daily observations were constantly relayed to whoever happened to be in yellow – in some ways his presence, constant yet intangible, became even more strongly felt than if he had been in the peloton. On this occasion, Merckx truly was unbeatable.

Fifth in the prologue behind Joop Zoetemelk – but at a mere 5" – Spain's correspondents noted something new about Ocaña: as well as his usual passionate, involved, intense self, he also seemed strangely happy.

Even after the prologue he came up to *MARCA*'s press car, smiling away and talking nineteen to the dozen about the 11 bikes (compared to the usual two or three for most pros) he'd ordered since the start of the season. All of them, too, were exceptionally expensive, ultra-light models made of titanium.

Could his upbeat mood be due to the absence of Merckx? For all he claimed it was not the case, knowing that in a sense he had nothing to lose given Merckx was not present must have given Ocaña a feeling of liberation. On top of that, if you discounted races when he had had to abandon, none of the other riders participating had managed to beat him in a major Tour in the previous two years. (Thévenet had finished third behind him and Merckx in the 1973 Vuelta and Ocaña had finished three spots ahead of Zoetemelk, third to the Dutchman's sixth, in the same race in 1971.)

Ocaña took the one option that was really open to him: he put his head down, ignored the constant questioning and focused on beating those rivals who were there. In any case, he was not the top favourite which, given his dislike of pressure, almost certainly favoured him: rather, *L'Equipe* argued that 'if it came to a gallop' Thévenet and Zoetemelk, who they considered more consistent, had the greatest chance of occupying Merckx's throne. Ocaña, meanwhile, was placed at a lower level because of his erratic performance in previous Julys.

Not everybody felt the same way. Raphael Geminiani, doing a round of the Tour's press room as the more venerable sports directors are still wont to do at the start of races, invited the French journalists to 'learn Spanish from their colleagues over there. A week from now, the only riders you'll be interested in will be speaking that language.'

Was Geminiani right, though? Ocaña was soon to find it wasn't just Merckx who could potentially mess up his Tour performances: in kilometre 18 of the first sector of the first mass start stage, a dog running out into the road on the outskirts of The Hague caused Ocaña to get entangled with another rider, fall and go flying. It was the first crash of the 1973 Tour and, in keeping with his infamous bad luck, it was already rumoured that he would have to quit.

Legend has it that Ocaña was the only rider of all 132 Tour starters to hit the deck, but that wasn't true: two domestiques, Dutchman Tino Tabak and Madrid-born José Luis Abilleira from Bahamontes' La Casera squad, who had swerved to avoid the dog and unintentionally caused Ocaña to crash, also went down.

However, it was certainly true that Ocaña was the only favourite to be affected so early on. And although X-rays after the second part of the stage, over several sections of *pavé* cobblestones to Sint Niklaas in Belgium, revealed no broken bones, Ocaña suffered severe bruising on his right side. If he recollected that Maurice De Muer had told him before the race start that 'your bad luck is officially over' it can only have rubbed salt into the wounds.

'That crash, so early, really damaged my morale,' Ocaña said much later on in the race. 'I pretended that my injuries weren't too bad, but things were very tough for quite a few days.'

Arguably even more worrying was the emergence of a rival barely mentioned in the French press as a possible contender, Belgium's Herman Van Springel. Already a top-three finisher in all three Grand Tours, the 29-year-old former diamond cutter from Antwerp was one of the few riders able to cross over between cobbled Classics and stage racing. He exploited this versatility to the full en route to Sint Niklaas, shooting ahead on the *pavé* alongside Ocaña's BIC team-mate José Catieau to gain a 2'16" advantage on all the other contenders.

The Spanish media were confident that Van Springel would lose ground in the upcoming Alps, but given that he only lost the 1968 Tour on the very last day to Jan Janssen, perhaps they were overconfident. Van Springel was one of the top 1970s Classics riders as well as a great stage racer, but he was usually almost completely overshadowed in Belgium by Merckx. 'You just give up [trying to beat Merckx],' he once said. 'You have no option.' In the 1973 Tour sans Eddy, though, Van Springel had a one-off chance to shine in cycling's biggest bike race.

After such an unexpected early blow by Van Springel, the peloton were far more attentive. The next stage across Belgium to the Roubaix velodrome on the French frontier, which included assaults on the Tour of Flanders' key climb and yet more *pavé*, failed to have its expected impact.

Stage three's 226-kilometre slog across northern France, Roubaix to Reims, on the other hand, was another story, and the first occasion in the race where Ocaña staged an ambush of which Merckx would have been proud. As *MARCA* bluntly put it in their headline: 'Nobody expected it'.

Running for the first 70 kilometres on what was essentially a reverse route of Paris–Roubaix, while a heatwave blasting northern Europe ensured the cobbled sections were at least dry, it could not stop the Classics riders from using them to break the race apart.

However, what nobody could have predicted was that when Guimard went on the attack after 70 kilometres in one of the toughest cobbled sections, no fewer than five BICs, including Ocaña, would be the quickest to follow. Or that when the break of 11 managed to sheer off the front, far from Ocaña telling his domestiques to keep a steady pace, instead the Spaniard, perhaps inspired by his first (and last) ever Paris–Roubaix performance that April where he finished 29th, went for broke and told them to ride hell for leather.

With such a powerful front group pounding across the narrow farm tracks and long, cobbled sections, it was pandemonium behind. Paris–Roubaix is one of the hardest races in which to organise a chase, and instead the peloton split into several chunks with another Spanish contender, Jose Manuel Fuente, bouncing around unhappily on the highly unfavourable cobbled terrain, in a third group a further 30" back.

Although the peloton cleared the cobbles – 'bad enough to make a bike rider lie on the side of the road for a bit, thumb a lift from the nearest car and go home,' wrote *MARCA*'s correspondent huffily – after another hour Ocaña had no intention of easing back. Only Guimard posed an overall threat in his group and, when the gap rose to nearly 6'00", it briefly looked as if Ocaña, taking part in his most audacious attack since Orcières-Merlette, had won the Tour outright.

BIC's Schleck and Sylvain Vasseur (brother of Alain) finally dropped back from Ocaña's group, but, as panic set in behind, the chasing groups began to shatter. Poulidor, inexplicably working hard despite having team-mate Guimard (who sat in) in the front group, drew clear in a small counter-attack. Fuente, having crashed, dropped to nearly 10'00" back. But from the favourites' point of view at least, as they pounded across the plains of northern France and Reims Cathedral's twin towers – the famous snail's horns – appeared on the edge of their vision, the main pack finally fused into one large group and they stood some chance of limiting the havoc wrought by Ocaña.

With just three riders – Ocaña, Mortensen and Catieau – working on the front, the gap dropped relatively quickly, but was still well over 2'00" as the break swept into the Reims velodrome. Guimard, having failed to collaborate, had enough strength to take the stage, while Catieau swapped the green of points leader for a spell in yellow. Ocaña, meanwhile, with his eye on more long-term goals – such as taking the yellow for good – could not fail to be satisfied with an operation that had nothing in common with his usual solo hell or glory attacks. This was a triumph in which he had leant heavily on his team, and they had responded perfectly.

In one fell swoop, in a break of nine, Ocaña pushed back all the favourites except Guimard to over 2'00", while Fuente, who had had a disastrous day, dropped out of the running altogether after losing 7'00". Fuentes' time loss was a bonus of huge proportions. Given that he was no time triallist, when it came to forming an alliance with Ocaña in the mountains, the Asturian climber was his preferred option.

Overall, though, the differences were not colossal – 2'30". But Ocaña's attack to Reims had achieved several objectives at the same time. It simultaneously intimidated his rivals by being so unexpected, gave him a time cushion going into the mountains, acted (because it had been a group triumph) as a huge collective boost to BIC's morale, and forced his enemies (like it or not) onto the offensive. In a race where the top name was absent, to have pulled off such a feat, particularly after his bad crash on stage one, gave Ocaña's move even greater resonance. (It also enabled him to regain all the time lost on Van Springel.)

Small wonder that Anquetil gave Ocaña the thumbs-up for the overall, pointing out that with climbers as talented as Joaquim Agostinho and Catieau now both racing for BIC, 'I can say that Luis is almost sure to win.' Even Guimard, who had fallen out with Ocaña, said, 'he's the big favourite now, even if it's still a very open race'.

Ocaña was curiously glum at the finish, despite the journalists congratulating him on his audacity, as well as being distinctly annoyed that Guimard had won. Apart from saying the gap could have been far greater, he remarked: 'If Guimard had helped us [BIC riders] just like he used to help Merckx in the Alps when I was in trouble … it's hard to understand the attitude of that man. How is it possible that men like him want to win the Tour without actually pedalling?'

Nonetheless he grudgingly recognised that eliminating Fuente from the running – 'the most dangerous rival in the mountains' – was his big objective and that was duly accomplished. 'I'll need these minutes and more,' he reflected. 'This is a race you have to win on all the terrain – flat, time trialling and climbing.' But in the one area where he had seemed most vulnerable, Ocaña had come out on top, even if he concluded, 'I'm surprised I did as well as I did. The pain from my crash has all gone.'

What probably got Ocaña so wound up about the stage, and was to prove decisive in the long term, was not just that an enemy like Guimard was basking in the limelight but that he, Ocaña, had done all the hard work. It could also have been for a rider with a total aversion to practical but unspectacular racing approaches like, say, Zoetemelk – 'he didn't care if he won by 20 minutes or one second' was how Thévenet described the Dutchman – that finishing eighth at Reims and moving up to fifth overall was a comparatively low-key conclusion.

Ocaña was perhaps right to think that, with more collaboration from Guimard, he could have opened up a far more significant gap. But it turned out that the Frenchman was suffering from the same knee injuries that had sunk him in 1972. Two days after Reims, as the race ground over the Jura towards its first rest day – with little significant change overall barring one late attack by Zoetemelk at Nancy, which netted him 30" advantage – Guimard lost almost 20'00". Guimard, the man who had matched Merckx in the mountains throughout the 1972 race before abandoning two days before the final in Paris, this time quit before the 1973 Tour had left the Alps.

Ocaña himself could not have been more content on the race's first rest day. After checking out one of the upcoming Alpine climbs, the Salève, as part of his training, the arrival of Josiane at the Tour combined with the rapidly healing injuries from his stage one crash put him in an upbeat mood. ('Every night of the Tour that year she spent the night with me,' Ocaña would later say, arguing that the benefits of sex during a race, 'was a question of each rider's organism. Sex stimulates some riders ... I've known riders who went like the clappers afterwards.') Certainly rather than go into a sulk when one Spanish journalist cheekily asked him if he'd brought a parachute for the descent off the Salève, he burst out laughing and said he had remembered an attack of haemorrhoids on the same climb in the 1969 Tour that had caused him to lose as much time as Guimard: 20'00".

'Some day this falling off has got to come to an end,' he added, grinning broadly, before saying he felt his 'morale was good enough to win the Tour. Actually finishing first is another thing, because you can't be too cautious. But I am in a good position and my team is responding well. They'll have to work harder if I lead, but they'll be happier, too.'

Half of the directors said that Ocaña was now the favourite, and only one seemed unconvinced of his chances. Having backed a Spaniard to win early on, Raphael Geminiani, usually one of the most astute observers in the cycling community, now predicted 'a Walkowiak Tour', a reference to the bizarre 1956 race, where, with leading star Louison Bobet absent, Frenchman Roger Walkowiak exploited the top contenders' excessive conservatism to take a totally unexpected victory. On paper, it was an entirely reasonable theory, given Merckx's absence. But in fact 'Gem' could not have been more wrong.

***

In 24 hours flat, Luis Ocaña went from being fifth overall and 2'00" down to leading the Tour by 3'00" on Joop Zoetemelk. In a single, nine-kilometre Alpine climb, the Salève, on the first sector of a two-part stage barely 86 kilometres long, Ocaña took a hold on the race to the point where – had he wanted – he could simply have sat back and waited for the time trials. The second, far harder, sector to a summit finish, Méribel, won in a downpour by Bernard Thévenet ahead of a handful of favourites, including Ocaña, merely confirmed the status quo.

'Controlling the controllables' is a modern catchphrase in the British Olympic and Team Sky cycling teams, and Ocaña had certainly done that. Having checked out the Salève – both ascent and descent to the finish at Aspro-Gaillard on the rest day, he had decided on the correct gearing for an all-out attack – for the record, a 44x13–23. He had thrown his rivals off the scent by hinting strongly in interviews on the rest day that he would play a defensive game – 'My objective is not to get dropped' – and saying that the race would not be over until the ascent of the Puy-de-Dôme in the final week. And on the climb, four kilometres from the summit, when he attacked, only Zoetemelk was able to respond. Forty-eight seconds over the field at the top, after a very cautious descent, his margin remained a solid 53".

That he should take such an advantage on a comparatively easy stage was one major source of encouragement. That he had followed up his 'ambush' on the road to Reims with a classic all-out mountain attack – and stage win – was another. It had been straightforward and, rather than attacking from the gun as he had done so often, his move over the Salève was a clinically executed, perfectly timed demonstration of power that was in some ways as unlike Ocaña as it could get. Right down to the clichés with which he described it all.

'There was a plan and it all worked out perfectly,' Ocaña said. 'If I hadn't attacked, then they would have.' Was it too early to take the jersey? 'It's never too early,' he responded.

'You won't get bored in the rest of the Tour,' Ocaña had promised the press on the rest day, but could it be that Ocaña was racing in such a calculating and dominating way so that they might? Fortunately, if Ocaña was acting more like Merckx than at any other point in his career, there was another rider out there who could provide some much needed instability in a Tour that otherwise looked as if it would be over two weeks before reaching Paris.

***

According to Spanish star climber Julio Jiménez, José Manuel Fuente was a 'rebel who refused to bow down to anybody'. 'He is driven by a mad desire for an impossible challenge,' claimed Eddy Merckx. 'A complete eccentric,' says his friend and fellow rider Luis Balagué, who recalls Fuente announcing halfway through the 1973 Tour de France to his team-mates that 'nobody should talk to him for a week' – and keeping his self-imposed 'vow of silence' for the full seven days. According to everybody who met him, Fuente was one of life's anarchists: a gifted climber whose outright refusal to calculate his attacks bordered on the unhinged at times, and who almost never, in any case, accepted when he was beaten. Introverted on occasions, but given to wild outbursts when he came out of his shell, he also had a fine sense of theatre: having once lost nearly half an hour to Merckx in the Giro, lying flat on his back at the finish he flung out one arm towards a nearby church and said 'my morale remains as high as that steeple'.

Apparently racing on pure instinct, Fuente's greatest moments of his career included two Vuelta wins, a podium in the Giro and Tour and attacks that allowed him to gain 9'00" on the peloton on a single climb in the Vuelta. It was largely fuelled – as he himself admitted – by a combination of amphetamines that wrecked his kidneys and saw him retire by the age of 29, plus a huge talent for climbing and – like Ocaña – excessive reck-lessness. There are numerous examples of this – like in 1975, when close to the end of his career and knowing that he would be tested (and found positive) at the end of a Vuelta stage, he loosened his bike wheels, crashed and feigned unconsciousness so that he would be taken away in an ambulance and thus avoid the testers. But that was Plan B. Plan A for dodging the testers was to throw himself and his bike down a ravine. 'However, as it was too foggy, I couldn't see how deep it was,' he said. 'So I had to abandon that plan.'

If Ocaña was famous for attacking for the sake of it, Fuente not only did that but he also wound his rivals up – intentionally. When Ocaña attacked on the Salève, Fuente – having said his Tour 'started at the foot of the first climb in the Alps' – then opted to do nothing whatsoever 'purely because I didn't want to cramp Luis' style'. (He then punctured on the descent, and told journalists that 'anybody with half a minute would have won that stage after that downhill, even [an out and out non-climber like] Walter Godefroot.') One of the few cyclists of his generation who smoked *during* races (and was happy to be photographed doing so), he went his own way in every way he possibly could. While Ocaña had spent the rest day looking at the Alpine climbs, Fuente spent the entire day in bed, hence his nickname *el Tarangu* – Asturian dialect that translates as 'the unconcerned one'. 'He was very deep,' says Balagué, 'one day he'd sit on your back wheel for miles and miles, the next he'd attack you. And you wouldn't have the slightest idea why.' 'He could talk the hind legs off a donkey,' says Agustín Tamames, 'but the quieter he got the more worried about him you had to be.'

If anyone could make Ocaña seem the personification of a consistent racer, it could only be Fuente. He was erratic to the point where Txomin Perurena, his team-mate at KAS, said that the Asturian was affected by lunar phases and attacked whenever a full moon was approaching. Both his unpredictability and his lunacy – in the archaic sense – are borne out by the start of the 1973 Giro, where in two stages he had lost 20'00" to Merckx. But he then bounced back, beating Merckx by 2'30" on the hardest stage of all, a four-col monster in the Dolomites, in which he attacked in the first hour and crossed the summit of each climb in first place. (And sure enough, the moon *was* indeed close to being full at that time.)

Fuente and Ocaña had rarely crossed swords before the 1973 Tour. In 1971, when Ocaña crashed on the Menté, Fuente – leading the stage – also went off the road no fewer than three times. On the third, he went over a parapet and had to be hauled back onto the road using an inner tube as an impromptu rope. But he then went on to win, both the stage to Luchon and the Superbagnères stage, the following day.

'He would go from 20 to 40 kilometres an hour in a single acceleration,' recalls Thévenet. 'Luis wasn't so sudden when he attacked, but his attacks were more sustained. Luis would need 300 or 400 metres. And after 300 metres of that kind of attack, you couldn't follow him. Fuente only needed a couple of hundred.'

Merckx was so impressed by Fuente that he predicted he would win the Tour, and referred to him as 'Spain's greatest climber since Bahamontes'. Now, though, he says, 'I knew I could get rid of him on the flat stages. In the Tour in particular, they were too fast for a rider like him.' Ocaña, on the other hand, as he had shown at Marseilles in 1971, could not be eliminated in the same way.

And if Merckx destroyed Fuente's chances of victory in the 1972 Giro on the long, flat stages across the north of the country, in the Tour Ocaña had already followed suit in the stage to Reims. But while Ocaña took on the mantle of Merckx in the 1973 Tour, Fuente took on Ocaña's: determined to attack at all costs, refusing to surrender, failing to calculate the odds. And on the second stage in the Alps, by far the hardest of the Tour and taking in the Madeleine, Télégraphe, Galibier, Izoard and Les Orres climbs all in one day – more than 100 kilometres in total – it was almost inevitable he should attack: after all, another full moon was less than a week away, on 15 July.

That Fuente should tear up the script was not unexpected – that was his usual response – but the second Alpine stage was dramatic even by his standards. As *ABC*'s cycling correspondent put it: 'If yesterday [the stage to Gaillard] was a noisy firework that formed part of a show which started in The Hague, today was one of those bombs that makes the whole of humanity's hair stand on end.'

The Madeleine, nearly a third of the day's climbing, went off quietly enough. But on the ascent of the Télégraphe, the stepping stone that precedes the Galibier, Fuente began to make one staccato dig off the front after another, a seemingly never-ending process of sharp little charges. In total, he made a jaw-dropping total of 27 attacks, if not an all-time record for one rider on one climb surely close to it. Each time, Ocaña responded, sometimes with Thévenet, sometimes alone with the Frenchman bridging up. At last, though, only Ocaña could respond to Fuente, and by the summit of the Galibier they had approximately 1'10" on Thévenet's chasing group, containing no more than himself, Spain's third GC contenders, Vicente López Carril and Mariano Martínez – a climbing domestique with GAN, born in Spain but who had taken French nationality. The rest of the field, though, were at 4'00" to 5'00". If the Tour looked more than finished after the Gaillard, the Galibier was the start of its devastating confirmation.

Fuente, in fact, had managed to begin to blow the Tour apart thanks to his multiple attacks – in Ocaña's favour. Normally when a rider repeatedly tries and fails to get away in the mountains, once he is reeled in there will be a drop in pace and the chasing pack will recover ground. But because Fuente had accelerated so hard, so often, there was no such room for recovery and the rest of the field dropped steadily back.

By the foot of the Izoard after the long, fast descent down the Lautaret Valley to Briançon, the duo's advantage was holding. But then came another key development: instead of attacking again as the road began to steepen, Fuente simply glued himself to Ocaña's back wheel. And for the whole of the 21-kilometre ascent, Ocaña – who knew he had a Tour to play for and Fuente at 7'00" – powered away at the front, while Fuente – conscious he was being given an armchair ride to second overall – did not take a single turn.

If Fuente had unwittingly set the scene for Ocaña's knockout blow, this interminable ascent of the Izoard was where, kilometre by kilometre, brick by painful brick, the Spaniard of Mont-de-Marsan turned his lead into an impregnable fortress. The Izoard is the kind of place that would have surely appealed to Ocaña's sense of drama, too – as the appropriate place for a Tour-winning ascent. 'The setting,' Geoffrey Nicholson wrote in his superb *The Great Bike Race* a few years later, 'calls for the kind of heroic action which most notably Coppi provided ...

'Alpe d'Huez is a rigorous climb with its mathematical progression of tight corners and steep inclines, but the Izoard is far more awesome, a rocky wilderness at 7,743 feet which needs only a few skulls at the roadside to complete its scene of devastation.

'It begins complacently enough [but] then a steep ladder of hairpins rises to the most imposing sight of all, the Casse Deserte, a ledge of road cut across a vast incline of small rocks like an arrested landslide.'

By the time the duo reached the summit of the Izoard, Ocaña was suffering so badly that Josiane, standing there at the top to cheer him on as he rode past, later said, 'I hope I will never see his face look like that again.' Yet the effort had been worth it: Thévenet and Martínez – by this point López Carril had slid back – were at triple the distance, while the main pack was now trailing along 10'00" behind. Barring disaster, the Tour was effectively Ocaña's to lose now.

Despite growing increasingly angry with Fuente – in part, surely, for threatening to steal some of the limelight of what could have been one of his most glorious days on a bike and in part for failing to collaborate and make their margin even bigger – Ocaña could not shake him off on the spine-chilling descent, finally a mechanical incident, a puncture for Fuente with 37 kilometres to go, managed it for him. Coming shortly before the foot of the last climb, to the ski station of Les Orres, Ocaña sped away for all he was worth, gaining over 2'00" on his former ally on the flatter ground before Fuente started the relentless process of squeezing down the gap.

After a total of eight hours in the saddle, by this point both lead riders were nearing complete exhaustion, as the yo-yoing time gaps between the two would suggest: 1'15" with 20 kilometres to go, 2'00" at the foot of Les Orres, 2'10" at ten kilometres to the finish and then – suddenly – the clocks were reversed again. Fuente showed he was still stronger at climbing at that point by finally halving his time loss on Ocaña, but it was not going to be enough. Instead, for the second time in two days of Alpine racing, at Les Orres the BIC rider crossed the line with his arms in the air, while Fuente finished 58" behind.

Beyond that, though, the opposition had been flattened, to the point where Thévenet and Martínez's loss of just under 7'00" – which would usually be described as a devastating defeat – came across as fairly respectable. For Zoetemelk, Van Impe and Van Springel, the next group home with more than 20'00" lost on Ocaña, such a time loss was beyond humiliation: it was the kind of difference that should – in theory – be compared in the history books to Merckx and Mourenx in 1969, or Coppi on Alpe d'Huez in 1952. And even they could be considered the luckier ones: 12 riders were thrown out of the race that evening for taking tows from cars on the climbs, and another five abandoned. Just two riders finished outside the time limit but, given that the time length of the stage was so great – and the percentage for the time cut correspondingly high – it was hardly surprising it was such a low number.

What Ocaña had achieved was arguably an even greater ride than to Orcières-Merlette two years before. True, Merckx was among his rivals in 1971 and Fuente did indeed do a huge amount of the spadework on the Galibier. But the distance Ocaña spent at the head of the race, from the summit of the Galibier to the summit of Les Orres, was 165 kilometres, 30 more than the entire Orcières-Merlette stage: as *ABC* put it, 'he has triumphed in brilliant, unquestionable and unreachable style over all who have tried to stand in his way'.

And yet, instead, Ocaña's 1973 Tour achievements would be underrated, permanently, by the absence of Merckx. As Jacques Goddet wrote, 'Ocaña's victory will forever suffer from the consequences of the defection of the only other rider in the current peloton who could have matched him.' In the relentless succession of Merckx victories from 1969 to 1974 in the Tour, 1973 is the only one with another rider's name on it. And what is most ironic of all is that, had it been Merckx, not Ocaña, who had ridden away with Fuente then destroyed the field on the toughest stage of the race, that Tour would surely have been hailed as one of his greatest stage race triumphs. Instead, thanks to Merckx's absence, for many fans the 1973 Tour has been written off as virtually irrelevant.

The riders themselves knew that should not have been the case. 'I finished second in Paris,' Thévenet said, 'but there was no Merckx. In any case it changes nothing. Except maybe I'd have been third.

'Really, that year, I don't see how Merckx could have beaten Ocaña.' Taking himself as an example, Thévenet says, 'I wasn't attentive enough on that stage to Reims and once my brakes broke on a descent I lost two or three minutes because of a cock-up and maybe six minutes in total as a result.

'But even so I finished up quarter of an hour down, and Fuente, who wasn't doing so badly, was maybe 18 minutes down on Ocaña. Luis was on another planet.

'Okay, so Merckx wasn't there, and one can't know what would have happened if he had been, maybe Luis would have given an even stronger knockout blow, maybe he would have made a mistake and Merckx could have benefited from it, you can't say.

'What you can say, is that that year, he was really, really superior to the rest of us.'

With a fortnight of racing still to go, in the subsequent stages all Ocaña could do was underline, again and again, his level of dominance, even if, as *MARCA* wrote, 'to pretend that anything interesting can happen from here [Les Orres] on is completely out of place'.

Fuente and Ocaña provided some of the headlines by failing to give any sort of impression of being united as Spaniards against the rest of the world – as the Spanish media strongly hinted would have met the approval of the Franco regime back home. Instead, Ocaña and Fuente began bickering about each other the minute the stage had finished, with Ocaña particularly resentful of Fuente's failure to collaborate from the Galibier onwards.

'His behaviour is not worthy of a Spaniard,' Ocaña spluttered, while Fuente was his usual sincerity personified and said: 'I didn't work with him because he wouldn't let me get away on yesterday's stage [to Méribel] but he did let Thévenet go. That's why I wouldn't help, it's logical.'

The division between Ocaña supporters and Fuente fans was not as intense as Bahamontes' rivalry with Jesús Loroño, the most famous conflict between two Spanish cyclists, but it was, as would be seen in the 1974 Vuelta, deep nonetheless. 'It was impossible for the fans to be Ocaña and Fuente supporters at the same time,' Thévenet says. He recalls Ocaña 'killing himself laughing when the Tour reached the Portillon in the Pyrenees and somebody had written on the tarmac: *Ocaña a secar la fuente.*' This is a play on Fuente's name, which means fountain in Spanish, and translates as a request to Ocaña to 'dry out the fountain'. But, orally at least, that was not going to be easy, because, barring the odd vow of weekly silence, 'Fuente never kept his tongue buttoned down and he kept on sounding off'.

'Luis could have a bad day, if we keep an eye on him, we could all attack him. And then we'll see who can handle me,' Fuente defiantly responded. 'I admire leaders, but I admire more somebody who can stretch Eddy Merckx's neck, like [Fuente did] in the biggest stage of the Giro to the point where Eddy looked like a giraffe.'

Asked by journalists on the long bus ride down to the start of stage nine if he considered Fuente to be a star rider, Ocaña answered, 'Him? Don't make me laugh. Finally there was some justice and that puncture allowed me to get rid of him.'

There was always the possibility, of course, that Ocaña could fall off, and not just because he had celebrated his victory at Les Orres by zooming around the ski station on a motorbike the same evening, then going out to dinner with his wife. But as the race moved across to the Pyrenees, Ocaña looked more and more secure, snapping up another win in the time trial at Perpignan and gaining nearly 1'30" on Thévenet and 1'39" on Fuente. And at the first summit finish, a comparatively inoffensive second category climb at Font-Romeu, he applied exactly the same tactic on Fuente that Merckx had used against Ocaña himself to such great effect the year before. After following him up the climb, Ocaña then darted ahead at the last minute to ensure there was not even a psychological gain.

The fact that the racing had been so hard played in Ocaña's favour. The day after the Les Orres stage, faced with a 224-kilometre stage, including a first-category climb and three second-category, the entire bunch staged a go-slow for the first three hours. The length of the transfers and stages had meant the riders had been getting up at five every morning for the previous three days and on top of that the heatwave showed no sign of ending.

'It's a massacre,' Ocaña said. With one rider, Vicente López Carril, allowed to go up the road for a lone victory, the pack eased back.

The Fuente–Ocaña war of words eased briefly, too, after KAS's owners made a special visit from Vitoria to the race to plea with Ocaña and De Muer for an end to the conflict between the two Spaniards. Things seemed to have quietened down to the point where Fuente gave Spanish journalists a lengthy speech about how Ocaña was stronger than in the Vuelta a España. Asked how he had gone back on his previous opinion that he could still beat Ocaña, Fuente cheerfully admitted, 'I had been lying to myself.'

However, an unwritten deal between BIC and KAS that Fuente would be allowed to take the King of the Mountains title was broken (the title went to Pedro Torres) and by the end of the Pyrenees the slanging matches had broken out again. By then, though, it was too late for Fuente to have much effect.

Merckx, too, continued to snipe at Ocaña from a distance, saying he was winning 'the Tour of Absences'. Ocaña took that in his stride, pointing out that 'only he and Gimondi are missing. I would have made Merckx suffer at Les Orres and Fuente is here, who's much more dangerous than Merckx.'

Tackling the Col de Menté again on stage 13 as part of an identical finale to 1971 was probably the most delicate moment psychologically for Ocaña, particularly as Fuente decided to 'do a Merckx' and attack going over the summit. But although the weather had cooled noticeably, the rain held off. Having caught up with Fuente, Ocaña vanquished the ghosts of the past with a counter-charge over the Portillon – the climb very near his old family home of Vielha – that enabled him to gain another 3'30" Thévenet and more than 4'00" on Fuente. And, rather than Ocaña, another Frenchman – the perennial Raymond Poulidor – suffered an appalling crash, on the Portet d'Aspet, that left him severely concussed but thankfully able to answer the phone next to his hospital bed when Ocaña called him after the race from next to the winner's podium.

'I owed a debt to Luchon and I think today I have paid it,' Ocaña said about his fourth stage win of the Tour and first in the Pyrenees, where news broke, too, that he had extended his contract with BIC until the end of 1975. 'I wanted to wipe out the terrible memories of two years before, secondly it was in this godforsaken place that I started to ride a bike and thirdly I wanted to be sure, once and for all, of winning the Tour.'

Ocaña only relaxed totally when the race left the Pyrenees for good the following day, with his first puncture of the Tour on the descent of the Soulor within 20 kilometres of the finish, a reminder of how precarious his luck could still be. But with the main mountain climbs behind them, Ocaña pronounced the 'nightmare is over' and Josiane finally summed up the courage to call a hotel in Paris to reserve a room for them both for the night after the race. Ocaña showed an unusual degree of caution, though, deciding not to head over to Mont-de-Marsan as the race passed by 'because you never know what happens when you drive too fast' – a statement that, coming from Ocaña, would have surprised quite a few people.

As ever with Ocaña, the moment he stopped living off his nerves fellow riders would be surprised at how laid-back he could become. 'There was a time trial at Bordeaux, one of the few big challenges left, and I met him before the start of it and asked him how he was,' Thévenet recalls. 'I couldn't believe it when he told me he'd been asleep up to half an hour before the race started.'

After taking no risks in the Bordeaux time trial, Ocaña put on two last demonstrations of strength before the race reached Paris, at the Puy-de-Dôme, the Tour's final summit finish and the last race against the clock at Versailles. Neither victory was at all necessary; both underlined his superiority and provided further fuel to the speculation that Ocaña would have won it even had Merckx taken part.

However, if such speculation was what Ocaña wanted, it backfired spectacularly. The more he won and the more people compared him to Merckx, the more important Merckx's absence became. In a race that had long become largely boring thanks to Ocaña's superiority, 'what if Merckx had raced?' was one of the few debatable points left on the long, long grind to Paris.

The comparisons reached ridiculous levels, to the point where one journalist reminded Ocaña in a press conference that Merckx had beaten Roger Pingeon in his first Tour in 1969 by 18'00" – and Ocaña promptly announced that he, too, wanted to beat whoever was the runner-up by an even bigger margin. (He did not succeed, though, failing by 2'03".)

Things got worse when he announced a post-Tour assault on the Hour Record – which just happened to have been captured by Merckx the previous winter. (This never actually took place.) Then, when Ocaña, now obsessed with the idea of winning by more than Merckx, attacked on the Puy-de-Dôme, it was four kilometres from the summit. This, as he pointed out to journalists, was 'exactly the same point where I attacked two years ago against Merckx. It was here where I started my journey towards the yellow in 1971 and it's here that I will hopefully have completed my last major effort towards winning it in 1973.' However, a quick glance at the overall classification showed he still needed a further 2'10" to beat Merckx's record-beating margin – and another all-out effort, in the 16-kilometre time trial at Versailles on his ultra-light, 6.8-kilo titanium bike, beckoned.

It was no longer only Merckx calling the race 'the Tour of Absences' either – more and more newspapers were following suit. And reminders of the previous occupant of the Tour throne came from even the most pro-Ocaña of newspapers. 'We won't be hearing cries of "Merckx! Merckx! Merckx!" in the velodrome in Paris but "Ocaña! Ocaña! Ocaña!",' *MARCA* pointed out two days before the finish. And after the race it republished a bogus front cover it had run in the paper on 18 December the year before, as part of its wish list for 1973, with the headline 'Ocaña wins the Tour, Merckx second – time trials were decisive'.

The other debate that intensified in the final days of the Tour concerned Ocaña's nationality. After several Spanish newspapers had published a quote from Josiane saying that her husband would take French nationality after the Tour, Ocaña furiously denied this, saying he 'had flown the Spanish flag [as national champion] proudly in France, and Josiane doesn't talk to the press. I'm more Spanish in France than you [Spaniards] are that live there. Why do people ask me these things?'

There was no escaping the questions about Merckx, though – indeed, Ocaña seemed positively to encourage them by racing in as similar a manner to the Belgian as possible.

'He's a great rider and I think this year with him the Tour would have been a different race. That said, I'm in better form than I was in 1971 when I last wore yellow.

'I have only thought about winning. The rest doesn't worry me. If he had been here, it would have been a good fight. Merckx is Merckx, I'm me, and the important thing is to win.'

Warming to his theme, Ocaña argued, 'They [Merckx and Gimondi] haven't come because strong guys are the ones that are here. It's not because he's raced more, I've done as many races as he has.' He then cited the Orduña climb in the Vuelta, where he had managed to drop Merckx and Fuente, and then did the same with the latter 'several times' in the Tour as a 'good point of reference'.

And it is true that the way Ocaña won – with six stage wins, all ten BIC riders completing the course and his squad winning the team prize to boot – all but converted the Tour into a one-man show. Spain, too, had reached a level of domination in the Tour that it had never previously achieved, with the overall victory, 13 days in the race lead, two out of three spots on the final podium, the King of the Mountains title and eight stage wins all taken by Spanish riders – even if one of them lived in France. After a 14-year gap between Spanish Tour de France wins, this was a comeback with a vengeance.

There is also the little known fact that Ocaña might have won the Tour in imperious style, but, as ever, he was racing on a knife edge. According to his close friend and future BIC team-mate Luis Balagué, 'he got an infection [from an injection] in the 1973 Tour, and if he'd gone on for another day he wouldn't have made it. They extracted a litre of pus from the wound and he was ill for seven or eight days. We missed a lot of the criteriums because of that.'

When they returned to the crits, it was business as usual with Merckx, particularly, as Balagué says, 'we weren't very bright and we went to Merckx's hometown in Belgium for the first post-Tour criterium, maybe eight days after'. Typically, given Ocaña's liking for sticking his head in the lion's mouth, he could not resist a chance to show off his yellow jersey in Merckx territory.

The atmosphere was, Balagué says, electric, with the crowd notably 'anti-Ocaña' and the Spaniards paranoid they were going to be physically attacked. Things got so hostile and nerves so jittery that Fuente, also racing there, started shouting that the crowd were throwing lighted cigarette ends at the Spanish riders during the race. He only calmed down when Balagué pointed out to him what he thought were cigarette ends were in fact the sparks coming from riders' pedals as they scraped the cobbles each time they took a corner at high speed.

Merckx himself was in a merciless mood. 'We asked him to go slowly because Ocaña wasn't well ... slow! They went flat out.' In revenge, Balagué 'sat on Merckx's back wheel and refused to take a turn when he broke away, but that was about as much as we could do. I wasn't letting him go anywhere.' Things got even more tense when 'they kicked Fuente out of the race for getting lapped, the organisers said they didn't like shirkers, they'd paid for champions'. Thankfully, the race passed off without further incident, but Merckx had made his point: as far as Ocaña and he were concerned, following that 'minor matter' of the 1973 Tour, the gloves were off again.

What Ocaña's victory achieved, in any case, was to raise their rivalry to a level never seen before. And in 1973 there was still an opportunity for one final showdown: at the Worlds.

***

With the exception of his GP Llodio solo ride to victory in his first year as a pro and his National Championships win in 1972, Luis Ocaña's track record in one-day racing can be summed up in one word: dismal. His best placings in any Monument – the five major Classics – were seventh in 1970 in the Giro di Lombardia and 13th in Liège–Bastogne–Liège in 1973. His most memorable performance in the Giro di Lombardia, perhaps the Classic that suited him the best, came in 1971, and concluded with him marked down and shadowed by Eddy Merckx's domestique, Jos De Schoenmaecker, as the Cannibal sped away for his umpteenth Classics victory.

Ocaña abandoned, fuming at his inability to chase down the Belgian, and later railed at Merckx's other rivals in the chase group that formed behind. Declaring that he was the only rider who would not submit to Merckx, he told them: 'You have more to gain by taking on Merckx than competing against me. Where are the anti-Merckx alliances that are announced at the start of each season? So many words, so few deeds.

'If I had ridden in the Tour as you seem to do, I would never have got rid of Merckx in the way I did. If you keep riding in this way, I wonder what interest there will be in bike races.'

However, much as Ocaña's single victory against Merckx in the Tour is remembered far more than his numerous defeats by the Belgian, on one occasion – the 1973 Worlds – he managed to get the better of him in a one-day race. And given that he was so ill at ease in the Classics, it is to Ocaña's huge credit that, when it came to beating Merckx in a one-day race, he managed to put all the pieces of the puzzle together at least once.

That Ocaña was able to take advantage of the Belgian team's infighting cannot be doubted. The 1973 Worlds, held on a very hilly circuit in Barcelona's Montjuïc Park, is still famous for being the year when team-mates Freddy Maertens and Merckx managed to bungle things so badly that neither of them won. They did not talk to each other for decades afterwards.

But Ocaña had his own issues with rivals, given that Fuente and Ocaña were by then at daggers drawn, and both were obvious leaders for Spain in the hills of Montjuïc. However, Ocaña resolved the power struggle in his favour. And in large part that was thanks to his old friend and colleague Ramón Mendiburu, who, as national trainer, decided to knock the selection question on the head before the race had started.

'It was very, very hard to sort out,' Mendiburu recalls. 'I went up to Paris after the end of the Tour and I found Fuente in some hotel somewhere in a … relaxed mood, let's say, and asked him about the Worlds. And basically he wouldn't pay me the slightest bit of attention.

'Ocaña, three or four days after the Tour, went down with an infection, a cyst, because of an injection or something he'd taken. Anyway, he had to stop racing criteriums to get the cyst operated on and he couldn't race for nearly a fortnight.

'So I went to Mont-de-Marsan twice to see him. Two or three days before that, Fuente had now said he would take part but only do 150 kilometres then quit. And at the same time I had the Catalan press on my back, wanting to build up the atmosphere for the Barcelona Worlds.

'The stress was really getting to me, and I was pushing Ocaña, who was going round [muttering], "the circuit [of the Worlds] this, the circuit that", he's [Fuente] saying he won't ride, he's saying he will. "I don't know, I don't know." So we're all going round in circles.'

When the moment came to name the selection, Mendiburu took a deep breath and named Fuente as reserve and Ocaña in what he felt was a solid team. Fuente was furious, but said he would come to Barcelona all the same.

But at the training camp, Ocaña then announced he would not stay in the team hotel but instead would stay in another in Castelldefels, called El Rancho. This was hardly a move designed to maintain the squad's sense of solidarity – on top of which Fuente, in an attempt to prove he could be just as wayward as Ocaña and get away with it, also announced he was no longer staying at the team hotel either.

With their two main riders refusing even to stay in the same hotel that the other one had previously been in, never mind actually stayed in, Mendiburu says he had a major task banging heads together – 'some guys insisting and insisting that they were okay, and then they weren't, it was a nightmare' – and fending off journalists, presumably chasing a juicy 'team-falls-apart' story.

'I had *el Butano* [the nickname of José Maria García, Spain's top sports radio journalist for over two decades] trying to get into Ocaña's room to interview him at midnight the night before the race. And things got so bad that the pre-race team meeting was postponed from the evening to the morning of the Worlds itself.'

Plumping for Ocaña had its risks. He had taken part in every Worlds bar 1972 since turning pro and failed to finish a single one. (He rode only one more after 1973, also failing to finish.) But, given their achievements in the Tour, Mendiburu had to choose either him or Fuente. What Mendiburu did not know – and it is perhaps just as well for Ocaña – was that the Spaniard had unwittingly nearly wrecked two key Spanish riders' race condition the day prior to the Worlds, riders without whom, as he recognised later, 'I would have possibly not got onto the podium at all.'

'We were lodging in a hotel at the top of the Tibidabo climb,' recalls Txomin Perurena, 'and Ocaña being Ocaña, he'd ordered some special frozen grapefruit juice the night before the Worlds. And given it was so hot, it really messed with my digestive system and I was, well, throwing up and on the toilet at the same time. All night.' Bored as well as severely ill, Perurena recalls, 'I ended up counting my visits to the bathroom and I remember in total I went to the toilet 21 times that night.'

Jesús Manzaneque was hardly in much better shape. 'We went out training the day before, Mendiburu had told us to do 80 or 90 kilometres easy. But in fact we'd only gone about five or six kilometres when we went past a watermelon stand. And Ocaña says, "Right, boys, training's over for today" and we all stopped and he bought us a watermelon *each*. I managed some of it, but Luis ate all of his. Obviously we didn't breathe a word about our short training ride to Mendiburu but God knows how Luis made it into the winning break.'

At the next day's race, Perurena says the only food he could trust his stomach to handle was 'four dried biscuits. I wasn't wasted, I was a total corpse.' However, he managed to bring the lead group down to seven – himself, Merckx, Ocaña, Giovanni Battaglin, Gimondi, Maertens and Zoetemelk – thanks to an attack which effectively decided the race in favour of the lead group.

'Merckx was obsessed with me,' he recalls, 'even though I was dead. He came up to me on one of those last laps and was talking away to me but I couldn't understand. I think he wanted to make a deal.'

The Spanish continued to make the running, with another attack by Perurena sparking the moves that eventually led to the break of four – Gimondi, Merckx, Maertens and Ocaña – going clear. That they should race so well is partly due to Mendiburu – the exclusion of Fuente from the team meant that Ocaña was given, as lone leader, 100 per cent top-flight support for his Worlds bid on home soil.

Perurena also confirms what many observers suspected – that Maertens, as a very young pro, 'was a total slave to Merckx that day. If he'd worked on his own account rather than driving himself into the ground for Eddy, Freddy would have won with one leg.'

As it was, three laps from the finish, Perurena made another drive which whittled it down to the four finalists, with Ocaña, dropped by a few metres on the main climb, able to claw his way back on.

At this point Ocaña's fixation with Merckx – who was in fact racing injured after a stone thrown up by another rider's wheel struck his left knee – cost him dearly. He opted to glue himself to Merckx's wheel and, as he put it afterwards, 'blindly accept that Merckx was the strongest, which was a mistake'.

But, in fact, given Maertens and Gimondi battled it out for gold while Merckx suddenly lost power and had to settle for fourth behind the Spaniard, Ocaña admitted he was 'surprised when it turned out that the other two were the strongest'. Given another 20 yards, he claimed, 'I could have been World Champion.'

Still, a bronze medal was his to take home, even if – yet again – there was a hint that, rather than what he won, defeating the Cannibal was what really motivated him. As he put it, 'beating Merckx is always a pleasurable experience'. But unfortunately for him, and Spain, that day there were two more riders who performed even better than him and his arch-rival.

Would the race have been different if Ocaña's team-mate had been in a better condition physically, able to soften up the opposition even further? It's tempting to think so, but neither Mendiburu nor Perurena are willing to go that far.

'Bronze was a great result,' says Perurena, while Mendiburu says, 'It was a sprint and an uphill sprint on top of that. He rode more than well.

'Finally it worked out very well, Luis got third, Pedro Torres finished sixth, Txomin was right up there in the breaks and made the winning break. And all the journalists, particularly the ones from Barcelona, who'd already half written their stories predicting a total disaster, had to start all over again.'

As for Ocaña, 'he was swearing and cussing, he always did, but underneath you could see he was pleased with bronze. And that's bearing in mind that he didn't like Classics, too much racing in crosswinds and with your elbows sticking out.

'Luis was no good in a sprint, even a small group sprint. If it was him against another rider, he'd always come second,' adds Perurena, 'which is why he was so pleased with a bronze.'

Even if neither won, Ocaña was for once able to put aside all the disastrous performances in previous Classics. That in itself made the 1973 Worlds a remarkable achievement. But nobody was under any illusions that it was ever going to get any better for Ocaña in one-day racing. The Tour, though, might yet have been a different story.

12

LOSING THE FIRE

Saturday 10 July 1976, stage 14 of the Tour, through the Pyrenees to Saint-Lary-Soulan, tackling several of the climbs that feature so much in Luis Ocaña's history: the Portillon, the Menté and the Peyresourde. The owner of Ocaña's Super Ser team, Ignacio Orbaiceta, has come to the race and is following with manager Gabriel Saura in the team car, and Ocaña, despite being more than 10'00" down overall, has promised he will win the Tour that day.

Fast-forward three or four hours and in fact it is Lucien Van Impe on his way to winning the race outright. Team manager Cyrille Guimard has nagged him repeatedly until he eventually agrees to break away over the Portillon with 70 kilometres to go. He passes numerous stragglers until he reaches the rider at the head of the race: Ocaña, racing alone and so strongly that he leads the Tour over the Peyresourde.

Instead of Ocaña trying to drop Van Impe, however, he openly decides to work for him, letting Van Impe sit in his slipstream until the point comes where Ocaña is exhausted and Van Impe then moves ahead to take the victory – and the Tour. So for a full 30 kilometres from the summit of the Peyresourde to the foot of the final climb to Saint-Lary, even as Ocaña assists Van Impe, the Spaniard knows that his boss is just yards behind him, watching helplessly from the car as his massive 40 million peseta investment in his cycling team – four times the budget of an entire race like the 1975 Volta a Catalunya – is wrecked by blatant treachery.

For Ocaña, after three largely fruitless seasons, it is one final gesture of defiance, a deliberate act of sporting self-destruction that causes Super Ser to fold at the end of the season. It is the third time in less than a decade that Ocaña has – wittingly or otherwise – helped bring down the curtain on a professional team, each time in more dramatic fashion. But this will be the last.

***

Given his usual relationship with misfortune, it would hardly have been normal for Luis Ocaña to have two spectacularly successful seasons in a row. And in fact after 1973, given that the last four years of his career represent a steady march downhill, it was almost as if he had used up whatever outstanding allowance of good luck he had left in one single season.

There were flashes of his old strength, most notably in the 1974 and 1976 Vueltas, but his total of two low-profile road wins, combined with crashes and injuries galore, served only to remind the world of his lack of success. At the same time there was a steady draining of his levels of ambition until, as Eddy Merckx puts it, 'After [the 1973 Tour win] he was no more a fighter … Luis ended up losing [his] fire' for good.

'The first problem,' recalls Luis Balagué, Ocaña's team-mate for the last season with BIC in 1974 and the following two in Super Ser, 'was the winter of 1973. A rider's season is won and lost in the winters, and you're living like a monk when everybody expects you to relax a little after winning the Tour. Luis had too many events to go to, celebrations and homages and whatever.

'It would be "just one day". But then "just one day" and "just one day" would mount up and eventually that'd be three or four weeks down the pan. Just like that.'

Then there was the question of Ocaña's bad luck, which – even if he tried to ignore it – still caused him an exceptional number of problems at the beginning of 1974. 'I remember we had gone down a few days in advance of the [early season warm-up race] Vuelta a Levante to the coast for training and we'd ridden 200 metres to a supermarket to stock up on some food.

'There was a zebra crossing and Luis managed to skid on it and fall off when his handlebars got tangled up. Then in the same year in the same spring, in the Setmana Catalana, he hadn't even started the race, he was on the team presentation podium when he fell off and broke a finger.' Even if Balagué says Ocaña 'was a rock' when it came to bad luck, he admits, with an ironic smile, that 'he never missed out on the chance to have some [misfortune]'.

If the bad luck continued apace, by the time he was 30 Ocaña's physical capacity was no longer what it once had been either. 'The rival teams would give him two minutes in a break and let him dangle out there,' recalls Super Ser team-mate and 1975 winner Agustín Tamames. 'He'd be as impulsive as ever, but it wouldn't work. He abused his strength.'

'I remember abandoning a race once and listening to the radio as I drove home how Luis had attacked from very early on and spent maybe 70 or 80 kilometres on the front. I took a bet with myself that he would get caught with 25 kilometres to go and in fact he ended up getting caught, thanks to KAS driving away, with ten kilometres to go.' But the lesson Tamames took from it was the same: 'you have to calculate your strength down to the last gram. Luis was too impulsive.' What had once been a reason for admiring Ocaña – his spontaneity and rushing into attacks – had become a millstone hanging round his neck.

However, there was one factor that endured until the Tour of 1976: Ocaña's ambition. And in 1974, flushed with success from his best year ever, he started the season at BIC by announcing that he would take part in all three major Tours, with the main focus on defending his title against Merckx in the Tour de France. But each time, he was foiled.

Under-rested and undertrained after an off-season involving too many celebrations, Ocaña had already started the season on the wrong foot, as Balagué has asserted. Rather than lowering his sights given that he was in very bad form, trying to race all three

Tours in one year represented a massive raising of the bar on Ocaña's part.

On paper, as the first Grand Tour of the season and the least prestigious, the 1974 Vuelta should have been the one in which Ocaña took the fewest risks, particularly as he had skipped Paris–Nice because of the theoretical amount of stage racing awaiting him in April and May. Instead, with his old rival José Manuel Fuente, *el Tarangu*, as the principal opposition, Ocaña initially failed to take the Asturian seriously. Then, when he tried to claw him back sufficiently closely to polish him off in the final time trial as he had done with Agustín Tamames in 1970, he ended up burning himself out.

'He wouldn't consider him to be a serious rival,' says Balagué. 'Then one thing after another would go wrong, then another, and Fuente would get one minute, then another.'

Ocaña miscalculated so badly that after the final time trial in San Sebastián, which he raced while sick, he ended up fourth overall. It was the first time, discounting abandons, that he had completed a major Tour outside the podium since his first Tour de France with BIC in 1970. On top of that, so much hard racing in the cold weather since his season debut in a rain-lashed Setmana Catalana had brought on another bout of bronchitis. He had ignored his doctor's advice to quit the Vuelta, saying he wanted to help team-mate Joaquim Agostinho win it (not to mention having a crack at victory himself!), and illness wiped out his chances of taking part in the Giro d'Italia. There was still the Tour de France, though, about which fans were rubbing their hands in glee at the thought of a repeat of his superb 1973 form matched against an equally in-form Merckx. But then disaster struck.

According to Bernard Loizeau's *Luis Ocaña, le soleil des pelotons*, in a bid to avoid testing positive for drugs while he got over his bronchitis, after the Vuelta ended Ocaña took a crash course of banned medicines and abstained from racing. His three-week spell out of the saddle ended when he took part in the Midi Libre, three days earlier than anticipated. But his knees could not handle the sudden acceleration of pace demanded by the abrupt return to racing at a time when other pros were in peak condition and, on stage four, in the middle of a snowstorm, he abandoned.

Ocaña had reached the middle of the cycling year with precious little to show for it – and in painfully inconsistent form. Any hint of success was due as much to his exceptional willpower as to his actual racing condition. His following race, the Dauphiné Libéré was a case in point. He lost 7'00" on a single climb, the Granier, to stage winner Alain Santy, then dug deep on the following day to charge away over the Dauphiné's toughest climb that year, the Luitel. Caught before the finish by some of the top favourites, he nonetheless finished sixth overall. If this was a testament to his innate talent, it was also a sign (given he'd won the Dauphiné for the previous two years) that even talent, without solid foundations of training stretching all the way back to the winter, had its limits.

'I have suffered greatly,' Ocaña said, 'but I would say I'm at about 70 per cent of my peak condition. Miracles don't happen, but the important thing is that I can be in top form for the Tour de France.'

Yet following his uneven start to the year, his crash course of more race miles to hone the top end of his condition had to continue apace – and Ocaña finally paid the price. At the low-key build-up to the race, the Tour de l'Aude, on 18 June, a rider's musette got jammed in his back wheel. He fell, and three riders immediately behind him also hit the deck. All of them managed to get back up again, except for – who else? – Ocaña.

Nothing was broken but, on falling, he cut his right arm so badly that his doctor at Mont-de-Marsan was adamant that he could not take part in the Tour de France, due to start a week later. With a minimum of two weeks' rest needed for a full recovery

Ocaña might – *might* – have been able to start had he been closer to peak condition. But with the antibiotics he had to take for the injury already acting as a physical brake, Ocaña was not prepared to risk starting the race against Merckx as defending champion and then getting dropped early on. (There was a clear historical precedent for this, which Ocaña wanted to avoid, too: Spain's previous defending champion, Federico Bahamontes, who, in 1960, abandoned the Tour after three days because he had failed to recover fully from a pre-race illness.)

'I never imagined the injury was so serious,' Ocaña, who initially thought he had fractured his elbow, said later, 'but I realised when I got home and the pain redoubled how bad it was. It was others who caused me to fall and I was the only one who didn't get up.'

Ocaña's non-participation in the Tour that year effectively brought his rivalry with Merckx to a close: Merckx's career began to go downhill after that season and Ocaña's, while also sinking, did so largely in different races. But there were other major knock-on effects such as the collapse of his relationship with the BIC management. The accident at l'Aude and Ocaña's non-participation in the Tour came at a moment when the Spaniard's relationship with Maurice De Muer had already hit a low point. As Mendiburu explains, by early 1974 the natural wear and tear of a relationship built largely on the adrenalin of ultra-aggressive racing had led to a burn-out point.

'There was a falling-out with De Muer because De Muer got fed up with having to advise him so much for this and for that. And Luis just did whatever he wanted,' Mendiburu argues. Perurena is more direct: 'He was really fed up with De Muer.'

Bereft of results – 'Luis said that he would have problems with BIC if he didn't do the Tour,' Balagué recalls – and with his key ally inside BIC no longer supporting him, the ripples of damage caused by Ocaña's non-Tour participation spread wider and wider.

Midway through the Tour, BIC announced that the team would fold at the end of the season, that they were terminating Ocaña's contract two years before it officially expired, and that De Muer and Ocaña, who in tandem had won a Tour, a Vuelta, three Dauphiné Libérés and countless other smaller races, would go their separate ways.

But if Ocaña expressed his dissatisfaction with one part of the BIC organisation with the Spaniards, with Cescutti he maintained a pretence that all was well. 'I never heard him criticise De Muer,' Cescutti says now. Josiane concurs, saying that, although the two fell out, 'The problem was not so much De Muer, but more with the upper echelons of BIC. He had far fewer [good] results in 1974 and on top of that he hadn't done the Tour de France.' When it is suggested to her that his previous good season should have given him some goodwill credit, with a flash of anger she responds, 'Yes, but sponsors are like that'.

One factor that remained constant, however, unlike the results, was Ocaña's vulnerability to illness. 'I interviewed him after a freezing cold stage in the Setmana Catalana in 1974,' recalls *El Mundo Deportivo*'s Javier de Dalmases, 'and as he was talking flecks of blood kept coming out of his mouth and landing on my face.' Ocaña's bronchitis was plaguing him again, 'and it did so for the rest of the year,' Dalmases adds. (As a rookie journalist, he mentioned this incident in his article, and was informed by a senior colleague that Ocaña, furious that his rivals could see that he was on the back foot, was going to beat him up. Typically, though, by the time the two crossed paths again a few days later, Ocaña had completely forgotten about the incident and greeted him like an old pal; indeed, after he retired, Ocaña not only became firm friends with Dalmases but also wrote a column for *El Mundo Deportivo*.)

The last period of Ocaña's time with BIC saw him continue racing throughout the autumn one-day races, despite his poor physical condition. One journalist wrote that his racing was 'similar to forced labour' after he took a lowly eighth in the GP des Nations. In a year in which the end of the season could not come too quickly, and with Merckx winning Giro, Tour and World Championships, Ocaña finally eased back at the end of October. By this point Merckx had won 38 races in a single season. Ocaña had won none.

Fortunately for Ocaña, Super Ser, a new team formed by Navarran businessman Ignacio Orbaiceta, were waiting in the wings. Unlike KAS, who wanted to sign both Ocaña and Balagué but were unable to agree on a contract, Super Ser's budget was so big they all but gave Ocaña a blank cheque, and he signed for what was reportedly between four and six million pesetas a year.

Apart from taking three French riders with him from BIC, Sylvain Vasseur, Jean-Jacques Fussien and Roland Berland, Ocaña also got to choose the riders he wanted from other teams. Unsurprisingly, Balagué, so close to Ocaña that according to Van Impe 'for fun, Ocaña used to tell Balagué to attack when everybody had stopped for a piss and he'd always do it', was one of those on the list. 'I'd been Luis' friend for years, right back in the Werner days in 1971 when our team was all paid backhanders by Luis to help him every day in the Tour – we were never going to do anything in the race there, after all,' Balagué says bluntly. Other top names included King of the Mountains Pedro Torres, Paris–Roubaix winner Roger Rosiers and José Luis Viejo, later to have a claim to fame as the protagonist of the Tour's biggest ever time margin of victory for a stage win: 22'50". Super Ser might not be on the level of Molteni, Peugeot or GAN-Mercier – by now a very distant relation of Ocaña's old Fagor squad, which it had ostensibly replaced – but it was certainly good enough for a serious crack at the Tour de France and the big Classics. Ocaña later called it 'the best team of all time'.

Whether or not this was Ocaña seeing everything through rose-tinted glasses, in any case there is general agreement that the team was logistically near-perfect. With an enormous budget, riders were blessed with everything from top bikes – 'Zeus,' Tamames recalls, 'and they were so good and long-lasting that I don't understand how the company didn't go bust' – to being the first ever cycling squad with a team bus.

'It had a shower, massage beds, a telly, everything,' Tamames recalls. Super Ser's management also paid the kind of attention to detail that has helped bring such success in recent times to British squad Team Sky. In what would be the equivalent in 1970 of Sky using a professional weather expert in 2010 to advise them where best to do their training, for their training camps Super Ser's management would telephone the Spanish state television weatherman and ask him to provide them with a personal forecast for the Mediterranean coast around the team's training hotel in plush Marbella.

However, the training camp was a disaster. 'It tipped down with rain the whole time and Ocaña would take us out on 200-kilometre training rides every day and treat them all as if they were races,' Tamames recalls. 'We never had any time to recover.'

The pressure to produce, according to Tamames, started to get to Ocaña, partly because of his bad 1974 season and partly because he was discovering that, as he approached 30, he was being superseded by a younger generation of riders.

'He'd get more and more nervous, marching up and down the team bus before time trials.' Tamames recalls Ocaña taking puffs of oxygen from the mask on the bus before going outside to warm up. 'I'd tell him to leave off and he'd say, "hey, it's just 20 seconds and then we're done". But' – as Tamames observes – 'pure oxygen doesn't do you any good, it's for sick people, for goodness' sake.'

For Ocaña, though, given to 'taking anything', in De Muer's words, that did not matter. And, as Cruz points out, riders at the time tended to assume that if your doctor gave you something, it was generally for your benefit in terms of performance.

There was a brief early upturn in Ocaña's fortunes when he took his first victory in over a year, a 28-kilometre time trial in the Vuelta a Andalucía, 15" ahead of a 20-year-old German who was set to become one of his country's greatest ever stage racers, Dietrich Thurau.

But then the remorseless downward spiral re-established itself, to the point where, for the second year running, Ocaña finished fourth overall in the Vuelta. And another negative pattern began to repeat itself: in 1974, despite making most of the running in the Spanish race, he'd ended up being over-shadowed by BIC team-mate Joaquim Agostinho, who came within 11" of beating Fuente; in 1975, Tamames went one better – and, again thanks to a splendid final performance in the last time trial, won the race outright.

To say that Super Ser were surprised by this particular outcome is no exaggeration. 'Luis was the favourite for the overall, and Super Ser's publicity rep told me they had printed thousands of posters of Luis as the winner,' recounts Ramón Mendiburu.

'At the final time trial in San Sebastián, it went completely wrong. I looked at Luis at the start of the race and his legs were completely swollen up, and I can remember thinking "what the heck is he on?".'

'It [1975] was supposed to be a resurrection after 1974, which went so badly, and it didn't work out,' Mendiburu concludes, while Orbaiceta was equally dismissive, saying 'our Vuelta win saved our season'.

In some ways, though, Ocaña was lucky that he even got that close, given that he single-handedly all but provoked a workers' strike at Zeus, the Basque bicycle-manufacturing company based in Eibar, to block the Vuelta on the nearby Urkiola Pass in the Basque Country. Leading the race into the final stages, Perurena states categorically: 'I could have won the Vuelta that day. Super Ser were using Zeus for their bikes and components, but Ocaña insisted on having Campagnolo [components] in the Vuelta. Doing that was very serious, it could sink a company and the workers at Zeus were on the point of coming out onto the climb and blocking the race in protest. And if the race had stopped there, it would have suited me.'

Instead the Vuelta continued and the Urkiola stage was witness to the race's most crucial development. Having won four stages, Tamames – who had replaced Balagué, allegedly because of a falling-out with the team management – was now 17" ahead of Ocaña. And at the foot of the Urkiola, Ocaña launched a searing attack that split the peloton apart.

Here versions differ widely as to what happened. According to Tamames, 'he'd tried to attack on Urkiola about four or five kilometres from the top and I didn't chase him down. But then when somebody else got across to him' – and Tamames was with that rival – 'Ocaña said to me, "look, go on [attack] because I'm stuffed, go on, [overall contender Mikel] Lasa's coming".'

Tamames duly attacked, taking a fifth stage. 'I'd been calculating all the way through, because early on in the Vuelta we'd made a mistake and let [KAS rival] Perurena get away and get five minutes lead when there were ten stages left to go.

'But then I started winning stages, pulling back a minute here, and a minute there on Peru', like on the [mountain-top stage finish to] Formigal. And I started thinking to myself, "my God, you're good enough to win".' And after taking that fifth stage win on the Urkiola, Ocaña was very much on the back foot compared to his team-mate, even if Super Ser, to judge by their publicity department, still thought he had it in him to repeat his feat of 1970 and win the event outright.

As Tamames tells it, the relationship between the two Super Ser leaders could not have been more harmonious. However, according to Balagué, Ocaña was not at all pleased that Tamames, Balagué's substitute in the Vuelta line-up, had ridden away from him on the Urkiola.

That evening in the team hotel, Balagué claims, 'Ocaña went around yelling, "who the fuck have you brought me here?" – to replace Balagué. On top of that, Tamames, previously at a professional dead end in a low-budget Portuguese squad, had been signed by Super Ser manager Gabriel Saura, his old amateur director, as a pet project and according to Balagué 'was given favourable treatment by him' in the Vuelta.

With a Vuelta win at stake and four riders who could still theoretically win it – Lasa, Tamames, Ocaña and race leader Perurena – the atmosphere on the last day's 32-kilometre time trial was electric. For Perurena, who'd already lost the 1974 Vuelta on the last day to Fuente by a mere 11", the thought of seeing the lead wrenched out of his hands by the bare minimum for a second year running must have been unbearable.

Tamames himself had a lot of emotional baggage at stake, too, given that in 1970, having led the Vuelta for six days, Ocaña had overtaken him on the final time trial. Now was his chance to turn the tables. As Tamames saw it, 'Luis wanted to win the race, too, and he was up there, but it's whoever strongest gets it.' Both opted for massive gears, too – Tamames using a 54 chainring, Ocaña a 55.

Tamames had a tough time of it on the hilly time trial course through San Sebastián, with no time references because the crowds were so dense that the following car could not reach him, and even going the wrong way in the pouring rain when he was misdirected at one point.

'I really didn't know what was going on, I'd lost ten seconds because of going the wrong way.' But in the Anoeta velodrome, where the finish was located, the noise from Perurena's supporters was so intense it was impossible for him to know that both Lasa and Ocaña had registered poor times and only Perurena stood between him and the lead. 'Finally [Super Ser team-mate Roger] Rosiers came up to me and said, "hey, you've won by ten seconds".' In fact, it was 11, but Tamames, after early years as a pro all but wrecked by a knee injury – in 1969 he raced only two months out of a possible eight – was not going to quibble.

While Saura smugly declared that Ocaña had overestimated his strength at Formigal and the Urkiola, for Tamames there must have been an element of satisfaction at overhauling the man who had beat him in 1970 and was Spain's most recent Tour champion, too. 'In 1970, I had no idea what had been going on. I'd been pushed too hard by my director and I had the wrong gearing. On top of that, I'd never gone flat out in a time trial before. This really made up for it.' The year before, as he pointed out, there had been no room for him in any Spanish team and now he had won the biggest Spanish race of all. For Ocaña, though, the Vuelta 1975 was another nail in his sporting coffin.

***

The 1975 Tour de France is rightly famous for being the one in which Eddy Merckx finally ran out of steam, blasting away over the Col d'Allos in the Alps towards Pra Loup but then being overtaken by Bernard Thévenet, Felice Gimondi, Joop Zoetemelk and Lucien Van Impe on the final climb. All his major Grand Tour rivals of the previous five years, in fact, managed to gain an advantage on Merckx that day – bar two, and they were both Spanish.

José Manuel Fuente had already failed to finish the 1975 Vuelta, where he had seriously underperformed, after discovering he faced a doping test – for which he would be sure to test positive – on the last day. But in the Tour of Asturias in June, his home race, he began to feel more permanently unwell. Then, at the Tour de France, Fuente finished over 18'00" down outside the time limit on the second day's second sector stage to Roubaix. Tests later revealed the extent of his kidney problems – after which he was refused a racing licence. His career was effectively over.

Ocaña's abandon was no less dramatic, coming when he was lying fifth overall, nearly 7'00" down on race leader Merckx after stage 12's seven-hour, 242-kilometre stage from Tarbes to Albi. (It was also three days before Pra Loup and Merckx's greatest defeat since Orcières-Merlette, four years previously.)

Ocaña's time deficit looked bad, but he was less than 3'00" down on a possible podium placing and with the Alps, the Puy-de-Dôme (where he had twice won) and a mountainous time trial at Morzine still to come, there was a lot left to play for. His Tour build-up had been patchy, though, to say the least. A lowly 16th place in the Dauphiné was explained away by Ocaña as fatigue caused by his super-intense training sessions prior to the race, one of which featured double ascents of the Pla d'Adet, Aspin and Aubisque – 90 kilometres of climbing in a single day!

After that had come a third place in the Vuelta a Asturias and a third place in the Vuelta a los Valles Mineros. At the Tour, having lost minutes here and there for little apparent reason early on – as well as 17" when the bunch split at the finish and he was blocked by a motorbike on stage seven's finish at Angoulême – on stage 11 Ocaña had been the second rider across the summit of the Tourmalet and third over the Aspin. But he abandoned – and it still remains a mystery exactly why.

Possible reasons ranged from a knee injury – according to Thévenet caused by the infamous nocturnal visit to Mont-de-Marsan, although Josiane categorically denies it – to having an open wound in the skin around his testicles, according to Balagué, that made it too painful to ride. 'He stayed up in his room that evening, so his team-mates wouldn't see how bad he was,' Balagué recalls, 'he didn't want to tell them he was going to abandon. His balls were wide open.' The team itself wrote his abandon off as being due to sunstroke, which, if possible given the extreme heat, sounds more like the first excuse the person handling the press' questions could come up with. Others doing the rounds included tendonitis (Radio Tour) and a drop in blood pressure (according to the Belgian media).

Like everybody else the Spanish press had no idea either what was going on, although the evening he quit they had their suspicions that all was not well and hinted strongly at an imminent abandon.

'We are writing in the same motor circuit where three [sic] years ago we saw Ocaña, wearing yellow, fight in a time trial against Merckx,' *El Mundo Deportivo*'s reporter pointed out. 'The possibility of the rider from Cuenca taking an overall win almost blinded us to the hell-like heat of that day.

'Today [9 July 1975], the only thing that has changed is his position overall. Now he's fifth, seven minutes back, but Luis says that the Tour … "has only just begun".

'But the [press room's] general opinion is very different to his. We saw him losing time on the Aspin [in the Pyrenees on stage 12] and thrashing around on the bike at Saint-Lary-Soulan' – where, after three Pyrenean climbs, Ocaña lost 89" to Merckx and over 2'00" to Thévenet.

'Ocaña was among the favourites and even responded well in the two time trials at Merlin Plage' – on stage six, where he was seventh, 53" down on Merckx – 'and at Auch' – on stage nine, where he again lost 1'00" to the Belgian. 'But in the mountains, previously his strong point, he has weakened without any excuses. I like his morale being so high, but I fear his words are just ways of avoiding the verdict that hangs over him.' *El Mundo Deportivo*'s gut feeling could not have been more accurate: less than 12 hours later, Ocaña was out of the race, his third Tour abandon in six years. 'Four years later, Merckx is still the same, albeit a little less strong,' commented the newspaper, 'but Ocaña is a shadow of his former self.' And the day after it was even harsher, saying 'Merckx had an injury in the same place as Ocaña and won the Tour … the Tour is decidedly not Ocaña's race, despite winning it in 1973. The only year Merckx wasn't there.'

It wasn't just the media who were increasingly unforgiving of Ocaña. Having been outshone by Tamames in the Vuelta then quitting the Tour for a series of reasons which remain hazy at best, Ocaña was growing increasingly isolated in his own team, to the point where some of his team-mates also seemed to be turning their backs on him. 'He had had the chance to pick the riders,' recalls Tamames, 'but he always seems to be alone at the crucial moments.'

At the low-key Vuelta a La Rioja in September, Ocaña moved into the lead after taking his second win of the season, a time trial. But on the final day's stage, as an Alfil agency report puts it, 'his team-mates failed to provide him with any support whatsoever, and Ocaña, fighting completely alone and unaided, finally succumbed to the blizzard of attacks from different rivals'. Ocaña finished fifth.

Worse was to come. At the Montjuic hill-climb that traditionally brought down the curtain on the Spanish season, Ocaña performed so badly that even the fans turned their backs on him – and after finishing seventh he was booed by the crowd. That they should do so at Montjuic, the same place where, two years earlier, he had managed to inflict his single one-day defeat on Eddy Merckx and had taken Spain's best result in that year's World Championships must have made the experience, coming at the end of such a long series of poor results, even more painful.

**

It is tempting to write off 1976, Ocaña's second year at Super Ser, as being nothing more than a continuation of the downward spiral of 1974 and 1975. But, in fact, Ocaña was far and away the strongest rider in the Vuelta that year and after two seasons of disappointment, a second Vuelta win and third Grand Tour in his palmarès would surely have put his career back on track.

Ocaña's third place overall in Paris–Nice when short on form, but which included being in the leading break over the Ventoux and again on the stage to Les Arcs (where he staged a rare perilous downhill attack from the village of Carcès), as well as a fifth place in the traditional final time trial up the Col d'Eze, was largely overlooked in the media. They were more impressed by another Frenchman, the up and coming Michel Laurent, winning the race outright at the age of 22. But it nonetheless strongly suggested that Ocaña was not finished yet. So, too, did taking ninth in the Basque Country and sixth in the Vuelta a Andalucía.

'With no Merckx here, our champion Ocaña should win, but he's not been himself for a long time now,' was *ABC*'s brutal analysis of the Vuelta's contenders. And, with the Vuelta strapped for cash to pay for Thévenet, Van Impe or Zoetemelk, and just 100 riders starting the race, there was a real power vacuum to be filled.

In the opening prologue of 3.2 kilometres, Ocaña began on the back foot, with a 16" time loss to ultimate winner Dietrich Thurau. Given the very short distance and the two Vuelta prologue victories in his palmarès, this looked to be way too much.

In Ocaña's defence was the short, technical nature of the course through the winding backstreets of the coastal town of Estepona, his being two kilos over his ideal race form and the fact that he had a cold. Or perhaps he paid too much attention to the nine-year-old Swiss boy, John, a Super Ser guest on the race after he had written to the team describing himself as 'Super Ser's number one fan' and who had told Ocaña, in perfect Spanish, to be very careful on the time trial circuit as it was 'extremely dangerous'. But whatever the reason, it was still too much time.

'I will take a little while to come through,' Ocaña said, 'I'm still not in as good condition as I was in Paris–Nice.' The good weather, in particular, was helping him polish his form 'and in a few days you'll see'. Defiant as ever, when asked if he could win the race, he replied, 'If I didn't think I could do something in this race, I wouldn't have come.'

Super Ser had brought a spectacularly strong team, spear-headed by Tamames – complaining he was suffering from flu and not in good enough form to win – and Ocaña, with other key team-mates the new Swiss signing, Josef Fuchs, Roger Rosiers, Balagué and Pedro Torres. KAS, on the hunt for revenge after Perurena's last-minute defeat in the 1975 Vuelta, had brought what sports director Eusebio Vélez claimed were five possible winners and all except two of their top riders, Francisco Galdos, second in the 1975 Giro, and Juan Pujol. Teka, meanwhile, were relying on Joaquim Agostinho.

But the squad that looked set to dominate the running was Ti-Raleigh, led by reigning World Champion Hennie Kuiper, Gerrie Knetemann – one of Holland's most gifted riders ever – and, with Thurau, already German national champion in his second year as a pro, clearly in good shape too. Thurau protested that the race 'was too long for me to do well in' but when they won the first stage with another rider, José De Cauwer, it was clear that even if Thurau lost ground, there were plenty of others waiting in the wings. And then on stage four, another Raleigh rider, German track expert Günter Haritz, took over as race leader, although a positive dope test later removed him from the record books. As if that was not enough, they had Peter Post, one of the most dynamic sports directors in cycling history, in the driving seat. (Post also had the well-earned reputation of being one of the most frightening drivers in the peloton and, despite numerous fines in the Vuelta he blithely – and one hopes unintentionally – continued to 'sandwich' riders, such as Spaniard José Enrique Cima, between his car and his rivals' vehicles.)

However, it was the sudden change in weather, with heavy rain turning to sleet as the race wended its way across the high mountain plateaux of eastern Andalucía, that caused the first major sort out. No fewer than 15 riders, including all bar one of the Belgian Splendor squad, abandoned in the appalling weather conditions, while Ocaña, his cold seemingly forgotten, remained just 1'30" back on Haritz.

It says a great deal about Ocaña's decline that his sixth place in a technical time trial, 20" down on former team-mate and new race leader Agostinho, which would have been considered a defeat a few years previously, was now held to be a sign of a comeback. But on the next stage, a seemingly inoffensive 125-kilometre dash across the flatlands of Cartagena and Murcia, Ocaña proved that there was some life left in the old dog yet. And, yet again, he did it on terrain on which he was least expected to strike.

In what *El Mundo Deportivo* called 'the hardest fought stage of the Vuelta to date', Ocaña placed Santiago Lazcano and Pedro Torres in a seven-man break early on. The other teams reeled that move in after a breakneck 70-kilometre chase where for a long time the break had been held at 2'00". But at that point, rather than let the tension ease back, Ocaña himself opted to go on the rampage, taking another five Super Ser riders with him, including Tamames. Although the second group was far bigger – 41 – the gap it gained by the finish at Murcia, of 5'00", was also more important, with two big names, Perurena and Spain's star first-year pro, Enrique Martínez Heredia (who would go on to win the Volta a Catalunya in his rookie season) caught behind. 'Nobody expected such a devastating move,' said Agostinho, who made it into the mass break, afterwards, 'I can only hope all the stages are not like this one.'

'We went for it when we saw Martínez Heredia had punctured,' Ocaña revealed. 'A real battle.' He named Agostinho rather than Kuiper 'as the real danger man of the race', but Ocaña himself had gained nearly 30 places and was now lying eighth down, less than 40" back on the Portuguese rider.

A week ground by and an already tiny peloton shrank to just 61 by the time it reached the northern city of Gijón with the first 12 riders still within 1'00" of Thurau, who had regained the lead. Barring a second positive dope test for a race leader in the Vuelta in less than a week – in this case the little-known Belgian Eric

Jacques – probably the most significant news was that Agostinho was suffering from a fever and Agustín Tamames, Ocaña's team-mate and rival contender, had smashed his head badly in a fall and was set to surrender.

Ocaña, still eighth overall, was enjoying a mini-boom in popularity. The Spanish press reported that he was the only pro to have posters supporting him from fans on the roadside, but the message on one of them, 'Ocaña, get in a break or go back to Paris', neatly summed up what seemed to be a widespread sentiment in Spain: he could either be good or be French, but not both.

Suddenly, as the Vuelta crossed into the mountains of northern Asturias, with just five days remaining, the race burst into life – and it was all thanks to Ocaña. His attack on the Fito, well known to cycling fans as the climb where, 20 years later, Indurain would finally throw in the towel and quit both the Vuelta and professional racing, was of such intensity that Thurau cracked. When Ocaña reached the summit, his attack had been so effective that he was provisional race leader, and in fact this became the last time Ocaña would lead a major Tour. However, eight riders caught the Super Ser leader on the long drop down to the finish at Cangas de Onís. The stage win went to Vicente López Carril, Agostinho returned to the lead, but with Kuiper at 9" and Ocaña at 31", there was little sign of the pressure easing on the Portuguese rider.

According to Kuiper, talking later, this was the stage in which Ocaña lost the Vuelta. 'If he had attacked just a little harder on the Fito, we would all have ended up like Thurau,' he said, 'and Ocaña would have won the race outright.' Instead Ocaña had sat up on the descent of the Fito because with four KAS riders, two Tekas as well as the Dutchman in hot pursuit, but once again no team-mates, he felt outnumbered.

Thurau, released from the pressure of leading a Grand Tour in his second year as a pro, bounced back with a vengeance the next day, winning at Reinosa. It was his third win of what ended up being five stage victories, a remarkable total for such a young rider. But the real battle was once again centred on Ocaña and his next target for elimination – his old ally from 1971, Agostinho.

On the first big climb of the day, the Sierra Collada, Agostinho was already in trouble thanks to Ocaña upping the pace and dropping the rest of the field. And on the second, the Carmona, after a furious but fruitless pursuit of Ocaña, Agostinho cracked. Ocaña, though, was also in trouble – his team-mate Fuchs, who had broken away early on, was unable to support him. And there were still 70 kilometres to go to the finish in Reinosa.

It was at this point that an Ocaña of yesteryear, alone and at the head of the field, would have been able to drive himself into the ground and win the Vuelta. But instead, as Tamames has observed, his rivals had gambled that the Spaniard's reserves were no longer what they were. On top of that, a strong headwind made racing solo a near impossible mission. For the second time in 24 hours, on the final descent of the final climb, the Palombera, Ocaña was joined by six riders, two of them – Kuiper and Thurau – Ti-Raleighs. Kuiper was still in yellow that night and Thurau had recovered, thanks to his stage win, from the pain of being humbled the day before. But, for all Ti-Raleigh's supposed strength, Ocaña was the king-maker in the race. 'I only ask that my strength continue responding,' he said.

After two days of eliminating rivals, if there had been any poetic justice in the 1976 Vuelta, Ocaña would have destroyed the field on the final mountainous stage, to the Santuario de Oro on stage 18. Instead, exhausted by his efforts of the previous two days, he cracked, to the point where he had to be pushed up the final segment of the climb. He was not completely out of the running, given Kuiper had also lost time, but after taking the race by the scruff of its neck, at the last possible moment Ocaña was fading.

Then for the third year running at a time trial finish in San Sebastián, Ocaña was unable to deliver the goods. Instead, he finished eighth, over 1'00" down on Thurau – the winner of the first and the last stages. It would have been little consolation to Ocaña that Kuiper suffered even more badly and ended up dropping to sixth. Instead, Ocaña finished second overall, sandwiched between two KAS riders, José Pesarrodona and José Nazabal, who had played exactly the same game as Tamames the previous year: using Ocaña's strength to polish off their rivals and maintaining just enough consistency to inch ahead. Not pretty, perhaps, but effective.

For the third year running Ocaña had lost the Vuelta on the last day possible. And 1976, arguably, must have hurt the most. He had told journalists in Bilbao he was convinced he could win and, even allowing for his relentlessly upbeat approach, there could be little doubt after the Fito and Palombera that Ocaña, this year, was the strongest rider in the Vuelta – and this was the closest he had come to winning a Grand Tour since the Tour de France three years earlier. In the sense that he had been responsible for blowing apart what had been a singularly dull Vuelta, he could even be described as the moral winner of the race. But Ocaña's strength was no longer such that his madcap breakaways could be as effective as, say, on the road to Les Orres in the 1973 Tour. Rather, it was his ability to organise mass attacks by his team, as he did en route to Murcia in the 1976 Vuelta (and to Reims in the 1973 Tour), which proved the more efficient weapon in his armoury.

Ocaña, in fact, was falling victim to his usual failing: whatever his heart told him he could do, despite all the odds he believed it to be right. Calculating his energy, as Tamames had done so effectively in 1975 and Pessarodona in 1976, was the card he needed so badly, and one that was permanently missing. But if on the Col de Menté it was his lack of skill at descending that let him down, in the 1976 Vuelta it was something even more irresolvable: creeping old age – at least, in terms of professional cycling.

***

Having started out with the goal of becoming the biggest team in Spanish cycling ever, by July Super Ser were already close to folding. 'They told me if I had won the Volta a Catalunya, rather than finish third, the team would have been saved,' Tamames says, 'and if I'd known that at the time I'd have gone a lot harder!' But, in fact, the torpedo that finally sank Super Ser came courtesy of Ocaña himself and his collaboration with Van Impe in the Tour, with boss Ignacio Orbaiceta watching from the team car close behind.

It had all looked so promising. Ocaña attacked on the Portillon, just as he had in 1973, and by the summit was all but alone. Yet, rather than keep going and blow the race apart, as he clearly had the legs to try to do – or at least fail bravely in the attempt – Ocaña waited for Van Impe, guided him over the Peyresourde, and then fell back in the final kilometres on the Saint-Lary-Soulan ski station, his 'work' done as well as any of Van Impe's domestiques. What the atmosphere must have been like in the Super Ser car during the 30-kilometre collaboration is anyone's guess. But Van Impe had, as *El País* put it, 'delivered the definitive knock-out blow for the Tour'.

'Disappointed with his leader, above all after the way he behaved in the Tour, he [Orbaiceta]] put an end to the team' is how an interview with the newspaper *Diario de Navarra* expressed it and as a former pro who had won a stage of the 1946 Vuelta, Orbaiceta could not have been hoodwinked when two riders from opposing teams were collaborating in front of him.

Although Perurena is adamant that Ocaña 'did not sell races', he hesitates when he recalls the 1976 Tour, and when it is put to him that the reason Ocaña worked with Van Impe was friendship, Perurena says, 'for friendship, and for the criteriums they'd have ridden afterwards' – where Van Impe would have taken Ocaña and the Spaniard would have received a large indirect pay-off.

'He made Van Impe win,' says Luis Balagué, not racing but watching it on television. 'He must have given him a lot of money because that day Luis was racing "without a chain"' – Spanish cycling argot for when a rider is performing seemingly effortlessly. The one problem, as Balagué admits, was that 'the boss was there'.

There were other factors that meant Super Ser was up against the ropes. In the Tour, the news had already broken that Ocaña's Super Ser team-mate Jesús Manzaneque had had the dubious honour of being the first rider to test positive, for 'stimulants'. A minor fine and losing 10'00" overall, as well as his third place in the Le Touquet time trial, might have been overlooked, except that he and Viejo had been the only Super Ser riders performing reasonably well.

On top of that Ocaña had tried and spectacularly failed in one of his long-distance solo attacks, on stage seven, a hard grind across the southern Ardennes outside Bastogne down into Nancy. Rather than panic, it was a sign of how his rivals no longer took him as a serious overall threat that they gave him a gap of 1'00" and then let him stew, for kilometre after kilometre, alone but clearly able to be reeled in whenever it was necessary.

The ultimate humiliation came when he was joined by Aldo Parecchini, a little-known Italian rider seven years his junior, on his stage seven attack and Ocaña tried to get him to take a turn on the front. Parecchini, a team worker for one of Ocaña's rivals – Ronald De Witte in Brooklyn – understandably refused and then darted away. Ocaña followed, but as soon as he reached the Italian, Parecchini sat up again. After much swearing and shouting, Ocaña finally left Parecchini to it – and the Italian went on to win the stage.

It had been a humiliating defeat for Ocaña after a pointless attack, and when the media asked him what had happened at the finish, he responded very badly. Rather than answer, he simply spat out the mouthful of water he had just taken and walked away.

Parecchini's post-stage comment, that 'Ocaña is a great rider with a very bad character' was widely quoted that day.

'The atmosphere was terrible,' recalls José Luis Viejo, responsible for Super Ser's one high point in the race, a long-distance breakaway that he won by the biggest ever post-war margin, 22 minutes and 50 seconds, on stage 11 into Manosque. 'Luis was a very nervous guy, he wanted me to share a room with him, and I did in 1976 but I didn't want to share with him!'

'Then his wife was always around which made it even more complicated and on top of that he would get really pissed off with her, yelling at her because there wasn't a kilo of cherries – cold, mind, they couldn't be room temperature – in the room after the stage.

'By that point Luis wasn't any good as a leader, even if he'd still got the character for it. I'd had to push him up the Izoard, he was in such difficulty.'

Viejo's win at Manosque allowed Super Ser some breathing space. But if Orbaiceta thought that Ocaña was – as he had told him before the Saint-Lary stage – back on form and getting ready for an all-out assault on the Tour, his expectations were shattered again. 'The day he escaped with Van Impe he was paid off very well,' says Viejo. 'That was the reward that Luis gave us, he got Van Impe to win the Tour.'

'He was driving away in the break with Van Impe and Orbaiceta was in the car and he was, like, "why is he riding so hard when we've got guys behind overall?".'

So he actually drove up and asked him and Luis didn't pay him any attention. If he'd gone on his wheel [forced Van Impe to work] then it would have been a different story altogether. And that's why the team collapsed.'

There are other indications that by that point Ocaña was growing cynical about cycling. Viejo claims, for example, that Ocaña told him in 1976 that his crash in the 1971 Tour 'was the best thing that had ever happened to him' because in the fans' eyes it maintained the suspense on the Merckx–Ocaña rivalry and Ocaña had told Viejo 'he couldn't have won the Tour that year anyway, he wasn't strong enough'. Given Ocaña's second place in the time trial the day before the Menté crash and the way, according to Thévenet, that he easily responded to Merckx's earlier attacks on the first Pyrenean stage, this comment hints far more at general growing disillusionment with the sport and the sinking realisation that his time was up, than anything else.

Fourteenth in Paris was hardly going to make up for the Van Impe debacle. Nor was taking the King of the Mountains prize – his last individual triumph, albeit not an actual road win – in the low-key Etoile des Espoirs stage race in the Bayonne region that autumn. And, sure enough, the next year Super Ser was reduced from being Spain's new team to one rider, cyclo-cross man Rafael González and an amateur team, 'which did give him [Orbaiceta] a lot of pleasure,' *Diario de Navarra* recalls.

For Ocaña, the 1976 Tour effectively spelled curtains for his career.

'Ever since he'd won the Tour, he went downhill' is Viejo's analysis, and Ocaña's sense of losing his own strength was compounded by increasingly difficult relationships inside what was supposed to be a 'dream team'. 'Saura was a good director, he knew how to take care of his riders, but Ocaña fell out with him because he was used to ordering everybody around. Ocaña wasn't popular because he didn't count in the team in certain races, we had other riders like [Eddy] Peelman or [Jean-Jacques] Fussiens who would go for it in sprints, and he didn't like having to work for them.'

Viejo pulls no punches when he indicates that Ocaña was losing the plot in other ways: 'Luis was rubbish when it came to splits in the bunch. I don't know how he managed but every time there was a split, he'd be out the back having a shit.'

Finally, in terms of 'medical assistance', Viejo says, the Spaniards were no longer able to keep up with the foreign opposition. 'In comparison the Spanish were at a level [of doping] that it made us laughable. We were falling back on that area, we'd be eating bananas to get over climbs, those bloody great bananas and the Dutch and Belgians would be barely carrying any food because of their *special nutrition*, their *energy drinks* and so on. In Super Ser they didn't know anything, the guy who knew the most about all the medical subjects was Ocaña, because he came from France, he knew about cortisone, Luis knew a lot.'

Although Ocaña signed for a Belgo–Dutch team, Frisol, in 1977, as Merckx puts it, 'he was no longer motivated'. He did stand on a winner's podium once more, when he formed part of the Frisol squad that took the Tour Méditerranéen's opening team time trial. But whatever pleasure the opening stage brought Ocaña was probably snuffed out when he crashed out after three stages – either that or Merckx finally winning the race outright.

'The men he will have to have help him seem to be very limited,' said *El País* in its pre-season analysis of the Frisol-Gazelle squad. '[Twice former Tour best young rider Andre] Romero, Dutch national champion [Jan] Raas, [Cees] Priem – sprinters of some quality, and that's it.'

Almost friendless in the team, with no Spanish riders and just one French team-mate, his training partner Romero, meant that for the first time in his professional career Ocaña was all but in a 'club of one' when it came to racing.

Nor had his bad luck abandoned him: apart from his Tour Méditerranéen crash and abandon, where a painful knee injury set him back two weeks, in the Setmana Catalana on stage two he lost all chance of winning the race when a rider – ironically enough Romero – was blown off his line by a helicopter's downdraught and collided into him. Rather than wait for his team, Ocaña then engaged in a 50-kilometre solo chase that left him exhausted for the final ascent, key to the race, into Andorra. As the effects of his injury – primarily to his back – took hold, Ocaña then abandoned before the final time trial. Then driving home through the province of Lleida from the race, Ocaña had another crash – this time in his car. Although lucky only to be slightly injured (his car was a write-off), doctors kept him under observation in hospital for 48 hours.

The two crashes, in fact, were probably the determining factor in his retirement at the end of the season, aged 32. Frisol, who had signed him as their GC rider, had agreed that the contract would only be renewed yearly depending on Ocaña's motivation. But the longer-term consequences of his back injury, perhaps the worst of his career, led him to decide that enough was enough.

In the 1977 Vuelta, after much toing and froing over whether he would start as a last-minute replacement for Frisol leader Jan Raas, Ocaña, finishing 22nd, was a shadow of the rider who had come so close to taking the outright victory in 1976. There were two near-misses regarding stage wins, his last possible chance to remind the public of his former greatness. But on each occasion, at Tossa de Montbui on stage 12, and more spectacularly after an 80-kilometre solo breakaway on the penultimate stage at the foot of the Urkiola, he was left to burn himself out before being reeled in by his rivals: the same bitter lesson that he was on the way out that he had had in previous Vueltas, all over again and, it turned out, for one last time.

His final real all-out effort, with his morale boosted by a third place in the time-trial segment of a small Pyrenean race, the Trophée des Cimes, that June, was the scenario for his first big win: the Spanish nationals. But with no Frisol team-mates for support, Ocaña was swamped by the big Spanish squads, KAS and Teka. When a three-man breakaway went away with one rider from each of those squads and began collaborating, given that the least they would take was a medal, Ocaña began a lone, furious, futile chase. He raced solo to fourth, a fine effort given the lack of team backing, but futile in terms of a podium bid – given that there were three riders ahead.

Then, in the Tour, having finished 25th – his worst finish in a Grand Tour since he was ill in the 1970 race – when news of his positive dope test for an amphetamine-like substance, pemoline, broke on the last day, the writing was on the wall: that it was time to go could not have been more clearly written. 'I don't deny I was positive,' he later said, 'but I am no more guilty than others.'

Ocaña's eighth and last Tour had been a race with cause for very little satisfaction in any case. On stage two, not even the pleasure of hearing that both Eddy Merckx and the Tour's leader, Thurau, his first big rival and one of his last, were dropped from the peloton as a result of Ocaña's long drive at the front end of the bunch on the lower slopes of the Tourmalet, could have provided much consolation. By the grimy ski station of La Mongie, halfway up the Tourmalet, Ocaña was dropped himself, and if he battled his way back onto a group containing Merckx on the descent, on the Aubisque he cracked completely. It turned out later he had made a mistake worthy of a rookie: caught up by his excitement at leading the Tour on the lower slopes of the Tourmalet, he had forgotten to eat on the descent. By Pau, he had lost 12'00".

Ruled out of the overall from a very early stage, Ocaña was once again very active on the front of the bunch on the lower slopes of some major climbs in the Alps – the Cou, the Forclaz and the Glandon. But these were more like brief cameo appearances by a former giant of the Tour before the real contenders took over, and the race's main feature began. When the final major set-piece segment of the race got underway, stage 20's 50-kilometre time trial at Dijon, not even such symbolic gestures were possible: before he started, Ocaña was informed he had tested positive on stage 18 – one of five riders to do so late in the race. He received the standard penalty for the time: 10'00" added to his overall classification.

If 1976 suggested that his motivation could switch towards the financial from results, Ocaña may not even have had that satisfaction at Frisol in 1977, given that riders were allegedly only intermittently paid. He struggled on, even so, to the GP des Nations on 2 October. On a blustery autumn day, he finished tenth in the 90-kilometre event, nearly 9'00" down on new French star Bernard Hinault. But there was a symbolic edge to choosing to finish his career in the same event as one of the other French greats, Raymond Poulidor, and where Ocaña had taken one of his greatest amateur wins ten years before. It was also a time trial, Ocaña's strongest individual suit. At least in that sense Ocaña had come full circle.

As a conclusion to his racing, it was hardly a worthy end of the road, but that tends to be the case for most riders: Fausto Coppi's last year had little to show for it, Miguel Indurain just climbed off midway through a Vuelta a España he did not want to race, and Federico Bahamontes quit after having one argument too many with a Madrid criterium organiser about prize money. Eddy Merckx would depart from the sport five months later, one of his last public appearances as a professional at a race start being to sign autographs at a chain store somewhere in French-speaking Switzerland. Ocaña's finale was equally unspectacular, but no less undignified.

A Spanish or French team might have signed him, given that he was just 32 and a half when he quit. But in one market there was no money, in the other no room: Spain was in the midst of an enormous sponsorship crisis and France already had a solid presence in stage racing, in the shape of Thévenet, and a future with Bernard Hinault, winner of the 1977 GP Nations.

Initially, at least, Ocaña seemed to have no regrets, with his wine business already set up in Nogaro: 'I had a bad time in the GP Nations, but when I came home and saw my vines, I knew I had a new task,' he said shortly after quitting. 'What my wife and my children expected of me was right in front of me, and at that precise moment all sentimentality was gone. My life on the bike was over but a new one was waiting for me. My vineyards were waiting for me.'

His decision to quit was, he said, principally due to feeling he had pushed himself too hard for too long, with the medication he had had to take since falling ill from bronchial pneumonia in the 1972 Tour, 'for which I had to take some serious doses' gradually taking their toll. 'It's true that I've had a lot of disappointment in the final years of my career, but it's dragged me down for years and it's finally been stronger than me.' It was, he insisted, 'nothing to do with amphetamines ...' although there was an indirect nod in their direction as possibly being responsible given that 'it was counterproductive for my body to take antibiotics and at the same time take the medication I needed to pedal'.

Defiant to the last, he still believed he could 'have won the 1975 and the 1976 Vueltas as well as the 1976 Paris–Nice. But I lacked the luck to do it ...'

The lack of a team, lack of decent results, shrinking financial rewards, dwindling physical strength, constant bad luck and – in terms of a bike rider's life – creeping old age, not to mention the strain of a life spent constantly on the road: all these would doubtless have combined. And it seems clear, at least initially, that Ocaña was keen to spend more time at home.

But perhaps the one factor that really counted in Ocaña's decision to quit was the most simple one of all: he had decided it was the right thing to do. Throughout his life, once Ocaña had made up his mind – be it to win a race or to throw it away – everyone recognised there was no swerving him from that path. Or as he once put it, 'my character blinded me from doing what my head was telling me was right'. Once he closed the door on his professional life, then, there was no hesitation – and no going back.

13

'I THOUGHT HE WAS SLEEPING'

France, January 2013, Josiane Ocaña: 'When it became clear he had hepatitis C, he knew that there was no more hope. It was the descent into hell and that was it, a descent into hell, I can't describe it in any other words.'

***

It says a lot about Luis Ocaña's career that 1978, his first long spell away from the bike in 25 years, was probably one of the most contented years of his life. He and Josiane had moved from Bretagne-de-Marsan on 15 December 1977 to his final home, around 30 kilometres further east, at Caupenne-d'Armagnac, near the town of Nogaro. Their new house, described by Josiane as 'a sort of castle' was vast – 600 square metres – and surrounded by 30 hectares of vineyards. With those vineyards Ocaña hoped to make a new, completely different career.

'For an entire year, he didn't even leave the house, he didn't go to a single race,' Josiane recalls. 'Nobody saw him, he didn't want to move around, it was like he was cutting away from his previous life.

'He wanted to be on his farm, he worked in the vineyards, he spent time with the labourers, he'd cut wood, basically he did what he liked.' But after a while, the lure of cycling proved too great – and Ocaña went back. With the considerable wisdom of hindsight, he perhaps could not have made a worse decision.

If Ocaña thought his ten-year run of bad luck would end when he stopped riding a bike, he soon found he had to think again. That was particularly the case when it came to car crashes, where it must truly have seemed that fate was playing a macabre game of some kind.

Ocaña had come through one bad car crash in 1977 unscathed, but the devastating crash in 1979 on the Tour's rest day, which he (and his co-pilot) miraculously survived, was followed by another one in 1983 with even worse long-term consequences.

'He was off delivering Armagnac very close to Mont-de-Marsan itself and a lorry cut across him and his car got caught up underneath it, he was trapped there,' Josiane recalls. 'It's funny, the first big crash he had was a plunge from the heights, this time you couldn't have got closer to the earth.'

Ocaña was hospitalised for four months with both legs badly broken and in harnesses. But if he ultimately recovered from those injuries, the consequences of his fractured skull were even worse. His hearing was so badly affected by one shattered bone that he needed a hearing aid for the rest of his life and, with a shattered eye socket and the eye itself forced inwards, his vision was also badly impaired.

It was as if, Josiane recalls, all his chickens had come home to roost at once. 'It's true that he was a professional for ten years and he never broke a single bone in his body. But from then onwards, right up to his death, he broke absolutely everything.' Even worse, the consequences – from nagging body pains to loss of vision and hearing – were ones that he had to live with every day.

For almost anybody, the subsequent scarring would have been hard to handle. In the case of Ocaña, who prided himself greatly on his physical appearance, it was even more traumatic.

'Seeing himself affected like that made him suffer enormously,' Josiane says, giving the impression she believes the series of accidents had a seriously negative effect on her husband's character. 'They had to remove a part of the eyebrow and his eye was completely cut open, and he was constantly demanding a mirror so he could see himself. And when he did, if things had been really bad before, then they got even worse afterwards.'

As if that was not all, Josiane is convinced that it is as a result of these two bad crashes that Ocaña contracted hepatitis, through an infected blood transfusion. Others might say, too, that Ocaña's body was already vulnerable to such illnesses after years of injections – administered, according to Balagué, in extremely unhygienic conditions – throughout his professional career.

'In cycling before, we didn't have disposable needles,' Balagué recalls about his BIC and Super Ser years with Ocaña. 'We'd each have our own needle and syringe, but [the soigneurs] would boil them up in the same water and same receptacle, with a glug of alcohol' – as a disinfectant.

While dismissive of the effects of doping except as a placebo – 'it's all in your mind, they'd tell you to attack and maybe you'd only have had an aspirin, if it was down to what you took, you'd all be champions' – Balagué insists anyway that the injections would be used only for 'vitamins B1, B6, C. An intravenous injection, maybe six in February and January.'

But he then goes on to talk about needles and injections as if they were a standard part of professional life, recounting the circumstances in which he found himself watching the needles being boiled up in the same cooking pot each day, and saying they could be mixed up, with 'one lot tipped out and the next lot bunged in'. As to the question of health, as he says, at the time – with cyclists seemingly at the peak of health in their twenties, when mortality tends to be the last thing on a young person's mind – 'who thought about that sort of thing?'.

As Balagué tells it, there were no blood transfusions at BIC and Super Ser that could have caused Ocaña to catch hepatitis. 'That was the Italians' game, we weren't up to their level.' But when it comes to the levels of self-deception he and his fellow riders would reach in their refusal to accept that there could indeed be future health problems with what they were doing in terms of 'medication', the Spanish were surely a match for any other nationality.

Balagué recalls one case in which he and six other Super Ser team-mates – Ocaña was not among them – undertook a routine health check in early 1975 and all of them were diagnosed with hepatitis, 'infected from needles'. Told to 'go to bed and rest', Balagué simply continued with his skiing trip and ignored doctor's orders, 'because,' he says blithely, 'it was the last chance I would get to ski all year'. A second check-up was carried out and when the results arrived in the post 'they were terrible for all seven of us, the doctor really insisted I rest … but I was feeling better. Then when I got a third analysis, the results were even worse. I went to the training camp with disastrous results, but finally everything was normal again.

'A cyclist's metabolism is different,' Balagué claims, as if that drew a line under his case and somehow explained his ability to recover. But ultimately years of living on the edge physically take their toll no matter how fit the person is and in Ocaña's case, his metabolism was, by the mid-1980s, no better than anybody else's – and soon, with the hepatitis slowly but surely weakening his body it was to take a serious turn for the worse.

Drawn back into the sport after his 'year off', whilst still working on his vineyards and producing wine, Ocaña accepted a number of jobs as sports director in the 1980s. They almost invariably turned out badly.

In 1983 he worked for the Colombian cycling federation when they sent the country's first ever national squad to the Tour. It had very limited success, with Edgar Corredor and Patricio Jiménez their top finishers in 16th and 17th place in Paris, while the real high point for the squad came when Jiménez led the Tour over the Tourmalet. It was hardly an earth-shattering performance in general, and after one season Ocaña – following the car accident that winter that once again saw him badly injured – then moved on to another team.

At the Spanish Teka squad, so busy were Ocaña and the rest of the management firing off accusations at each other that he barely had time to undertake his duties as sports director. Employed by the Cantabrian team for a single season, 1984, the curtain finally fell at a spectacular press conference in November at which Ocaña lambasted his co-directors. Armed with a tape recording of conversations and a suitcase full of documents that he claimed proved his case, Ocaña refuted accusations that he had betrayed the squad, saying: 'I am charged with being disloyal, unethical and treacherous, but I am going to prove the opposite. They have even said that they felt sorry for me, that my financial situation was a disaster and as good as said that they stopped me from starving. It was France and my father that saved me from going hungry, but it's hard to read that sort of rubbish.' Claiming he and some of the riders had not been paid for several months, Ocaña concluded by saying: 'The only decent thing they've got in this team is the bus.'

Teka's Santiago Revuelta fired back later that when they had signed Ocaña, 'we respected everything we had with him and then during the Tour I found out that he was signing riders for Fagor. So we threw him out of the team.' Whatever the truth, the next year Ocaña had moved on, to his old squad.

'He was very nervous, talking either a heck of a lot or saying nothing at all,' recalls Belgian Classics specialist Fons De Wolf, part of the line-up that season at Fagor, 'and the riders didn't like him for that reason as a director. Then the team got rid of him and it all started to go better.'

As a person, De Wolf says, it was another story altogether – that Ocaña was hugely popular, 'because even though he was either up or down, never in the middle, he was a really nice guy. Quite special. When I had to sign my contract, I remember he came all the way from Mont-de-Marsan to Brussels by train because he said he preferred it to flying.

'But we also went to a party at his home that lasted for three days solid, red wine and white wine and Armagnac and all the farmers there.' Asked if (and how) everybody could stand such a lengthy drinking session, De Wolf grins and says, 'Whatever Luis started, he always went through with it to the end.' On or off the bike, then, some things did not change for Ocaña.

As ever, Ocaña's temper got the better of him all too often, such as when he tried to crash his car into another sports director's – that of José Miguel Echavarri, his former team-mate at BIC – during the 1985 Vuelta. His refusal to accept some unwritten rules of the sport, such as not attacking when riders were picking up their food bags at the mid-stage feed station, also earned him some enemies.

'I remember during one Vuelta [a] España, in 1985, on a long, flat, straight section of road he came up to us waving a bidon in his hand' – on stage 16 from Albacete to Alcalá de Henares in the plains of central Spain – 'and told us to attack,' De Wolf recalls. 'The entire team, plus [rivals Pedro] Delgado and [Pello Ruiz] Cabestany, and a bunch of Russians, we all went for it.

'We got about two minutes or so after ten kilometres and they had to go flat out behind to catch us. I told Luis he should have told us about it beforehand, so we could have been ready. Instead, he'd just agreed it with Delgado.' Asked why he would do that, De Wolf smiles and replies, 'I guess he did it for Spain.'

After leaving Fagor, Ocaña announced the start of a new team, Bordeaux-Aquitaine-Sports, for 1986, that never saw the light of day, but in 1987 his and De Wolf's paths crossed again when Ocaña was a sports director at a small Belgian team, ADR (later to become famous as Greg LeMond's squad when he unexpectedly won the Tour de France on the last day of the race in 1989).

'They took him just for the races in Spain,' De Wolf recalls, 'but he was not so nervous then [because] he didn't have so much responsibility.'

'He was only there a little bit,' adds Dirk Demol, another ADR rider that year who later went on to become a director with the Discovery Channel and RadioShack. 'The boss wanted to bring in some big names to impress people.

'What I can remember about him was that he wasn't particularly effective. That's often the case with big champions, they can't understand why bike riders aren't as good as they were and often get too easily annoyed with them.'

Demol's theory is backed up by almost everybody, with Benito Urraburu pointing out that 'his qualities as a rider made him a disaster as a director. He was constantly furious with them.'

'It's a typical failing. I was working as a sports director in teams at the same races as him and he didn't exactly stand out,' concurs Txomin Perurena. 'Basically, he was a bit nuts.'

Ocaña's last attempt at directing was in a Cuenca-based squad, the tiny Puertas Mavisa outfit, from 1989 to 1990, which rode 'Ocaña' frames – produced by a bike manufacturer and then licensed under Ocaña's name – and which was sponsored by a local company that made doors. Mavisa was a former amateur team with a 90 per cent Spanish line-up, possibly its most exotic rider being Pascal Kohlvelter, the 1990 Luxembourg national champion. But with no major contenders, barring its eye-catchingly garish yellow and black team kit, it never made a huge impact. In Ocaña's time, Puertas Mavisa's biggest success was a stage in the Basque Country in 1990 and the Hot Spots Sprints competition and a transition stage in the Vuelta a España.

Ocaña's popularity was such that simply having his name associated with a local squad like Puertas Mavisa was a huge plus for them – to the point where, given he was both cycling star as well as a director, one of the team's publicity postcards showed a wanly smiling, slightly chubby Ocaña wearing a team shirt. 'People would come round to see him at races and hotels, he was so popular he'd have to get me to bring the car round the back so I could get him out of there,' his Cuenca childhood friend José Luis Romero recalls. Indeed, in Cuenca he ended up having a one-day bike race, now defunct, named after him along with the municipal sports hall.

But the crashes continued, too. 'He had a terrible thing about speed and cars. I can remember one bad crash he had about 100 kilometres from here in Tendillo, driving to Madrid early in the morning and he skidded on a frosty corner, taking the car right off the road.' By 1991, in any case, Ocaña's bike frames were no longer being used by Puertas Mavisa; Ocaña had left, too, and his time as a sports director was over.

In the period that followed – where he combined working his vineyards with temporary contracts for top races as a radio and TV commentator – on the other hand, Ocaña was highly valued. It turned out those qualities that made him so poor a sports director served him very well as an analyst. For nearly four years, from 1991 to 1994, he would be part of a Spanish radio station's analysis panel. Being opinionated and harsh on the field, under those circumstances, was exactly what radio producers seemed to want from Ocaña at the time.

'He'd go straight to the point and sometimes he'd be too tough on the riders, but his analysis was very hard-hitting,' recalls Ramón Mendiburu, by then working for the Vuelta. And, as Perurena adds, he made linguistic mistakes that Spanish radio audiences would find amusing and endearing; when he was excited, for example, 'he'd mix his French and Spanish up, start saying [in French] *c'est incroyable!* [it's incredible!]'.

'As a journalist he was great, really articulate,' adds Jean-Marie Leblanc, a former reporter himself who had seen Ocaña as both director and a commentator when directing the Tour de France. However, as a director Leblanc had the same concerns as Urraburu and Demol, saying 'When he was a sports director, nothing was ever right – the riders didn't go well, they didn't attack enough.' A little like the most infamous firebrand of all French sports directors, Marc Madiot? 'Worse, worse,' says Leblanc.

Ironically enough, Leblanc sees parallels between Ocaña in retirement and his number one rival. 'He's a bit like Eddy Merckx. Whenever Merckx goes on a race he wants all the riders to be champions like him – classy, attacking. And Ocaña was the same. But they couldn't. Not everybody's Ocaña and Merckx.'

However, after retiring, whenever he slung his leg over a bike Ocaña continued to think and act like the star rider he was, with the same degree of competitiveness. Bernard Thévenet recalls one Tour de l'Avenir on which he worked with Ocaña as a commentator, when the two decided to go out for a bike ride afterwards for old times' sake.

'He went absolutely nuts, he was riding like a madman. It had been at least five years since I'd hung up my wheels, he'd been retired for seven or eight and I said to him "fuck, we've not got the kind of age to be doing this …". Well, Ocaña thought he still had: he went all out. All out.'

Ocaña was also not averse to immensely long bike rides to go and see his old team-mates. 'He'd ride all the way here on his bike and come and buy stuff from my ironmonger's shop,' says his former Fagor team-mate Luis Otaño, who had advised him on his contract back in 1969. 'Have a chat, buy old bits and pieces of furniture.' It was some trip: from Nogaro to Rentería and back is around 400 kilometres – 80 kilometres more than the Milan–San Remo, cycling's longest one-day race of all, which takes around seven hours for professionals to complete.

However, there were signs, too, that his character was changing with time – and not for the better. 'He seemed to be a little bitter about everything in the cycling world,' Thévenet recalls, '[made so] by … I don't know, by life in general. There were good moments, too, just like when he raced, and one day he'd be okay and the next he wouldn't. But if something annoyed him, he'd criticise absolutely everything.'

'We'd meet up but he'd really changed,' says Michael Wright.

'He was directing some team and he came to Liège–Bastogne–Liège', near where Wright still lives. 'There was a guy who used to drive him a lot – a kind of private chauffeur – who had been killed, and I knew that Luis was going to see his parents, who lived near here.

'So I went to see Luis, it was great to see him, but he wasn't happy any more. I think he had problems already, but he was very different. He was bitter. When you're used to joking around a bit when you see another old team-mate and remembering the old times, something like that – it's sad.'

Politically, Ocaña moved in a bizarre direction, too, becoming an active supporter of the extreme right-wing French nationalist Jean-Marie Le Pen, in the 1990s. In a lengthy interview with *El País* in 1988, Ocaña said that he and many other big names in French sport were invited to meet Le Pen, but he was the only one who went.

It is possible to interpret Ocaña's interest in right-wing politics as arising because he believed that Le Pen somehow represented the old-school rural values of *la France profonde* where Ocaña felt most comfortable. Ocaña said he liked Le Pen, too, because he had also found – as so many exiles do when they return to their former homeland – that Spain had changed beyond recognition. With democracy, and all the upheavals that followed, the country no longer retained the old secure warmth that a pastoral upbringing like Ocaña's might seem to have contained for him – once the memories of hunger and cold had been consigned definitively to the past.

'I don't think Le Pen really believes everything he says,' Ocaña argued in the interview … 'all the other candidates are trying to stir us up with [the issues of] Europe and 1992. But he's the only one who still talks about morality and customs. I know that it makes you sound old-fashioned when you talk about old principles, but Luis Ocaña doesn't care about seeming old-fashioned.'

While he pooh-poohed the idea that Le Pen was synonymous with dictatorship – 'they're finished in Europe and just as well' – Ocaña said he did not see a contradiction between being a foreigner and supporting Le Pen. 'My country is France, and that's where I'll live for ever, but everybody knows that I am Spanish. A piece of paper wouldn't change that,' he said. Spain, however, had become a country in his eyes where 'it's sad to see how mucked up it's become. If you have a good car, it'll get scratched. If your wife wears jewels, they'll rip them off her. In the squares, you'll see the young people taking drugs. Not just in Madrid, but in the whole country.'

For Ocaña the solution was a return to the kind of agrarian utopia so beloved of extreme right-wing politicians, from Hitler to Le Pen. In Ocaña's rural Arcadia, the 35-hour week was abolished and the school-leaving age reduced back to 14 because, he thought, everybody benefited from hard work – and some from no higher education – from a young age. This would be a selective Garden of Eden, though: according to Ocaña, illegal immigrants (as his father, ironically enough, almost certainly had been in the 1950s in France) would be kicked out, along with 'terrorists and delinquents', because there was not enough work for the French 'who should have priority over the foreigners … If a neighbour comes to fuck up your garden, you kick him out. That's normal.'

All in all, the picture Ocaña paints is as revealing of himself as it is of his political vision. He comes across as an ageing, small-town ultra-conservative, who sees what he thinks are negative changes coming remorselessly into his community and feels helpless to prevent them from happening. Bogeymen like 'foreigners', under such circumstances, are easy to blame. Or, as Ocaña puts it in the interview: 'I am scared someone will rape somebody in my family, or burgle my house, or blow off a friend's head in a [robbery in a] department store.'

No such misfortunes are actually known to have happened to Ocaña in his lifetime – notwithstanding the time he tried to break into his own house, if Thévenet is to be believed, prior to abandoning the Tour in 1975. However, as the hepatitis took a stranglehold and the harvests continued to be poor, Ocaña found that he was heading for a final, irrevocable stroke of bad luck.

'He did the first tests in December [1993],' Josiane recalls, 'because for quite a while he'd been really bad, he suffered everywhere ... really I think it was too late, he must have had metastasis everywhere. Sometimes he'd get up in the middle of the night, he'd be screaming, his legs were really painful and he'd be yelling with the pain. It was terrible, I was very frightened and I'd call the doctor every time but I was living through some terrible moments.

'He was taking an injection every two days, and the day that he would do it [inject himself], he was really, really unwell and then the next day that would be a bit better and then the following day he would have to start all over again. That was terrible, terrible, terrible, and I think that all that, that's what did it, it was impossible for him to get over it.'

'He was operated on very badly after his accident [in the 1979 Tour] and suffered very badly when he returned,' adds Cescutti, 'and on top of that he had the financial problems caused by two years of bad harvests, frost and hail. He couldn't stand all his failures. He wanted everything to go well, and everything was going badly.'

Ocaña did not make his illness overly public, telling a few close friends – like Balagué. But there were times, as Jan Janssen – an acquaintance but not as close as Balagué – found out, that Ocaña would hint strongly that something was up.

'I remember Luis rang me up one time in that spring [of 1994] and asked me if I could help him out finding a dealer for his Armagnac and wine in Belgium and Holland,' Janssen recalls. 'So he came up here with a few bottles of his wine, took them round to one of the biggest dealers in the country that I'd previously contacted. And it was all agreed. Ocaña was to send a container lorry with his wine – it was table wine – and so we left. I asked him if he would stay with us and he said no, he had to get down to Carcassonne right away for some tests because his stomach was giving him a lot of grief and he needed to check it out. And those were the tests he needed to do.' The tests revealed what turned out to be a virulent strain of hepatitis.

By this point, Ocaña was growing increasingly aware that his body was giving out on him, and in the 1994 Vuelta, the last race he covered in situ for a radio station and which finished on Sunday 15 May, the signs of his hepatitis were becoming more and more obvious – and public.

'I'd seen him in the Vuelta, and I'd said to him: "Luis, what's wrong with your hands?" They were all white,' Tamames recalls. 'And he said, well, it's an illness that either goes or it doesn't … and he said, "fuck it, if it doesn't sort itself out, one day I'll go out and …"' Shoot himself? 'That's what he said. He was due a definitive diagnosis in ten days and I was joking around and I said to him, "well, it's better to shoot yourself than hang around with these buggers".'

Macabre jokes apart, the knowledge that something was seriously up with Ocaña was spreading, and not just, as Perurena points out, 'because he had to deal with some very aggressive treatment for his illness during the Vuelta'. Not that it stopped Ocaña from living life in the fast lane.

'On the Monday before that Vuelta, he came down to my factory and we had a meal in Mieres,' recalls Balagué. 'We had dinner – him, *Tarangu* and me and we were out partying until half past four in the morning. He had just made some champagne in his vineyards – I remember it was all really nicely done out because Luis was a real one for detail, a real perfectionist – and he wanted me to come down to the presentation of the champagne in Madrid.'

During their lengthy drinking session – Ocaña presumably slugging his favourite tipple, whisky – at some point Balagué noticed that 'He had a sticking plaster on his body and I asked him what it was for and he said it was over [the incision for] a biopsy for his liver. He was waiting for the results. He said he was worried about hepatitis, and I told him to stop thinking about stupid things like hepatitis C.

'Then, on the day he said goodbye to the Vuelta, after the race had finished, I couldn't help noticing that the way he spoke on the radio it was like he was saying goodbye for good to the people. It was as if he had it already in his head.'

Josiane confirms that Ocaña's thoughts were already heading inexorably towards an early end. 'My husband had suffered terribly seeing how his father wasted away and suffered from his prostate cancer. It had been terrible to see. He [Ocaña's father] had found out that he had prostate cancer when he came to see his first grandson in hospital and he made the most of the hospital visit to see a doctor. Two days later he went into hospital and he never came out until 31 August, the day he died. And he died suffering really, really badly, a ghastly physical decline that just didn't seem real and my husband would say, "if I ever know that I have that, in any case I won't accept it, and I will do what I have to do".'

By the time the results from his hepatitis tests came through, Ocaña's mental stability was suffering badly. Financial difficulties were affecting the farm, thanks to a series of freak storms destroying his crop year after year, to the point where, as Perurena, recalls, 'he had to sell his tower house in Cuenca to pay the taxman'. Although not facing ruin, Ocaña was calling in favours as best he could, from Janssen to Eddy Merckx, to help out his business. Fuente, too, said that when he and Balagué met up, one of the main topics of conversation was how to resolve the vineyard's problems. On top of that, although they remain unconfirmed, there were persistent rumours that he was having a full-blown extra-marital affair, although radio presenter José Maria García, who employed Ocaña at the Cadena Cope station at the Vuelta and wanted to do so again in the Giro that started six days later in Bolonia, later told *El País* that any problems with Josiane 'were halfway resolved'.

The conclusion that Ocaña reached seems to have been taken in as impulsive a manner as in the rest of his life, given that the morning of his death, he had – according to Cadena Cope sources – confirmed to their headquarters in Madrid by phone that he would drive down to Bolonia on the Saturday, two days later, for the Giro. There is speculation that the illness, above all, seems to have been what destroyed his will to go on living. But it is impossible to know for sure – especially in such a tumultuous, unstable individual. Only one thing is certain: as ever, when Ocaña decided on a particular course of action, there was no turning him aside.

***

Josiane Ocaña, January 2013: *'In my personal opinion, given the character of my husband, I never thought he could do something like that. I was the first person to be surprised, but surprised isn't exactly the word because, of course, he often told me he'd cut things short if something similar happened to me ... and then in the last part of his life, he'd say, "I want to finish it all, I'm done for, in any case I don't want to live any longer."*

'I paid a great deal of attention to that. Each time I'd call the doctor, and even two days before his death he had tried to do it [commit suicide]. I called the doctor – they [the local health service] were keeping a close eye on him – and he warned the police and the gendarmes came and, well, because he had guns, he had hidden them because I had tried to hide them and the police arrived in time.

'And then they tried to boost his morale, saying, "yes, Mr Ocaña, because look at this and think about that", and they stayed with

him for two or three hours. I was in the kitchen, they were in the living room.

'And then they came back in: "Madame Ocaña, we're leaving, don't worry, we've talked to your husband for a long time, that's going to be fine, don't worry, that's going to be fine." But I said to them, 'you're leaving me ... but you know, my husband, he's not totally ... you're there, there's a façade but when he's with me, he's somebody else and you can't imagine the things he's saying to me." So [they said] "don't worry", and so on and so forth and I was terrified of being alone with him and I even said to one gendarme – and he'll remember this all his life – "don't you realise the situation, if something happens to him, you'll be responsible, my husband puts on a show, he doesn't show what he's feeling".

'So they left, they left me alone with him, and he did it two days later, in the middle of the day. The first time was in the evening and 19 May happened at around two in the afternoon. He was in his office and ... he had a huge nervous crisis and I tried to call the doctor so he would come. But he didn't want me to pick up the phone, he stopped me, he was saying, "I forbid you to call my doctor." Because, as the gendarmes had come two days before ... he followed me around so that I wouldn't telephone because at that point there were already cordless phones ...

'And then suddenly, just like that, he says, "will you let me go to the office?" And I said, "of course, why do you ask me that – go, go". And then I said to myself, if he leaves for the office, I'm going to call the doctor to tell him what's just happened. And Luis went off to his office, which was just opposite the house, there was a track which separated the two of them. And I called up the doctor straightaway telling him what had just happened and the doctor told me, "I'm coming, I'm coming, don't worry, I'm coming."

'And then in a single moment, you know, there are feelings that you suddenly get and I suddenly said to myself, "it's not normal that he said that to me" and so I thought, "I'll go and see, I'll go and see, I'll go and see."

'But maybe five minutes had gone by, not even that, and I got there and there were these huge bay windows in his office and he was sitting there, he was ... I'll get there, talking about it makes me ... he was sitting in his armchair and my first reaction was to say to myself, "ah, he's fallen asleep", I said that to myself, "he's resting". And then I got closer, you know, these are completely unreal situations, just talking about it I can see it clearly again ... and I get closer and closer ... and afterwards when I saw the carnage ... I had telephoned my doctor and the gendarmes and the doctor arrived very soon afterwards.

'And within all that misfortune, [at least] I wasn't with him alone for a long time, to see that sight, because that's one of the biggest reproaches I make to him is that seeing that, that breaks a person for ever. And that's what I'll always hold against him, making me see a thing like that.'

14

'STRONGER THAN FATE'

'I always thought more about what I'd lost than what I'd won' – Luis Ocaña, October 1977

Ocaña's funeral was held in the Chapelle des Cyclistes at Labastide-d'Armagnac, the same chapel where he and Josiane had married nearly 30 years before, less than an hour's drive from Mont-de-Marsan and Nogaro. Back then the happy couple had posed for photos under the metal gantry capped by bike wheels that stands over the narrow, single-lane approach road: in May 1994, the fields of lowing cattle that surround the chapel, which stands alone in verdant, rolling countryside, witnessed a much bleaker spectacle.

'It was packed for the funeral,' remembers Ramón Mendiburu, who drove there from the Basque Country with Txomin Perurena. 'His son gave a very moving farewell speech.' Later, Henri Anglade, a former professional who finished second in the 1959 Tour turned stained-glass-window maker, would create the chapel window dedicated to Ocaña: at full-speed, clad in yellow, with his curved back, battling on a time trial bike.

The tributes poured in, but probably the most perceptive one came from – unsurprisingly – the rival who defined Ocaña's career: Merckx. 'Despite being my most tenacious rival,' he said, 'I valued him for his strength of character. He was very difficult to beat, his will was unbreakable and he had huge class.'

Thévenet, for one, the rider who knew Ocaña the longest of his fellow pros, is firmly convinced that Ocaña's decision to commit suicide was partly due to a natural refusal to conform. It was, he says, as if Ocaña refused to be beaten by what he would have considered to be the injustice of a terminal illness. And there was only one way to beat it and simultaneously wave his fist in defiance at the gods one last time.

'I'm sure that he hadn't wanted fate to decide when his time had come. He wanted to be stronger than fate,' Thévenet says.

'I think that, with hindsight, Luis was made to have a dramatic end,' says Jean-Marie Leblanc. 'His life was all drama, with highs and lows. Among the highs were winning the Tour de France. You win the Tour and you're not an ordinary man.

'[But] He was like a hero of a modern novel. In French we say *brûler sa vie* – burning himself out. All those decisions he took were never considered. It was all too fast, too generous, too much of a hurry, too excessive. There was a point when he could have died in a traffic accident because he drove so fast and so nervously. His destiny was always going to end up being some kind of *drame*.

'He was a born loser,' says Leblanc – but this is no criticism; rather, he has a curious mixture of respect and sadness in his voice, 'right up to when he lost his life.'

As for Cescutti, perhaps his biggest regret of all about Ocaña has nothing to do with bikes. It is that Ocaña did not listen to him and build the hotel in Mont-de-Marsan 'on the banks of the [River] Midouze' instead of investing heavily in the vines he grew after retiring – and which left him in deep financial trouble. 'If Luis had only listened to me about that hotel,' Cescutti says softly and with a bitter laugh, 'maybe he wouldn't have killed himself.'

***

The ride up the last climb where Luis Ocaña wore the 1971 Tour de France leader's jersey starts easily enough. The Col de Menté's official starting point – announced, as ever, by a sign with the initial altitude (720 metres above sea level), the finishing altitude (1,346 metres above sea level) and average gradient (7 per cent) is halfway up a deep, thickly wooded Pyrenean valley. In the gorge below on the right of a narrow A road that twists and turns so violently you feel it is on the point of buckling, the clear water of the River Ger gurgles over dark rocks; on the left, if you had an extendable neck that would allow you to see above the canopy of oaks and pines that shadows the road, an interminably long ridge of low mountains towering almost vertically above would be visible, reaching into the main, glinting, snow-capped mass of the Pyrenees.

After three fairly uneventful kilometres along the cramped valley floor that do little more than bring you to the village of Ger-de-Boutx, the climb begins in earnest. The woods fall behind on the series of hairpins as neatly folded on top of each other as a coiled ship's cable, while more pinewoods rear up on the opposite side of the widening valley.

Following a straighter, much more exposed, section leading up to the summit, even without the apocalyptic conditions of 12 July 1971 it is easy to see that the final kilometre of the ascent would be the perfect spot for an attack: the road dives back into a series of silver birch thickets, changing direction constantly. It also steepens by a few more degrees – imperceptible when starting a climb, a possibly critical difference at the top.

Then, at the top, once past the monument to local rider Serge Lapébie (son of Guy, the 1936 Olympic double gold medallist and nephew of Roger, the Tour de France winner), there would be no time to draw breath or reflect for more than an instant – as Ocaña presumably did not – on whether to follow Merckx. The descent starts immediately, inviting a snap decision: to follow your attacker, or not to follow?

On the descent, around half a dozen hairpins need to be negotiated in less than a kilometre: all are badly cambered. The road is far more exposed, running across a far steeper, emptier mountainside than on the ascent, ensuring riders would have felt the full impact of any stormy conditions. 'It's a really nasty descent,' recollects former British pro Graham Jones, who pedalled down the same roads in the Tour less than a decade after Ocaña and Merckx, 'very tricky all the way.'

Each of the factors, regardless of Ocaña's skills – or lack of them – as a descender would have contributed to the odds being stacked against him. But the knockout blow, rather than the bend itself where he crashed, is perhaps the approach to it. After the initial thread of hairpins following the summit of the Menté, in the final segment of road leading towards 'Ocaña's bend', it continues to twist but, for 500 or 600 metres, there are no serious corners. Riders would, then, have been building up to full speed again and perhaps lulled into a relatively false sense of security by the lack of corners, maybe to the point where they imagined the worst – as in the most technically challenging – part of the descent of the Menté was behind them.

Approaching at perhaps 60 kilometres an hour allowing for the poor weather, there is the corner itself: long and fairly shallow, but a full-scale 170-degree turn and again badly cambered, with just a tiny ledge of gravel and stones on its outer lip where Ocaña lay after his crash. As if that was not bad enough, the road does not broaden out more than a fraction, leaving riders nowhere to go if – as appears to have happened – Ocaña blundered out into the middle of the road immediately after crashing, an umissable 'target' for Agostinho and Zoetemelk.

On top of all that, just as Van Impe said was the case 40 years earlier, there is fencing on the bend now. But as is so often the case on mountain bends in France, it is not placed at the apex of the corner – which is where Ocaña skidded off – rather on the far side. (The logic presumably being that that is the point where a car, if it braked too late, would reach: the fence is therefore placed where it would save most lives.) Merckx, therefore, could save himself, but Ocaña's slightly different line – and puncture – left it too late for his initial fall. It was, as a commemorative plaque to the accident, on the cliff wall on the bend's upper side, states in a few bald lines, a 'terrible accident in appalling weather conditions'. Ocaña's crash was also, with all these factors combining, the height of bad luck.

And just to add insult to injury, after the corner where he fell there is only one more seriously difficult hairpin on the descent of the Col de Menté. Had Ocaña got through that last real obstacle, it could well all have been plain sailing – perhaps all the way to Paris.

***

It feels wrong, somehow, to remember a rider more for how he lost a Tour than how he won it – even if the extent of the misfortune that Luis Ocaña suffered throughout his career takes the meaning of the concept of 'bad luck' to a whole new extreme.

But there are two good reasons for doing so, and why losing, in this case, is to be admired as much as winning. Firstly, there is the man Ocaña lost against: a rider whom the vast majority of the 1970s peloton thought was unbeatable, yet only Ocaña was foolhardy or courageous enough to challenge. Secondly, there is *how* Ocaña lost: essentially, as a result of his own recklessness, the very quality that had driven him to inflict the greatest ever defeat on cycling's greatest ever rider at Orcières-Merlette.

But there are other ingredients in the mix – and other defeats: the perpetual, relentless blows of misfortune that to someone more superstitious than Ocaña would perhaps have battered his morale far more irreparably. All of that bad luck reached a point on the descent of the Col de Menté where all the possible factors – the storm, the changes in the terrain, the puncture, Merckx's superior descending skills – combined to sink the one man who had refused to accept the apparently God-given, unwritten decree that Eddy Merckx, the invincible, race-gobbling Cannibal, was going to have the run of the show in whichever race took his fancy. One of the most convincing psychological portraits of Merckx has it that he was driven to win races by an overwhelming fear of failure, rather than actually enjoying it. That he, too, might well not have enjoyed or entirely controlled his race-winning impulses almost adds to Ocaña's misfortune of coming up against him so often as a rival.

It would be inaccurate, though, to say that Luis Ocaña's career is *all* about losing. His 1973 Tour, in which even Merckx admits he would have had problems beating him, is grossly underrated because of Merckx's absence. That it was written off at the time as irrelevant is understandable, given how inescapable a reference point the Cannibal had become. But 40 years on, there is a strong case for revising the standard history of that particular Tour, which is all too often dismissed glibly as an insignificant anomaly.

The same goes for Ocaña's time trialling, where his ability to destroy his rivals in races against the clock was second only to Merckx at the time, and unequalled for decades before or after in Spain. But while *Maître Chrono* Jacques Anquetil remains the undisputed benchmark for time trialling in France, in Spain Ocaña has been completely overshadowed by Miguel Indurain – arguably cycling's greatest time trialler of all time. (Ocaña's thoughts on Indurain were as uncompromising, incidentally, as they had been about a certain Belgian: 'Nobody dares to attack him. I'd have attacked him until I died, just like I did with Eddy Merckx.')

Quite apart from his time trialling, extreme bad luck and all but fruitless opposition to Merckx, there are other reasons why Ocaña was the exception to the rule. Conventional sport abounds with theories about how athletes learn more from their defeats (or injuries or illnesses) than they do from their victories. Injured pride is – on paper – more memorable in the long term than inflated pride, and the ensuing learning curve and depth of training brought on by resentment at losing ensures that the 'bounce back' by an athlete is even more powerful and impressive than any initial success.

But what makes Ocaña different, again, was that he did *not* learn. He applied identical tactics – attack and be damned on the road stages, and flat-out, full-on concentration in the time trials – regardless of the result or how many times it failed or worked.

Perhaps the most revealing moment of Ocaña's Le Pen interview came when he was discussing how he felt racing had changed since his day. Modern society, he felt, had its equivalent in modern bike racing, which in turn became a harking back to the 'good old days' when anarchic attacking was more widely accepted.

'Previously, when you raced, you stopped working [in normal jobs] and became a professional,' he said, the implication being that you retained your natural youthful aggression. But not any more. 'Now, in the cycling schools for young riders, you learn how to economise, how to use the rest and wait for support. You learn to be a cheat and when you sign your first [professional] contract they're already professionals, right down to their fingernails.' Ocaña's reason for signing a professional contract – throwing a hammer at his boss – was, as ever, based entirely on feeling, with zero calculation involved. And he did not learn how to 'cheat' ever – at least not in terms of saving his strength.

But compare that to the great British cyclist Tom Simpson's racing philosophy, which he once expressed in a letter he wrote: 'the thing is not where you finish, how much [money] did you make [sic].' There is no following question mark: this is a statement of fact. In comparison, Ocaña's failure to weigh up the benefits of one strategy or another was one more reason why he was, and remains, so appealing a racer. No odds were ever too high for Ocaña not to believe it was possible to win, as Urraburu recalls when he cites the case of a journalist sharing a car with Ocaña during the Tour (on which he later commentated) and the road was blocked by strikers. 'There must have been around eighty of them, but Luis got out, fists at the ready, prepared to fight the lot of them to get through.'

From start to finish, Ocaña was fuelled by brute emotions, unadulterated impulses, total involvement. Small wonder that, after his racing career was over, he was overwhelmed with a sense that whatever life gave him afterwards it would never provide him with the same extremes of joy and passion that he felt when racing. 'If I could start out my career as a professional again, I would happily accept dying the day after my last race,' he said in the same interview. 'With no regrets.

'It's not that I am unhappy in my life now, but I know it'll never equal the tension and feelings I had on the bike.' And, given how completely Ocaña lived for his sport when he was on his bike, he was probably right, too.

***

On a shelf immediately opposite the entrance to Josiane Ocaña's home, there is a trophy her husband was awarded by his old Stade Montois club. The inscription reads: 'In honour of Luis Ocaña, winner of the 1971 and the 1973 Tour'.

Yet even if Pierre Cescutti's assertion that by rights Ocaña should have won the Tour in 1972 as well as the previous year may be a little hard to swallow, the idea that Ocaña is the 'moral winner' of the 1971 Tour has its backers, and not just in Mont-de-Marsan.

Part of it has to do with the human tendency to back the underdog. But there were plenty of those in Merckx's day. Perhaps what appealed most about Ocaña was that, although he failed to learn, he came back for more defeats, more suffering, more bad luck. It wasn't just that he refused to lie down and be beaten that made him likeable; what made him most human of all was that he kept on making the same mistakes, tripping over the same stones. Ocaña partly inspires sympathy for the same reason that Raymond Poulidor, 'the eternal second' who never won the Tour, was far more appreciated than five-times Tour winner Jacques Anquetil. But it is also surely partly because, however hard Ocaña tried, no matter how much he railed against life's (or sport's) injustices, such as having to live in the same era as Merckx, his own personality both helped him gain ground in what was an unequal struggle, but it also betrayed him – time and time again.

As a rider, there could be no doubt that Ocaña enjoyed his role as the head of the anti-Merckx rebellion. But curiously enough, if an innate refusal to race for second smacks of independent thinking, for Ocaña that was not the case: it was fate, he believed, just as it was fate that had caused him to be so good in the Tour de France. 'He once told me that the victory that he most treasured was when he won the Spanish National Championships in 1968,' José Miguel Echavarri once said, 'because nobody had expected it. When it came to the Tour, he was fated to do well there.' Hence Ocaña's total bewilderment, perhaps – muttering *pas possible, pas possible* as he lay in his hospital bed – when the 1971 Tour was wrenched from him.

And the argument over whether he would have won it, of course, will probably continue to rumble on. 'He used to say: that bloody Merckx, he knew I couldn't descend, so that's when he attacked,' Agustín Tamames recalls, and even Merckx is willing to admit, 'It was a pity for him and for the Tour, for everybody', before pointing out that 'the year afterwards I beat him also'. In other words, he proved, yet again, that he was stronger. Merckx also has little sympathy for Ocaña making mistakes like chasing him too hard on the Menté because, as he says, everybody makes them, even the Cannibal himself. 'He was sick [in 1972], too. But it's like me, the biggest mistake of my career was to go on in the [1975] Tour with a broken face' – a double fracture in his upper jaw and a trapped nerve caused by a crash in the Alps – 'and when I had that punch in the kidneys' from a spectator on the Puy-de-Dôme. As Merckx sees it, everybody makes mistakes. It's just how quickly you can recover from them that makes a great champion.

However, it is perhaps easier to be so uncompromising when you are Eddy Merckx and have won everything than when you are on the other side of the divide. Balagué, on the other hand, believes that 'Ocaña had that Tour more firmly in his pocket than when he won in 1973. The only thing that did for Luis in 1971 was his bad luck. If he hadn't been so unlucky he'd have beaten Merckx all the time.

'Don't forget that he rode for 150 kilometres on that Les Orres stage [of the 1973 Tour de France] with Fuente on his wheel, without him taking a single turn on the front, and then when Fuente punctures, he couldn't catch him. Luis was anything but a normal bike rider.'

And Balagué puts his finger on Ocaña's appeal to the public when he says 'however weak he was, he was always fighting Merckx, he was convinced that he was beatable. The fact that he had done it at Orcières was what kept him going.'

Equally unresolvable as the question of the 1971 Tour de France is whether Ocaña has his rightful place in French or Spanish cycling culture. Both have reasons to claim him, but Ocaña himself believed that he 'would never have become a champion in Spain'. Without Cescutti, in fact – not to mention that hammer he flung at his boss – Ocaña would almost certainly have failed to learn even the most basic of racing strategies. On the other hand, his personality and his racing style had far stronger Latin roots than anything that formed his character on the northern side of the Pyrenees.

If anything, Ocaña is a reminder of how arbitrary and fallacious divisions by nationality or race really are – in his case, as with so many exiles, that square nail really will not fit in either particular round hole of a specific country. Rather than focusing on what he might or might not have won, or whether the flag on his race number should have been red, white and blue or red and yellow, we should remember that Ocaña, above all, was – and remains – inspirational, and without him great cyclists on both side of the frontier might not have flourished as a result, in some cases very directly.

'He was my role model,' says Thévenet. 'He turned pro in 1968 and when he'd won the GP des Nations I was third or fourth, so our careers were almost parallel. So I said, what he had done I had to do, too.' Given Thévenet won two Tours, will for ever be remembered as the rider who first sank Eddy Merckx for good in a Grand Tour and was the pioneer of a new generation of local riders such as Bernard Hinault and Laurent Fignon, that alone makes Ocaña an exceptional figure for French cycling. But he had the same effect in Spain, too.

'In my childhood I always followed him. He was a Spaniard who won, and I thought I'd like to be like him,' said Pedro Delgado after Ocaña's death. 'As kids, we'd even have street battles between *Merckxistas* and *Ocañistas*. And I was always on his side.' And it was not just among the greats that he managed to strike a chord. If you are looking for gestures of loyalty, the way that Perurena and the other Fagor riders pushed him for kilometre after kilometre in the Tour de France 1968 and all the way up a major climb like the Ballon d'Alsace says it all.

The media were either enthralled or offended by him, but Ocaña never committed what is perhaps the most heinous crime for a reporter: being boring and so not providing column inches. 'Luis Ocaña, *Monsieur Panache*, was never one for half-measures,' *Le Dauphiné Libéré*'s head of cycling, Thierry Cazeneuve, wrote in his obituary. 'For that reason, for the majority of us reporters, he was and is a reference point.'

Some newspapers, like the almost perennially critical *El Mundo Deportivo*, pointed out when he quit that 'the champion that was Luis Ocaña died when he received the last bouquet of flowers on the final podium of the 1973 Tour. The last four seasons have been a martyrdom for him: he was desperate to please the public, but his physical strength was no longer there.'

But it had not been, even *El Mundo Deportivo* recognised, entirely Ocaña's fault. 'Perhaps the greatest Spanish cyclist of them all has had to face the toughest twilight of a career of any of the most important legends of sport out there.'

***

'Everything he did,' says José Miguel Echavarri, later Indurain's director, 'was tinged with heroism and tragedy.' And it is certain that two images of Ocaña linger the longest in the memory. The first is of the illusion of success, his head bowed en route to Orcières-Merlette, and the second is a picture of total despair, his mouth open with a howl of pain at the cruellest of defeats, on the Col de Menté, as what would have been one of the greatest sporting victories of modern times then slipped through his fingers. Its back story is equally poignant: a reminder that a split-second wrong-headed impulse can wreck months or years of perseverance and effort.

Other tragedies of sport – the death of Fabio Casartelli on the descent of the Portet d'Aspet in 1995 took place just a few kilometres before, on the same road tackled by Merckx and Ocaña in 1971 – are far more disturbing. But they are shocking for their rarity as well as their outcome. Rather than the issue of mortality, which thankfully only raises its head occasionally in sport, Ocaña's rise and fall in the 1971 Tour poses questions that remain constantly in the background of almost everybody's daily lives: the enormity of what we could have achieved – and have not – contrasting with the feeble gains that an unjust existence has ended up doling out to us. Or, as Ocaña put it himself after retiring, 'I always thought more about what I'd lost than what I'd won. My defeats mattered more than my victories.'

What gives Luis Ocaña the champion his most human quality, in fact, is exemplified by his return to racing after the Col de Menté defeat: when he made the same mistakes again and again but remained as determined as ever to struggle against his own limitations and failings with a degree of recklessness few, if any other, athletes have ever been capable of producing. And that furious, fate-defying, tragic recklessness is also what makes the title of *Monsieur Panache* one by which Luis Ocaña the bike rider fully deserves to be remembered.

LUIS OCAÑA: RACE RECORD

Place of birth: Priego (Cuenca), Spain
Date of birth: 9 June 1945
Date of death: 19 May 1994
Turned professional: 1968
Retired: 1977

1968 TEAM: FAGOR
Wins
Vuelta a Andalucía: stages 1, 2 and 6
Spanish National Championships (time trial)
GP Llodio

Selected placings
Giro d'Italia: 32nd; stage 19, 2nd
Vuelta a España: stage 8, 2nd
Volta a Catalunya: 4th
GP Nations: 4th

Grand Tour abandons: Vuelta a España, stage 10

1969 TEAM: FAGOR
Wins
Vuelta a España: prologue; stage 16 and stage 18 second sector
  (TT) and King of the Mountains (KOM)

Midi Libre: overall
Vuelta a La Rioja: overall and stage 3 first sector (TT)
Setmana Catalana: overall and stage 5 second sector (TT)
Vuelta al País Vasco: stage 3

Selected placings
Vuelta a España: 2nd; stage 14 second sector (TT), 2nd
Subida a Arrate (TT): 3rd

Grand Tour abandons: Tour de France: stage 8 second sector

1970 TEAM: BIC
Wins
Vuelta a España: overall, prologue and stage 19 second sector (TT)
Tour de France: stage 17
Dauphiné Libéré: overall and stage 5 second sector (TT)
Volta a Catalunya: stage 7 second sector (TT)
Setmana Catalana: stage 5 second sector (TT)

Selected places
Tour de France: 31st; stage 20, second sector (TT), 3rd; stage 23
    (TT), 2nd
Paris–Nice: 2nd
Escalada a Montjuïc: 2nd
Setmana Catalana: 3rd
GP des Nations (TT): 3rd
Giro di Lombardia: 7th

1971 TEAM: BIC
Wins
Vuelta a España: stage 12
Tour de France: stage 8 and stage 11
Subida a Arrate (TT)

Vuelta al País Vasco: overall and stage 4, second sector (TT)
Volta a Catalunya: overall and stage 5, second sector (TT)
A Travers Lausanne: overall, stage 1 and stage 2 first sector (TT)
GP Lugano
GP des Nations (TT)
Trofeo Baracchi (TT) (w. Leif Mortensen)
Dauphiné Libéré: KOM

Major placings
Vuelta al Levante: 2nd
Dauphiné Libéré: 2nd
Tour de France: stage 13, 2nd
Vuelta a España: 3rd; prologue, 3rd;
Paris–Nice: 3rd

Grand Tour abandons: Tour de France: stage 14

1972 TEAM: BIC
Wins
Spanish National Championships
Dauphiné Libéré: overall, stage 4 first sector, stage 5 second sector
  (TT) and KOM

Selected places
4 Jours de Dunkerque: 2nd
Paris–Nice: 3rd
Tour de France: stage 5 second sector (TT), 3rd; stage 8, 3rd;
  stage 11, 3rd; stage 12, 3rd

Grand Tour abandons: Tour de France: stage 15

1973 TEAM: BIC
Wins

Tour de France: overall, stage 7 first sector, stage 8, stage 12 first
    sector (TT), stage 15, stage 18 and stage 20 first sector (TT)
Dauphiné Libéré: overall and stage 6 second sector
Vuelta al País Vasco: overall and stage 4 second sector
Setmana Catalana: overall, stage 5 first sector and points jersey
Volta a Catalunya: stage 3 second sector (TT) and KOM
Regional Spanish Championships

Selected places
Vuelta a España: 2nd
Vuelta a Cantabria: 2nd
GP des Nations: 2nd
Tour de France: stage 12, second sector, 3rd
World Championships: 3rd
Escalada a Montjuïc: 3rd
Volta a Catalunya: 4th
Paris–Nice: 6th

1974 TEAM: BIC
Selected places
Vuelta al País Vasco: 3rd
Vuelta a España: 4th; stage 18, 3rd
Dauphiné Libéré: 6th
GP des Nations: 8th
Volta a Catalunya: 10th

1975 TEAM: SUPER SER
Wins
Vuelta a Andalucía: stage seven, first sector (TT)
Tour de La Rioja: stage two, second sector (TT)

Selected places

Vuelta a Andalucía: 2nd

Setmana Catalana: 2nd

Subida a Arrate: 2nd

Vuelta a Asturias: 3rd

Vuelta a España: 4th; stage 7 (TT) 2nd; stage 14, 3rd

Volta a Catalunya: 7th

Paris–Nice: 9th

Grand Tour abandons: Tour de France, stage 13: DNS

1976 TEAM: SUPER SER
Wins

Etoile des Espoirs, KOM

Selected places

Vuelta a España: 2nd

Tour de France: 14th

Paris–Nice: 3rd

Vuelta al País Vasco: 9th

1977 TEAM: FRISOL-GAZELLE
Selected places

Spanish National Championships: 4th

Vuelta a España: 22nd; stage 12, 3rd

Tour de France: 25th

GP des Nations: 10th

BIBLIOGRAPHY

Many thanks to all those who were willing to give up their free time to be interviewed for their valuable insight. In alphabetical order:

Jesús Aranzabal, 18 January 2013
Luis Balagué, 29 January 2013
Thierry Cazeneuve, 28 December 2012
Pierre Cescutti, 17 January 2013
Emilio Cruz, 29 January 2013
Javier De Dalmases, 1 February 2013
Miguel Indurain, 11 January 2013
Jan Janssen, 19 April 2013
Jean-Marie Leblanc, 14 2012
Ramón Mendiburu, 15 January 2013
Eddy Merckx, 7 February 2013
Josiane Ocaña, 16 January 2013
Luis Otaño, 14 January 2013
Txomin Perurena, 15 January 2013
José Luis Romero, 27 January 2013
Agustín Tamames, 27 January 2013
Bernard Thévenet, 27 December 2012
José Luis Benito Urraburu, 14 January 2013
Lucien Van Impe, 20 September 2012
José Luis Viejo, 13 May 2013
Michael Wright, 14 December 2012
Joop Zoetemelk, 13 December 2012

BOOKS
(Published in English)

Fallon, Lucy and Bell, Adrian, *Viva La Vuelta*, Mousehold, 2005

Fotheringham, William, *Put Me Back on My Bike: In Search of Tom Simpson*, Yellow Jersey Press, 2002

——*Roule Britannia: A History of Britons in the Tour de France*, Yellow Jersey Press, 2009

——*Merckx Half Man, Half Bike*, Yellow Jersey Press, 2012

Friebe, Daniel, *Eddy Merckx: The Cannibal*, Ebury Press, 2012

Moore, Richard, *In Search of Robert Millar*, HarperCollins, 2007

Nicholson, Geoffrey, *The Great Bike Race*, Hodder & Stoughton, 1977

Voet, Willy, *Breaking the Chain*, Yellow Jersey Press, 2001

(Published in Spanish)

Bodegas, Javier and Dorronsoro, Juan, *Con Ficha de la Española, 1960–2003*, Urizar, 2003

——*Historia del Campeonato de España*, Urizar, 2003

——*Historia de la Vuelta al País Vasco*, Urizar, 1996

Dorronsoro, Juan, *Historia de la Volta a Catalunya*, Urizar, 2007

Garai, Josu, *Ciclismo de Norte*, Recoletos, 1994

Molero, Juan Carlos, *Historias del Arco Iris*, Unipublic, 2005

(Published in French)

Guilleminet, Roger, *Roger Pingeon*, Alan Sutton, 2004

Loizeau, Bernard, *Luis Ocaña, le soleil des pelotons*, Herault de Maulevrier, 1978

Ocaña, Luis and Terbeen, François, *Pour un Maillot Jaune*, Calmann-Lévy, 1972

Terbeen, François, *Merckx–Ocaña duel au sommet*, Calmann-Lévy, 1974

Various – *Tour de France 100 Ans*, L'Equipe, 2002

NEWSPAPERS, MAGAZINES, WEBSITES AND NEWS
AGENCIES
(Published in English)
Procycling
Velo News
Cyclingnews.com

(Published in Spanish)
MARCA
Meta 2Mil
El País
El Mundo
ABC
El Mundo Deportivo
Urtekaria

(Published in French)
Le Dauphiné Libéré
Le Soir
Sud-Ouest
L'Equipe
L'Equipe cyclisme magazine
Alpes Loisirs
AFP

ACKNOWLEDGEMENTS

First and foremost, my greatest thanks is to Naomi, for (again) making this book both possible on all sorts of levels, for her patience, insights and collaboration while it was being written and, finally, for making it worth doing. And to Mar, particularly for the drawings to keep in my suitcase.

This book would not have happened, either, without much good-natured badgering from my brother William at its inception. From that point he was a constant source of encouragement, phone numbers, a mine of information about 1960s and 1970s cycling in all kinds of areas, and came up with lots of general, sound advice. Many thanks.

Barry Ryan's insights, dryly humorous and otherwise, and his willingness to have umpteen ideas bounced off him, made writing this book less stressful and the end result a better one. Many thanks, too, to Stephen Farrand, for his constant encouragement and support as well as some patient explanations, not for the first time and probably not the last, about the mysteries of bike gearing.

From the moment he grinned and all but whooped with enthusiasm when I first tentatively put the idea of an Ocaña biography to him to providing original material and background information, French cycling journalist Philippe Bouvet was of considerable assistance and a major inspiration. In the Basque Country and out of it, a huge *Eskerrik Asko*, too, to Karlis Medrano of Karlistudioa.com for his photos, his time, his fine cooking and his hospitality. And equally to my editor Charlotte Atyeo of Bloomsbury, a byword for enthusiasm, professionalism and invariably on-the-nail advice.

Javi Bodegas, Spanish cycling's top historian, once more proved invaluable for contacting former bike riders while Pierre Carrey also went out of his way to provide contributions and ideas. Thanks to Philippe Court for sacrificing his time to give me access to the back files of *Le Dauphiné Libéré* on a freezing late December afternoon; to Jacinto Vidarte for hospitality, ideas and phone numbers; to Phil Sheehan for his hard work with some state-of-the-art sound technology in deciphering a particularly important, scratchy tape recording; to Lionel Gauzere and the Stade Montois club for the warmest of welcomes and practical assistance in Mont-de-Marsan and to Benito Urraburu for his insights into Luis Ocaña. Finally, a big thank you to my agent Mark Stanton of Jenny Brown Associates, for once again efficiently sorting out the tedious background bits of converting a book from vague concept into something on a bookshelf.

Thanks, too, (in alphabetical order) to: Daniel Benson, Marie-Hélène Boudé, Thierry Cazeneuve, Richard Collins, André Darrigade, Dirk Demol, Fons De Wolf, Dan Friebe, Josu Garai, Marc Ghyselinck, John Herety, Nick Humphrey, Graham Jones, Raymond Kerckhoffs, Alain Laiseka, Jane Lawes, Richard Moore, Catherine Murray-John, Dave Prichard of Metro Books, Granada, Jorge Quintana, David Randall, Manolo Saiz, Stéphane Thirion, François Thomazeau, Graham Watson and Johnny Weltz. A special mention, too, of my ongoing indebtedness to the late Geoffrey Nicholson. Apart from being an invaluable account of the 1976 Tour which I used as a reference work here, his *The Great Bike Race* remains a benchmark whenever I'm writing about cycling.

I cannot end this section without mentioning my father, Alex, who indirectly sparked my interest in cycling and whom I know would have been as enthusiastic about this book as he was about my writing the previous one. *Míle taing, a bhodaich chòir.*

INDEX